THE
IMPATIENT
GARDENER

THE IMPATIENT GARDENER

by
Jerry Baker

America's Master Gardener

Ballantine Books • New York

Copyright © 1983 by Jerry Baker
Illustrations copyright © 1983 by Lauren Jarrett

All rights reserved under International and Pan-American Copyright Conventions. Published in the United States by Ballantine Books, a division of Random House, Inc., New York, and simultaneously in Canada by Random House of Canada Limited, Toronto.

Library of Congress Catalog Card Number: 82-90905

ISBN 0-345-30949-9

Cover design: James R. Harris
Cover photo: Brignolo/T.I.B.
Author photo: Joe Naras
Book design: Gene Siegel

Manufactured in the United States of America

First Edition: March 1983

20 19 18

To
Ilene
my wife, my life, my love
and
my children
Sue, Diane, Pat, Jeff, and Kassie
my pride and joy and hope

Contents

Acknowledgments

In preparing this book, I am fortunate to have had the assistance of many friends and colleagues without whose knowledge and generosity this book could not have been.

I'd like to give special thanks to Bob and Doris Tunstra (brother and sister) who are a legend in their own time. They have one of the most successful, beautiful, and imitated garden center operations in the country, The Fruit Basket, Flowerland of Grand Rapids, Michigan.

I am indebted as well to Ethel Daniels, the first lady of garden writers, of the Ross Daniels Company.

For the use of their vast research information and staffs, I thank Northrup King Seed Company, Stouffer Chemical, Lord and Burnham, The Dutch Bulb Institute, and the U.S. Department of Agriculture.

Special acknowledgment must go to Jim Greene, Norm Milley, and Rocky Meldrum. They know what it takes.

Foreword

Ten years ago I wrote my first garden book, *Plants Are Like People*. It was an incredible success, selling well over a million copies. I wrote the book as a result of the fan mail I received from my weekly appearances on Dinah Shore's TV show, *Dinah's Place*. As the program's garden expert, I approached indoor and outdoor projects with basically the same solutions and treatments as I would use for similar people problems. I still feel that plants are like people, and I try hard to treat them with the same respect and TLC I would one of my children. Some of my best friends grow in my garden.

In ten years I have seen a great change in society. Everything has to be right now; people want instant results, they can't wait, don't want to miss anything. I admire this determination to live life to the fullest, but I am a little disturbed at the impatience that goes along with it. My friends, let me remind you, it still takes nine months for a baby to bloom; you can't rush Mother Nature!

The people in this Roadrunner (beep beep!) Society still want their little corner of the world to be green and clean (and by all means on *their* side of the fence); but they don't want to do any more work than is absolutely necessary to ensure it. If that describes you, this is the gardening book you need.

Those of you who know me through my books, TV shows, and radio visits know that I don't just sit back and watch you stub your green thumb (if I can help it). I try to give easy, practical advice that will start showing results today. You need to slow up just enough to smell the roses.

I have kept my advice to the point, but not always brief. If I think a fact is important, it's here even if it doesn't seem important to you. But you aren't going to find a lot of theory here. I'm a graduate of "Hard Knocks University," where you don't miss a lesson. This book is written totally on the KISS (Keep It Simple, Stupid!) theory. It takes you through your gardening chores step by step, describing the procedures in the order you should do them, from earliest spring to the dead of winter. It will also make you chuckle, laugh, and enjoy reading what, as a rule, is a dull subject.

You will find many a homemade formula for sprays and concoctions; try them, you may be pleasantly surprised. I am not one to mince words or hold back on recommendations on how to save money and speed up results—after all, that's what you're looking for, right?

I also have a reputation for scolding listeners and viewers who have heard me give the same advice several times and have gone and done just the opposite; that is the serious side of Jerry Baker. There's nothing in this book that doesn't work, so you might as well start off on the right foot and follow my instructions to the letter. Sooner or later you'll end up doing it anyway.

CHAPTER 1 Lawn Care

Lawns Don't Have to Be a Pain in the Grass!

For the past couple of years I have kept a record of my neighbor's comings and goings in the garden. Every year, around the end of April, spring fever hits him. He starts to plant, prune, sow, and fertilize like a madman. Gradually the great bursts of activity peter out, until finally I see his wife or kids behind the wheel of the lawn mower. Almost to the day, this event occurs on my birthday, June 19. I have asked several of my growing friends to do a little research for me in other parts of the country. They concur with my findings—45 days is the limit for the average person's enthusiasm for gardening.

My objective is to stretch out those 45 days over the entire season. Pushing a lawn mower over a half-acre patch will burn off more calories than a five-mile bike ride or a one-mile swim—and it does wonders for your blood circulation.

It's All in the Timing

I wish I could tell you that anyone can have a prize-winning lawn with little or no effort—that when the mood moves you, you can fertilize, seed, water, or mow; but I can't, and I won't. Unless you do certain jobs at certain times of the season, you can just give up your dream of greener pastures.

In the foreword, I promised that I would make your growing job easier. As silly as my suggestions may sound, I want you to try them just once. You, your lawn or garden, and your neighbors will be happily surprised.

1

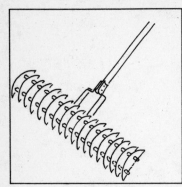

Lawn groom rake

There is no way that I can possibly list each job day by day, week by week for every city, state, or country in the world; so my first bit of advice for all of you impatient gardeners is to take a drive by the closest golf course in your neighborhood and check out what the greens superintendent is doing. Then, go home and do the same thing.

I know what you're wondering: How will I know what he's doing? Well, I don't know one professional gardener, greens superintendent, or forester who is too bashful to ask questions! So, be like the pros—ask!

Below I describe some of the most important jobs that you have to do in the proper sequence. If you're in doubt about the exact timing for your area, by all means call your local county agricultural extension agent. You will find his phone number in any phone book. (Be sure to tell him I said, "Hi!")

At the end of this chapter you'll find my thirteen basic steps to a beautiful lawn. Follow them, and you'll be amazed by the results!

Early Spring Care

Thatch Is Slow Lawn Death

Roughly 75 to 80 percent of all lawn problems are the result of thatch. Thatch is the accumulation of grass clippings and other natural debris that collect between the blades of grass during the growing year. When thatch is not removed, it becomes a breeding place for lawn diseases, insects, and weed seeds. A buildup of thatch prevents penetration of water, fertilizers, weed controls, fungicides, and insecticides. The result is a disappointed and discouraged homeowner.

Unless you have one of the nongrass ground covers used in the south, southwest, and Hawaii, you must dethatch your lawn at least once every two years before any other lawn job is attempted. If you don't, you and your lawn are going to lose. You are going to lose your time, money, and effort; and your lawn—oh, only its life.

Dethatching is no joy, that's for sure, but certain methods are faster and easier than others. You can remove thatch by hand, with a rake designed specifically for the job, called a cavex or lawn groom rake. That's the hard way. Or you can rent a power dethatcher, a much faster but more expensive way. Finally, you can purchase an Arnold power rake dethatcher blade; it converts your lawn mower into a power dethatcher. It's the least expensive, fastest, and easiest method.

The best time for dethatching is the early spring (when you first start on your gardening craze), or early fall (late August through September). Doing it at both times will give super results.

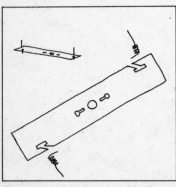

Power rake dethatcher blade

Power detnatcher

Rake up thatch after dethatching, and clippings after mowing

Don't throw thatch away, it's money! Thatch is raw compost; unless you have used a weed killer within three weeks, throw it into your compost maker or on top of your unspaded garden. We'll talk about that in the chapter on vegetable gardening.

Spring Scalpings Don't Hurt

As soon as you have dethatched, install a newly sharpened, balanced lawn mower blade—well oiled all over with Pam cooking spray or any silicone spray—on your mower and drop the blade so that it is just above the new green grass plants but not deep enough to gouge into them. Collect all of the clippings and remove them to the compost pile or unspaded garden.

Mow closely in early spring

Never use a dull blade; it can do more damage than most insects and diseases. It's a good idea to begin the season with two blades so that one is always sharp. The Arnold Manufacturing Company makes high-quality replacement blades for most lawn mowers on the market today.

Don't Let Crab Grass Make You Crabby

Crab grass is an international troublemaker that can be controlled early in the spring before the early spring shrubs bloom. Use any turf chemical that states it kills crab grass *seed*. These chemicals are called pre-emergence controls, or premerge for short. They work by killing the seed before it germinates. Purchase any inexpensive brand; there's no need to pay for packaging. If you are planning to overseed, however, you can't use a premerge because it will kill your new grass seed. Don't worry, though; crab grass is an annual grass, so this year's plants will die at the first frost. So at

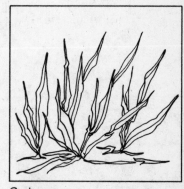

Crabgrass

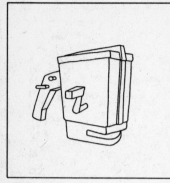

Whirly spreader

worst you'll only have one year of crab grass before you can use the premerge again.

Most Well-fed Lawns Are Starving!

Are you now wondering how a lawn could be well fed and starving at the same time? It depends on who is judging the menu and quality. Most of you probably feed your lawn early in the spring and a few, very few, feed in the fall. You may think that's adequate, but neither your lawn nor I consider that being well fed.

After you have dethatched and mowed, feed your lawn your brand of lawn food at *half* the recommended rate. Use a spiral or whirly type spreader (save up your pennies or ask Santa for one). The spiral spreader is the best professional machine available, but an Ortho whirly hand-held spreader will do fine. Apply the lawn food over the entire area—but remember, at *half* the recommended rate. You'll do this again in the fall. In between you'll use either a dry or a liquid lawn food every three weeks at 20 to 30 percent of the recommended rate.

Here is a guide to the feeding frequency needs of most grasses in the country.

	Jan.	Feb.	Mar.	Apr.	May	June	July	Aug.	Sept.	Oct.	Nov.	Dec.
Bahia					X							
Bermuda			X								X	
Bent			X						X			
Bluegrass				X					X		X	
Carpet grass				X					X			
Centipede				X					X			
Dichondra						X						
Fescue			X		X				X			
Zoysia			X							X		
St. Augustine			X						X			

The x's indicate the months when it is necessary to feed your lawn at half the recommended rate with a dry lawn food. Make sure you start at the right time this spring.

A Good Meal for Your Lawn

It's no secret that a well-fed lawn is thicker, tougher, and greener. Also remember that a lawn consists of millions of individual grass plants, crowded together, all competing for

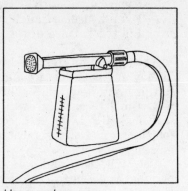

Old-fashioned push spreader   Hose-end sprayer

their share of food, water, and air. When we mow it short for the sake of appearance, we cut down the lawn's ability to manufacture its own food. To make up for the damage mowing does, we must give the lawn a helping hand. A good fertilizer is one that has the basic nutrients that grass depends on: nitrogen, phosphorous, and potassium. In addition to these three, your grass needs sulphur and iron. Look for lawn foods that contain these bonuses.

The real confusion comes when you try to figure out how much fertilizer to buy to cover your lawn area. Here is the formula that greens superintendents use:

> Measuring the area in feet, multiply the length by the width. Next, divide the answer by 10; now divide that answer by the amount of nitrogen (first number on the lawn food bag) in your choice of fertilizer. This will tell you exactly how many pounds you will need to buy to cover the area.
> $$L \times W \div 10 \div N = \text{pounds to buy}$$

Time for a Tonic!

My Grandma Putt, the lady who taught me most of what I know, always said that people, plants, and pets need a good tonic to get growing. Lawns are no exception. After you have dethatched, mowed, fertilized, and seeded in the spring, add this mixture to a hose-end sprayer (one that has a 15- to 20-gallon capacity or adjusts to 20 gallons—see the note below).

Grandma Putt's Spring Grass Tonic:

1 cup Epsom salts
1 cup Listerine mouthwash

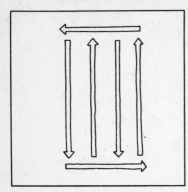

Spray or feed in this pattern for even coverage

1 cup liquid soap
1 cup household ammonia
Fill the balance of the quart jar with beer

Now, spray up to 2,500 square feet of lawn with the tonic in May and again in late June. You can use it to water after fertilizing to help the fertilizer soak into the soil. This tonic will stimulate early growth and encourage any thatch that was missed to begin to decompose and become organic food for the turf. Don't get carried away; a drunk lawn is disgusting!

Note: The hose-end sprayer is a very handy garden tool, one that you'll hear a lot about in this book. It is a quart jar that attaches to the nozzle end of your hose. It siphons the solution in the jar into the flow of water through the hose at a fixed ratio. In this case, you want to pick a sprayer that will control the ratio of solution to water so that when 15 to 20 gallons of water have passed through the hose, the one-quart solution of tonic will be gone. The most versatile models adjust so that you can change the ratio of solution to water simply by turning a dial.

Don't Wait for April Showers

Ever wonder why the grass is always greener at the end of the sump pump hose? (Did that sound like an Erma Bombeck line?) Grass loves a fairly regular drink and shower, and the sooner it gets a drink in the spring the faster it will turn green. Begin to water as early in the spring as you can. As the warm days approach, it will be necessary to water daily. Let each area covered by your sprinkler get 45 minutes to an hour of water each day before 2:00 P.M. Never water in the evening unless you are rich and foolish—fungicides cost a fortune!

There Are Good Lawn Sprinklers and Bad

No, I don't think you're dumb! Yes, if water comes out, it's good and if not, it's no good. That's not what I am referring to. It's how much water and in what pattern it is released that matters. The best method of watering a lawn area is an underground sprinkler system. It's the best for two reasons: first, you don't have to drag a hose around; and second, it applies the water in a uniform, cover-all pattern. Underground sprinkler systems come in a broad range of prices, so you should be able to find one to fit your pocketbook. As far as the ordinary sprinkler that fits on the end of a garden hose, I have found that the impulse head is far and away the hardest working and gives the best results. If you want to

Simple sprinkler

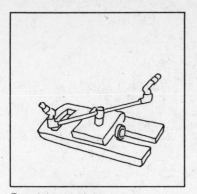

Revolving sprinkler

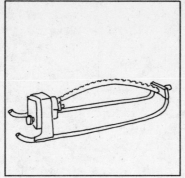

Oscillating sprinkler

Impulse-head sprinkler

get even more out of a sprinkler, set it up in the air. An impulse sprinkler at ground level covers about 3,000 square feet and at 5 feet in the air covers 8,000 square feet.

One Brush Cut a Season Is Enough

You can screw up a lawn quicker with a lawn mower than a thousand bugs at a lawn banquet. Improper mowing is a major reason for poor, scraggly lawns. Proper mowing not only keeps a lawn dense and neat, but also aids in maintaining the health of the grass so it can ward off diseases, insects, and weeds. Removing too much of the grass blade at one time shocks the plant's physiology, causing root-system reduction, as well as severely reducing its food manufacturing capacity. Lawn clippings that are too long do not filter to the soil surface where they can decompose naturally, but remain suspended within the living leaves to form a thick and often injurious layer of thatch.

Grass cut too tall does not produce a dense turf. When grass is cut too short, the plants weaken and thin.

For best results, a lawn should be mowed as frequently as necessary so that no more than one-third of the blade is removed at one clipping. Cut more frequently when grass is growing rapidly; less often when growth slows, in midsummer and when temperatures are cool. If grass becomes very long, mow it once at a 3-inch mower setting (no lower). Three to four days later, mow again at the desired height.

For best results:

- Use a sharp mower. A dull mower damages leaves, leaving ugly dead tips, which soon turn brown.

Late Spring and Summer Care

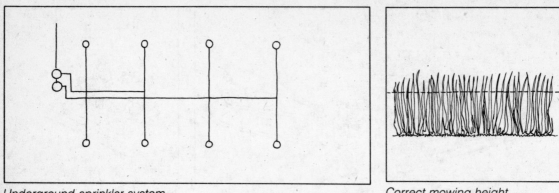

Underground sprinkler system

Correct mowing height

- Mow at the right height:
    Bermuda, centipede grass, bent grass
    and dichondra...................... ½ to 1 inch
    Kentucky bluegrass, fine leaf fescues
    and perennial ryegrass............. 1 to 2½ inches
    Tall fescue and Bahia grass......... 2 to 3 inches
- Never mow the grass when wet from rain, dew, or hose watering.
- Mow after 6 P.M.
- Pick up *all clippings*.
- Mow high enough to shade rhizomes.
- Change mowing pattern from time to time. A criss-cross pattern is best.
- Always mow *before* you feed, seed, or use chemicals.
- Never mow within 24 hours of feeding, seeding, and chemical treatment, and make sure you've watered at least once after these procedures before mowing.

Maintain maximum suggested mowing height when the weather is hot, in shade, during drought, under low fertility conditions or when wear and tear is a problem—in short, whenever the grass is under stress. Lower the cutting height when the weather is cool.

Note: When mowing a bluegrass lawn where Bermuda grass may be a problem, never mow lower than 1½ inches. This will reduce the possibility of an invasion by the lower-growing Bermuda grass.

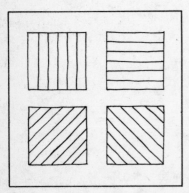

Good mowing patterns

Weeds Are a Lawn's Best Friend

Any good turf expert will tell you that where weeds grow, grass will grow better. However, your neighbors would prefer grass—and so would you. The most common troublemakers belong to the broadleaf family. The more common broadleaf weeds are:

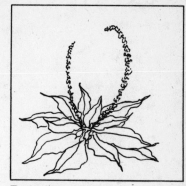

Typical broadleaf weed

Bedstraw	Knotweed	Ragweed
Black medic	Mallow	Sheep Sorrel
Buckhorn	Morning Glory	Speedwell
Buttercup	Lamb's-quarters	Shepherd's Purse
Chickweed	Lespedeza	Thistle
Chicory	Oxalis	Spurgis
Clover	Pepper Grass	Wild Carrot
Dandelion	Pigweed	Wild Garlic
Dock	Plantains	Wild Lettuce
Ground Ivy	Poison Ivy	Wild Onion
Heal-all	Poison Oak	Yarrow
Henbit	Purslane	

As their name suggests, they are recognizable by their broad leaves. They can *only* be controlled when they are growing vigorously. Don't try to zap them early—it won't work. Liquid weed controls work best, but the spray can drift to other plants in your yard and kill them. I have found the most effective liquid control of most broadleaf weeds to be a combination of 2, 4-D, MCPP and Banvell. I buy it in the Super K-Gro label at K Mart. It can be used on both northern and southern lawns.

Dry "weed and feeds" are easier and safer than liquid weed killers, but they're only partially effective. If you use them, fine, but don't bother with them before the weeds are growing strongly, and don't expect them to provide a real meal for your lawn.

I have found that the plastic hose-end sprayers are reasonably cheap and a good way to apply liquid lawn killer. Make sure everyone knows that this particular sprayer is for *weed killer only*; you don't want someone using it to spray the rosebushes and killing them off! You can paint it red or some other bright color to make it stand out from any other sprayers you keep around.

Never spray weed killers on a windy day, even on a lightly breezy day. Otherwise you'll kill your whole garden. And for Pete's sake, keep the sprayer down below your waist. Spray out in front of you and down as close to your feet as possible. This little trick will prevent the spray from drifting and killing innocent plant bystanders.

Liquid Lawn Food, a Chlorophyl Cooler

I receive thousands of letters weekly, and again and again I am asked, "Is liquid lawn food better than dry?" Well, guess what—your lawn doesn't really give a darn what kind

Label sprayer used for weed killer

Point sprayer away from you and down

you feed it. But frequency and blend do have a great deal to do with the final appearance and health of your lawn. Assuming that you've applied a dry lawn food at one-half the recommended rate in the early spring as described on page 4, you can safely use a liquid lawn food during the late spring and summer for supplemental feedings. In the fall you will have to give another feeding of dry lawn food at one-half the recommended rate (see the chart on page 4). A straight liquid diet over a prolonged period of time (two or three years) will weaken and eventually destroy a lawn.

If you opt for the liquid food, Rapid-Gro or Ortho-Gro is a good choice, and Frank's and K Mart both have an excellent product. They can be applied with one of the lawn and garden sprayers that attaches to your garden hose. The Burgess Lawn Feeder that attaches to your sprinkler and automatically feeds your lawn while you go about your other garden chores is also an excellent applicator. If you decide to use the dry lawn food, apply it with one of the small, handy Ortho whirly spreaders at the number 2 setting. (This little spreader is a must in any gardener's tool shed.) Either type of food should be applied at 20 to 30 percent of the recommended rate.

Punch Up Your Lawn

Since you are interested in saving money, time, and effort and ending up with the greenest scene on the block in front of your house, I suggest that you give your lawn a little punch in July and early August. Hook up the hose-end sprayer again and fill with household ammonia and spray over 5,000 square feet. It doesn't smell great, but your lawn loves it.

Bug Out Your Lawn

Geezo Pete! The way you waste money on lawn chemicals, you folks must all have a fortune buried in mason jars in the backyard. No, I know that's not true—I mean about the mason jars, because you bury them upside-down! Did you know that Americans spend better than $16 million a year on lawn and garden products, two-thirds of which are not necessary? So just use your common sense and save the copper.

Most lawn insects can be controlled with a chemical called Diazinon. It is packaged under many brand names, so be smart and shop for the best price. Apply it after you have done all of the jobs previously mentioned, but only if you actually had bugs last fall. Always punch or poke holes into the soil in the area to be treated before you apply lawn chemicals for insects and disease. Golf spikes, track shoes, garden spikes or a board with nails driven through and a handle attached will all do nicely. Repeat again in mid-September if they showed up this summer. I find that a granular form is more effective.

If mosquitoes are a problem, then spray the grass with Methoxychlor. Again, shop! Methoxychlor is the safe substitute for DDT and can be used to destroy gypsy moths, inch worms, Japanese beetles and many more. Dursban and Aspon are also very effective for cinch bugs and other soil insects.

The most common lawn insects are:

Ants	Clover Mites	Leaf Hoppers
Billbugs	Crickets	Millipedes
Chafer Grubs	Cutworms	Sod Webworms
Chiggers	Grass Thrips	Southern Armyworms
Church Bugs	Japanese Beetle Grubs	Spring Tails

Lawn Diseases Drive You and Your Wallet Nuts!

If you think medical bills for your kids or pet are high, just let your lawn catch what science refers to as a turf disease. Here are the most common, and the recommended controls:

Fungus Diseases and Organisms

Diseases	*Control*
Brown Patch	Acti-dione, Benomyl, Bayleton
Cottony Blight	Acti-dione, Benomyl, Bayleton
Dollar Spot	Acti-dione, Benomyl
Fading-out	Acti-dione, Captan, Zineb
Fairy Rings	Fore

Fusarium Blight	Bayleton (prevention), Benomyl (cure)
Grease Spot	Acti-dione, Captan, Zineb
Leaf Spot	Acti-dione, Captan, Zineb
Powdery Mildew	Bayleton, Fore
Rust	Acti-dione, Maneb, Zineb, Bayleton
Slime Mold	Acti-dione, Captan, Zineb
Snow Mold	Bayleton
Toadstools	Liquid dishsoap

Since we both know you are not one to do heavy research, my suggestion is to clip or dig up a small sample of a suspected disease and take it to your local garden center operator for identification.

Fusarium Blight

Fusarium blight is the number-one turf disease. It is caused by pathogens and fungi that attack the lawn grasses. Because turf grasses vary in their susceptibility to diseases, occurrence is sporadic and varied, depending largely on environment and growing conditions. Chemical control requires application of fungicides, which are expensive, and there are no fungicides that control all diseases. Here is an explanation of this disease, its characteristics, and possible controls, both cultural and chemical:

Active Time of Year: Late spring to early fall.
Signs and Symptoms

- Small, scattered light-green patches of turf turning reddish brown and later light tan. Shapes of patches are elongated streaks or areas.
- "Frog-eye" patterns in turf of healthy grass surrounded by border of dead reddish brown grass.
- Diseased grass found in exposed areas subject to heat and drought stress.
- Lesion on grass blade begins as light-green blotch; later turns straw-colored with uneven brown border and streaks of brown.

Conditions Favoring Disease Development

- Dry, exposed turf, particularly on southern exposures, or near paved areas subjected to heat and drought.
- Excess thatch
- Compacted soil
- High temperatures (80° to 95° F) and high humidity
- Excess soluble nitrogen during summer months
- Pure stands (only one variety) of susceptible turf

Comments: Fusarium blight is most often a problem with grasses on compacted soils or on exposed areas subject to drought. Sodded lawns of 'Merion' and 'Bensun' (A-34) are very susceptible, particularly if peat-grown sod is laid over heavy clay without providing a transition between the two different soil types. The peat-clay interface prevents proper penetration of water and chemicals, encouraging surface rooting and rapid drying. Seeded lawns rarely have this problem. Aerating the soil will aid penetration, and the lawn should be watered thoroughly during dry periods. Fungicide applications alone have little effect on Fusarium blight. Ideally, the soil should be wet before applying a systemic fungicide such as Tersan 1991 and the chemical should be thoroughly drenched into the root zone with 300 to 600 gallons of water per 1,000 square feet (½ to 1 inch of water).

Culture Control

- Keep grass growing vigorously, but do not encourage rapid succulent growth in summer.
- Aerate compacted soils.
- Do not mow when turf is wet.
- Remove excess thatch.
- Mow frequently at recommended height or slightly higher.
- Seed or sod with resistant turfgrass varieties (refer to the county agricultural extension agent for your area).
- Water thoroughly during dry periods.

Chemical Control: If Fusarium blight is a problem, a chemical called Bayleton, manufactured by Mobay Chemical Company in Kansas City, applied in early spring will prevent it from appearing. A summer application of Benomyl, packaged under many brand names, will stop it from spreading. Keep your lawn well watered, well fed, and cut at the right height during the hot, dry periods and you should be safe from worry.

Let Your Lawn Work Up a Good Lather

If I am known for any one piece of advice that people really think is nuts, until they try it, it's my recommendation to use soap on the lawn. That's right—plain, old-fashioned soap. Spray your lawn with dishwashing soap every two or three weeks through the spring and summer. In hot, dry periods it is even more important. Soap improves penetration of water in the dry soil; it removes airborn pollution from the blades so osmosis can take place. It makes bugs sick and lawn diseases (as well as toadstools) wish they never were born. Add a cup or two of any liquid dishwashing soap (cheap, cheap,

cheap) to your hose-end sprayer (15- to 20-gallon size) and let it rip. Don't doubt me, try it!

Summer Tonic

Even with all of the modern techniques, chemicals, and products available for maintaining a good-looking lawn, I still find that Grandma Putt's lawn tonic in late July ensures my lawn's devoted friendship. This tonic is sort of a picnic for my lawn—an extra bonus for keeping my little corner of the world green. Into the jar that fits on to my garden hose (15- to 20-gallon capacity) I add:

Grandma Putt's Summer Grass Tonic:

1 cup of household ammonia
1 cup of Epsom salts
1 cup of Listerine mouthwash
½ cup of liquid soap
2 cans of beer

Spray this solution over 2,500 square feet of lawn after you have mowed it of an evening. Let the neighbors laugh; the results will let you have the last laugh and the greenest grass!

Fall Care   Don't Give Up Yet!

A great number of you folks are probably so discouraged by now with the looks of your lawn that you don't give a hoot about this time of the year. You have tried every fertilizer there is, spent a fortune on weed killers and fungicides, mowed until *you* turned green and your lawn brown. I guess I can't blame you; most of us have been through your frustration until we learned the art of *doing the right thing at the right time*. Mix this with a few good tricks and a shortcut or two and you will be off, growing and crowing again.

Let's begin with a little knowledge that will help you get in the right frame of mind. The first day of spring is August 15. No, I'm not stupid! What I mean is that Mother Nature sows her seeds at this time of the year. Fruit drops to the ground and the seeds are released. If you sow grass seed between August 15 and September 30, no matter what region you live in, you will be so surprised and proud of the results that your buttons will pop right off your shirt. If you didn't get rid of the weeds that marred your lawn, now is the time—even better than April or May. Now sit back, relax, and rest because you are going to need it, and I am going to take you through fall lawn care step by step.

Step 1. *Dethatch*

You must remove thatch from your lawn area. If you don't, you will just be wasting your time, money, and effort. Once you dethatch, get in the habit of picking up your grass clippings each time you mow. Spray your lawn in May and July with Grandma Putt's grass tonics. You should get away with five years in between dethatching.

Step 2. *Mow low*

In late fall drop your lawn mower blade as low as you can without scalping your lawn or straining the mower. This one-time low mowing will get rid of the tall grass that bugs and disease hide in over the winter. Be sure that you pick up the clippings.

Step 3. *Fertilize*

If you've had trouble with weeds and you do not intend to overseed this fall, go buy the least expensive bag of weed and feed you can find. There should be tons of sales right now (don't be afraid of broken-bag bargains). To figure out how much of this product to buy for your lawn, see page 5.

If you are going to overseed, forget the weed killers, dry or liquid, and just use dry lawn food.

If weeds are no problem, feed dry lawn food at half the recommended rate. Use a broadcast type spreader for efficiency and speed.

Step 4. *Soil Conditioning*

Spread lime now! I don't care what others tell you, try it my way. If you want a super green, healthy lawn next season, no matter where you live—north, south, east, or west—spread Sof'n-Soil lawn and garden gypsum (a U.S. Gypsum product) this fall, right along with your lime—50 pounds per 1,500 square feet. In the north, along with all of the other good things it does, gypsum will prevent rock salt damage and dog waste damage. In the south it will also constipate cinch bugs and aggravate any others.

Step 5. *Overseed*

If necessary, overseed between August 15 and September 20. In the north use 70 percent Kentucky bluegrass and 30 percent fine-blade ryegrass. In the south use the turf-type ryegrasses at 10 pounds per 1,000 square feet. Use the little Ortho whirly hand-spreader.

Step 6. *Mist*

Lightly mist new seed and young grass until you have cut it three times.

Step 7. *Top Dress*

Lightly dress with *sharp sand* that has no weed seed in it. (Sharp sand, also called builder's sand, has larger particles than beach sand and resists compacting.)

Step 8. *Fall Tonic*

In late September or early October make a solution of

> 2 cups Epsom salts
> 2 cups liquid soap
> 3 tablespoons baking powder
> 1 cup tobacco juice*
> Fill balance of quart jar with water

Use a hose-end lawn sprayer of 15- to 20-gallon capacity to spray the tonic over 1,500 square feet.

Step 9. *Debug*

Spray with Diazinon as recommended (look for bargains—Diazinon is Diazinon). More than likely you will have little or no insect problems next season.

Step 10. *The Last Supper*

In both north and south feed in late October/November with an organic lawn food like Milorganite or other sludge-based lawn food. This is what the greatest and brightest bunch of turf experts in the world (golf course superintendents) do to prevent winter diseases from rearing their ugly heads next season.

Step 11. *Keep On Mowing . . .*

After you've followed all ten steps above, move your lawn mower blade back up to normal height and continue to mow till the grass stops growing.

That's it folks! Grow to it.

---

*To make tobacco juice, tie three fingers of Beechnut chewing tobacco in an old nylon stocking and soak it in a pint of hot water overnight.

What if you've tried to do everything right and your lawn still looks lousy? Cheer up; poor lawns can be improved. Healthy grass plants can increase in density and produce good lawns. The first step toward improving your lawn is to determine what went wrong with it. This handy list can help you pinpoint the problem and the likely solution.

First Aid for Lawns

Symptom:

Thin or bare spots in lawn.

Problem:

Compaction. Caused by heavy traffic or change in soil structure due to aging.

Cure:

Aerate to open up soil. Aeration is the process of penetrating the soil to below the root area to allow expansion and get oxygen to the roots. Spikes attached to a light roller, golf shoes or gardener's spike shoes, a hand-pulled spiker all will help to do this necessary job. If a lawn roller is used, it should only weigh enough to press the grass plants into contact with the soil.

Reduce traffic if possible. Good healthy grass can withstand a surprising amount of wear. In some areas, however, it may be impossible to prevent very heavy traffic, resulting in bare or thin spots.

Try creating a pathway by paving the worn area with a few pieces of flagstone or brick. Then seed around the stone or brick with a mixture containing the new fine-leafed perennial ryegrasses, which are noted for their wear tolerance and establishment ability in compacted soil.

Symptom:

Grass appears thin and covered with white powder.

Problem:

Lack of light or poor air circulation.

Cure:

Thin tree canopies to allow a sprinkling of sunlight. Trim trees higher and open up hedges to allow more air movement. If the lawn doesn't respond to this new treatment, you may have to introduce new shade-resistant strains of grass into your lawn. Fine-leafed fescues are very tolerant to shade and blend well with other grasses.

Symptom:

Grass blades become very dry and thin.

Problem:

Lack of water.

Cure:

Increase watering frequency and water deeply. Adequately fertilized grass is more efficient in its use of water, so make sure you are feeding properly. Cut grass taller (the longer blades provide shape to help prevent moisture loss).

If watering restrictions are a yearly problem, you can adapt your lawn to lack of water in several ways:

• Seed or overseed with grasses that require less water. Both tall and fine fescues fall into this category.
• Mow at the maximum desirable height for your variety of grass.
• Fertilize regularly, but do not exceed the fertilization schedule recommended in this book.
• Water deeply (8 to 12 inches) whenever you can.
• Water before 2:00 P.M. to prevent loss from evaporation.
• Control weeds. They use water too, and often thrive under drier conditions to the detriment of your grass.

Symptom:

A heavy buildup of decaying grass clippings between the blades of grass.

Problem:

Excess thatch.

Cure:

Remove thatch. Rent a mechanical rake or dethatcher, or rake the lawn by hand. Mow more often. Pick up clippings after every mowing.

Symptom:

Grass appears yellow or grayish in color.

Problem:

Lawn is too acid, too wet, or improperly fertilized.

Cure:

Correct soil condition with an application of lime. Don't water lawn after 2:00 P.M. Feed lawn regularly with a fertilizer especially designed for turf. Pick up all grass clippings so that fertilizer can penetrate the soil.

Symptom:

Crabgrass or broad-leaf weeds.

Problem:

Improper weed control, thin lawn, or overly vulnerable varieties of grass.

Cure:

Use pre-emerge weed controls on crabgrass *before* the crabgrass germinates. Use liquid weed killers or "weed and feed" on broadleaf weeds *after* they are growing vigorously. Thicken lawn by overseeding and fertilizing. Introduce hardier varieties of grass if necessary.

Symptom:

Recurrence of lawn diseases or pests.

Problem:

Low resistance of turf to invasion and stress.

Cure:

Use a mixture of grasses to obtain a broader range of disease and insect resistance and to improve the adaptability of the lawn to climatic and management variables. Lawn diseases tend to attack one variety of grass at a time, leaving the others unharmed. By planting a quality mixture of improved varieties, you are reducing the chances of lawn areas being wiped out by a single disease or pest.

Often you'll find that your lawn problems will respond to just a little more attention. But sometimes it may be that you are growing the wrong kind of grass or that your lawn is too unhealthy to come back. If that's the case, you'll have to either repair or completely reseed your lawn. Which solution you choose will depend on the extent of the damage to your existing lawn. If 50 percent of the soil or more is bare or covered with weeds, it is best to start over. If more than 50 percent of the lawn is covered with good grass, renovation is usually possible. Either way, before you do anything, you'll have to figure out what kind of grass seed you should be sowing.

Know Your Grass Seeds! Or Else . . .

Or else you may have a real collection of weeds or unattractive varieties of grass growing in your front yard. Some grass varieties are really meant for hay fields, not front lawns.

Northrup King Seed Company, one of America's largest seed firms, in their bulletin LS-507-8, gives the inside infor-

Varieties of Grass

mation on how not to get stung buying grass seed as well as what to expect from each variety. The bulletin states that grass seed is not just grass seed. Each kind represents different species and each specie has different growth characteristics. Each specie is further divided into individual cultivars (varieties) with more specific characteristics. Properly combined, mixtures of these grasses can produce superior lawns. Here are the most common kinds of grasses found in commercial mixtures:

Cool Season Grasses

These grasses seem to perform best north of the Mason-Dixon line. They prefer cool nights and moderately warm days. Mostly fine textured, they make an attractive, dense turf.

Kentucky Bluegrass. Often called the queen of grasses, it's by far the most popular for home lawns. Bluegrass is very durable; it bounces back well from drought and heavy traffic. It spreads through underground rhizomes (rootlike stems that produce new plants) and develops a thick, tough root system. (It is the primary grass used to produce sod.) Bluegrass requires moderate care to maintain its beauty. A number of improved varieties are available with specific adaptation to shade, poor soils, etc.

Perennial Ryegrass (fine-leafed types). This is a recent development in lawn grasses, combining the narrow blades of bluegrass with the rapid establishment of the old, coarse-leafed ryegrasses. These grasses can produce an especially tough turf that resists wear and tear, recovers quickly from damage, and increases the versatility of lawns for recreational purposes. Vigorous root growth penetrates even compacted soils and makes these grasses great for overseeding old and thin lawns. These perennial ryegrasses are compatible with bluegrass and fine-leafed fescue in mixtures.

Perennial Ryegrass (coarse types). These unimproved ryegrasses have coarse-textured leaves that do not blend well with finer grasses. They are semipermanent, each plant living for two years. The plants that remain after one year often produce a weedlike appearance.

Annual Ryegrass. This grass is coarse-leafed, but fast-growing and tough. Often used, especially in inexpensive mixtures, for quick cover and to prevent erosion on slopes. Generally lasts only one season. Not overly aggressive with other grasses.

Bent Grasses. These are especially adapted to humid areas (seacoast, etc.). They spread by aboveground rhizomes. Very aggressive, they require frequent mowing and dethatching, and have high fertility requirements. While often used on golf courses, bent grasses are not recommended for home lawns.

Tall Fescue. This grass is adapted primarily for lawns in the middle section of the United States, where neither the cool season grasses, like Kentucky bluegrass, nor the warm season grasses, such as Bermuda grass, will do well. While coarse bladed, it provides a year-round turf not obtainable from other species. In areas where finer-bladed grasses can be used, tall fescue is considered unattractive and weedlike. It grows under low fertility (as little as 25 percent of recommended levels), but requires moderate fertility (75 percent of recommendation) to maintain density and avoid thinning out.

White Clover. Sometimes added to lawns to enrich soil, as clover replaces nitrogen used by grasses. Clover, however, chokes out desirable grasses as it spreads, and the white flower can detract from the rest of the lawn.

Warm Season Grasses

These grasses are used in the southern portion of the United States, as well as in other subtropic regions around the world. A great number of southern grasses can be grown from plant materials only, but these often are regarded as weeds in other parts of the country. Only those that can be propagated from seed are listed here.

Bermuda Grass. This is the preferred grass for use in most southern and southwestern states. Very fast growing, it spreads by aboveground stems. It provides dense cover that chokes out weeds and competing grasses. Withstands wear and tear; a good choice for recreational lawns. Needs full sun and continuing care for good results.

Centipede Grass. This is a low-maintenance grass for southern lawns. Does well in acid soils. Medium leaf width, produces a relatively low turf.

Bahia Grass. Produces a coarse, open turf. It is used for low-maintenance lawns. Moderately tolerant to shade, grows rapidly.

Dichondra. Not a true grass at all, but a low-growing relative of the morning glory used extensively as ground cover in the west and southwest. It has a rich green color; spreads by underground runners. The large leaf area shades ground, preventing drying out by the sun. Dichondra does well in sun, and is adaptable to partial shade.

How to Read a Grass Seed Label

Fine-textured Grasses. This category includes bluegrass, fine-leafed fescues, and bent grasses. A good rule of thumb: Use grass seed mixtures that contain at least 60 percent fine-textured grasses.

Note: The fine-leafed perennial ryegrasses have been developed since this category was established and must, by regulation, be listed as coarse-textured grasses on grass seed labels. They are, however, as narrow bladed as Kentucky bluegrass, and the manufacturer's label will advertise them as such.

Coarse-textured Grasses. These broad-bladed grasses are not usually considered desirable for attractive lawns. This group includes both annual and the older perennial ryegrass and tall fescue. These grasses do not blend well with the fine-textured grasses in a lawn, and persistent plants often give a weedy appearance to turf.

Contents/Percentage. Indicates the percentage of the total mixture made up of the listed species and brand names of grasses.

Germination. Indicates the percentage of live seeds of each species and brand name of grass in the mixture. Obviously, a higher germination percentage increases your chances of obtaining a successful seeding. A percentage above 85 percent is acceptable.

Crop Seed. Expressed in percentage of total mixture. Look for a low number (2 percent or less). Crop generally indicates very coarse productive grasses unsuited to home lawns, rather than the decorative grass you desire. Not all crop seeds are a problem, but a significant number of some types can ruin the looks of a good lawn.

Weeds. Expressed in percentage of total mixture. Many weeds will disappear from a lawn during the first season's mowing. However, others can be more permanent. Look for a low number when purchasing seed. Premium quality grass seed mixtures carry very little weed seed.

Inert Matter. A percentage of the total contents not consisting of seed. Should be as low as possible, but it is often difficult to mill out completely bits of plant leaf, dirt, and chaff. Because of its small seed size, Kentucky bluegrass is especially difficult to clean. Mixtures with a high percentage of Kentucky bluegrass will often have a correspondingly higher amount of inert ingredients.

Origin. Indicates the locality where seed was produced. For named varieties (e.g., Baron's Kentucky Bluegrass as opposed to Kentucky bluegrass in general), the area of production has no bearing on the adaptation of the seed for planting a lawn in another part of the United States.

Test Date. Indicates the date when the mixture was tested to determine percentage of each variety and germination percentage. Look for current test dates on labels (although under proper storage conditions, grass seed maintains its germination percentage very well).

Poa Annua (annual bluegrass). Often listed separately or under the heading "noxious weeds," this undesirable relative of Kentucky bluegrass grows vigorously and seeds itself in one season. Quality grass seed mixtures should be virtually free of Poa annua seeds.

Seed Size. Grass seed mixtures are sold by weight. The percentage of each kind and variety of seed is listed on the package. However, grass seeds are not all of the same size. For example, Kentucky bluegrass has a very small seed compared to varieties of fine fescue. Therefore, there are many more bluegrass seeds per pound of mixture than fine fescue seeds. Premium mixtures are usually formulated to produce a balance between grass plants, once the lawn is established, so the seed size will vary.

Starting a New Lawn from Seed

If you decide that your lawn needs to be started over from scratch, you're taking a big step. How you start a new lawn will influence its performance and the satisfaction you will receive from your outdoor living space for years to come. A little extra time and money spent in lawn preparation and quality grass seed will pay big dividends. Here are a few things to keep in mind.

Aesthetic Considerations

- Plan a sweeping, open lawn.
- Grade the lawn downward from the house, both for appearance and to keep the foundation dry.
- A sloping or undulating lawn is more graceful than one that is absolutely flat.
- Complement your lawn with gently curving beds of shrubs, trees, and flowers. But don't clutter the middle of your lawn with ornamental plantings.

Technical Considerations

- Stockpile your topsoil for use after the subgrading has been completed.
- Sandy loam soils often produce better lawns than heavy clay soils. Sandy soils can be modified to hold more water and fertility. Spread 3 to 4 inches of peat or peat moss and not more than 1 inch of clay over the area. Spade or rototill this layer into the soil 6 to 8 inches deep. Little can be done with heavy clay soils except through the use of surface grading to increase drainage. Sometimes drain tile (a kind of clay pipe sold in garden centers) will help.
- Because phosphate and potassium do not move readily through the soil, these fertilizer elements need to be worked into the top 6 to 8 inches of soil with a spade or rototill before preparing the final seedbed.
- A loose seedbed soon produces an uneven and, therefore, unsatisfactory lawn. Thorough settling of the soil before seeding is very important. Either let it settle for a week or two before seeding or roll it with a half-filled lawn roller.
- No one grass is perfect for all conditions. Plant a mixture of grass species, choosing them carefully for your area. It is more difficult to add improved grasses at a later date. Spending a few dollars for quality grass seed will pay off later.

When to Plant

The best seasons for establishing a new lawn are late summer (July 4 to August 15) and early fall (August 15 to September 20), or as early in the spring as possible. Annual weeds are much less aggressive in late summer than in spring. Moderate temperatures during this period encourage root growth.

Steps in Lawn Preparation

Step 1.

Control weeds. Get rid of persistent weeds such as quack grass, orchard grass and Dallas grass. They will cause you perennial trouble if not eliminated. Fallowing and digging may give partial control. Herbicides should be considered. Use chemicals that control persistent weeds without leaving a residual effect in the soil, such as any broadleaf weed killer.

Spray to kill weeds before preparing new lawn

Step 2.

Remove debris and stockpile topsoil. Do not bury lumber, tree stumps, etc. Waste wood is a source of a disease called fairy ring. Also, as wood rots, soil will settle, causing unevenness. Topsoil should be saved to be placed over the new subgrade.

Step 3.

Cultivate the subgrade with a rake to loosen and to allow regrading to meet your contour requirements. Subgrade should follow planned final grade. Minimum slope away from the buildings should be 1 percent.

Step 4.

Ensure adequate drainage. On heavy soils, install subsurface tile drainage. Consider the new plastic drainage tubing as an easy solution.

Step 5.

Spread topsoil to a uniform depth of 4 to 6 inches. If subsoil

Remove debris

Cultivate and regrade the subsoil

Spread topsoil evenly over subsoil

Spread fertilizer

Rototill the fertilizer into the topsoil

and topsoil differ significantly in composition, mix 2 to 3 inches of topsoil with 2 to 3 inches of subsoil before adding the remainder of the topsoil.

Step 6.

Fertilize. Work a high phosphate fertilizer into the top 6 inches of soil. If your area is naturally low in potash (ask your lawn supply dealer), add potash as well. Soil tests can aid in determining proper balance. In lieu of a soil test, add 4 pounds of a 5-10-5 formulation fertilizer, or equivalent, per 1,000 square feet. Rototill the fertilizer into the top 6 inches.

Step 7.

Complete the surface grade by raking and rolling, or drag a weighted ladder over the surface to level high spots and fill low areas. *Note:* Often the top 1 or 2 inches pack down, leav-

Level the surface grade by rolling

Loosen surface soil to allow for seed coverage

ing a loose subsoil to settle over the next few months. For best results, thoroughly soak the soil to fill the loose pockets: then loosen and redrag the surface when it has dried.

Step 8.

Prepare surface soil. Loosen top ½ to 1 inch of soil to allow for seed coverage. Soil clods or lumps of ½ to 1 inch are okay. They help keep the soil from crusting.

Step 9.

Spread seed. Use a high-quality seed mixture and a good lawn fertilizer, following manufacturer's directions on the packages. For best results, use a mechanical spreader. Distribute one-half of the fertilizer and seed over the area from north to south, and the other half from east to west. This procedure prevents your missing any spots.

Step 10.

Cover the seed and the fertilizer. Use the back of a leaf rake, or fashion a drag from an old carpet remnant weighted with 2 × 4's. For best results, do not cover the seed deeper than ⅛ to ¼ inch. Twenty percent of the seed remaining on the surface is okay.

Step 11.

Mulch. Consider adding an organic mulch after you've covered the seed. The mulch will rest on the surface, keeping it from drying, and may aid germination. However, keep the mulch thin enough so some light penetrates to the surface. Light aids the germination of grass seed.

Spread seed in a crisscross pattern

Drag to cover seed

Water enough to keep the surface moist

Step 12.

Water. While establishing the lawn, sprinkle water to keep the surface always moist, but never saturated. Two or three light sprinklings a day are better than extended soakings at this time. Continue this practice for two to three weeks or until the grass seedlings are well established.

Postestablishment Treatment

- Fertilize using a high nitrogen–low phosphate lawn formulation at one-half recommended rate when the grass is approximately 2 inches tall.
- When the grass reaches about 2½ inches in height, begin mowing, setting the cutting height at 1½ inches.
- Water when needed. Reduce frequency and increase depth of water penetration at each setting. Surface should dry between waterings.
- Weed control. Most weeds will mow out during the first season. To speed the process, broad-leaf weeds can be controlled with herbicides. Perennial weeds must be dug or selectively controlled by herbicides. See your lawn products dealer for his recommendation. Follow label directions when applying any lawn chemical to avoid damage to grass and shrubs.

What to Expect from Your New Lawn

The first few weeks after planting a new lawn may be disappointing. Depending on the type of mixture used and the weather conditions, here is what you can expect during the first month or six weeks.

First Two Weeks. You won't see much; depending on temperature, availability of moisture, and fertility, the first seedlings will begin to poke through the soil. A little trick to reassure yourself is to kneel or lie down with your eye as close to the surface of the ground as possible and look across the seedbed. A faint green sheen will indicate the appearance of the first seedlings. Expect a few weeds. All nonfumigated soils contain weed seeds. (Fewer weeds will germinate during fall establishment than during spring establishment.) Good quality grass seed will contain few weeds, and none that will be troublesome after the first season.

The Third and Fourth Weeks. Some lawns will be ready for cutting. Mixtures containing ryegrasses and fine fescues will establish faster than the bluegrasses. However, some varieties of all species are faster establishing than other varieties.

The times given above are approximate. Cool weather can delay sprouting by many days. Infrequent and inadequate watering will also result in seedlings dying and, consequently, producing a thin stand. Overwatering and high temperatures often bring diseases, which thin grass. Don't be discouraged. Many lawns may look thin at six or even eight weeks after planting and yet develop into a beautiful and sturdy turf.

Repairing an Old Lawn

If you don't need to start your lawn all over, but you still want to do a little renovation, first correct any problems in your lawn management program; then follow these suggestions:

When to Overseed

Overseeding means broadcasting or spreading grass seed over an existing lawn without elaborately preparing the seedbed as for a new lawn. It is the best way to thicken a lawn or introduce new varieties of grass.

Overseed in early fall or early spring. If you have any serious seeding to do, the ideal time is between August 20 and September 20. If you missed the growing train last fall, get the seed on the ground by April 15. Trust me; this way works best!

You can spot-seed all season but you have to fool the seed a little. Add one cup of tea to each pound of seed, cover and place in the refrigerator (not the freezer) for 36 to 48 hours. After the refrigeration cycle, spread the seed on a dry concrete surface (the concrete helps take moisture out faster) to dry well enough to handle. Rough up the soil area to be seeded and spread the seed. Cover lightly with a thin layer of soil and press down with your foot or appropriate weight and then run like hell—'cause it's going to grow the same way! This method of seed treatment can be used on fall-sown seed to speed up sprouting time, but it's not necessary then.

Seed Variety	Needed Rate per 1,000 Square Feet for Full Stand
Bluegrass	1½ pounds
Fine fescue	3 pounds
Bent	¾ pound
Fall fescue	8 pounds

| Ryegrass | 4 pounds |
| Poa trivialis | 2 pounds |

Grass Variety, Planted by Plug	Number per Foot
Bermuda	1 plug per foot
St. Augustine	1 plug per foot
Zoysia	1 plug per foot

Eleven Easy Steps to an Almost New Lawn

Each of these steps can be done by hand, but mechanical help is also available through your lawn seed dealer or a rental equipment company.

Step 1. *Dethatch*

Use a mechanical or hand rake to remove the dead, thatchy layer from the soil surface (seed must be in contact with the soil to ensure seedling establishment).

Step 2. *Mow*

Cut the grass as short as your mower will allow and remove the clippings. This reduces the competition from the old grass plants and will give your new seedlings a head start.

Note: If your lawn consists of patches of undesirable grasses and weeds, you may wish to kill the old lawn. Chemicals are available to make this job easy. Use a chemical that does not leave a residual effect in the soil (the label will tell you if it does).

Step 3. *Loosen Soil Surface*

This is done by hand raking or by setting the mechanical rake to cut grooves ¼ inch deep in the soil surface (seed falling into grooves has a better environment for germination).

Step 4. *Spread Seed*

Uniformly spread seed over prepared seedbed. Use a quality seed mixture. The new fine-leafed perennial ryegrasses have the ability to start fast and penetrate old soils. Take this opportunity to introduce improved fine-bladed fescues and Kentucky bluegrasses, if they are adapted to your area, to upgrade the quality of your lawn.

Step 5. *Cover Seed*

Lightly cover seed by raking, top dressing with soil or peat moss, or running a mechanical rake at right angles to the direction of the original grooves. Some seed should remain on the surface.

Step 6. *Mulch*

Consider applying a thin layer of organic mulch to aid surface moisture retention. *Caution:* The layer of mulch must be thin enough to allow a little light penetration to the surface.

Step 7. *Roll Surface*

If the prepared soil is loose, it may be necessary to firm the surface with a light roller. If firm, this step can be skipped.

Step 8. *Water*

Begin light waterings to keep the surface moist, but never soaking wet. Continue until seedlings are well established.

Step 9. *Mow Regularly*

Keep lawn cut short until new grass plants are well established. Then raise mower to normal maintenance height.

Step 10. *Fertilize*

When the new grass plants are old enough to have been mowed two or three times, an application of lawn fertilizer can be made to stimulate their development.

Step 11. *Maintain*

When the new grass is well established, follow normal maintenance procedures.

Repairing Bare Spots

When localized bare spots develop, they can be quickly repaired by hand. This can be done in the early spring or early fall.

1. Loosen the soil surface with a cultivation tool or rake.
2. Apply lawn fertilizer and quality lawn seed to the surface. *Note:* Use a preplant fertilizer, not a standard formulation for established lawns.
3. Lightly cover the seed with soil by topdressing or raking.
4. Apply a light layer of organic mulch.
5. Firm the surface by gentle foot pressure.
6. Keep the soil surface moist until the new seedlings are well established. Maintain the lawn in a normal manner.

Touch Up

Often a lawn requires only a little extra bolstering with seed. Analyze the situation, then follow those steps listed above that seem useful. Lightly reseed thin areas with an appropriate quality seed mixture.

Lawn Sod

Why Use Sod?

Sodding is unquestionably a superior way to make a new lawn: There is no waiting, and it may be done at any time from May to November. In the warm climates this job can be started at almost any time. Bluegrass, as a rule, makes the best lawn for sod in the cool climates and is most suitable for full sun or very light shade. For shaded areas, you will get the best results from seeding a fescue blend. Sod is easy to establish on banks. If you have had difficulty with shade areas in the past, you might consider the use of a ground cover.

How Much Sod?

If you are in doubt as to how many rolls of sod you will need to cover your area, here is the simple mathematical formula. Multiply the length (in feet) by the width of each area to be sodded and then divide by nine; this will tell you how many rolls to buy.

$$L \times W \div 9 = \text{rolls to buy}$$

Soil Preparation

Good topsoil must be *at least* 4 inches deep. Rake out the surface to level and remove stones: The soil surface should be settled ¾ inch below normal grade. Roll, water, and roll again, as for a new lawn. A footprint less than ¼ inch deep should result if soil is properly settled. Shallow depths will show up early as discolored patches in the lawn and will start to brown.

Spread a layer of complete fertilizer (labels prescribe amounts for new lawn) on the soil and rake it in.

Prepare all areas to receive fresh sod in advance of purchase. Be ready to unroll the sod at once in its final place. If an unforseeable delay occurs, unroll the sod, grass side up, and sprinkle lightly with water. Sod left rolled in a stack over a weekend will heat and fail to revive.

Roughen the topsoil slightly   Unroll the sod

Placing the Sod

Use a steel rake to roughen the topsoil surface slightly, just before placing sod on it. Unroll sod across a slope, not up and down. Stagger the roll ends, like bricks in a wall. On very steep grades, pin the sod in place with 6-inch wood stakes, 15 inches apart along upper edges. Press each successively laid strip snugly up against the one next to it. After laying sod, smooth out small ridges and complete contact with the topsoil bed. Use a hand tamp for small areas. For larger areas, it is best to sprinkle first, then after the moisture has settled out and sod can again be walked upon without displacement, compact with roller half filled with water.

The New Lawn

An organic fertilizer will hasten the growth of contact roots

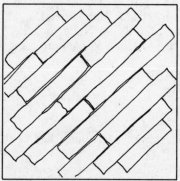

Stagger the roll ends

Trim excess if necessary

Smooth the sod with a roller

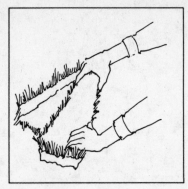

Spot-patch with sod

if applied shortly after the sod is laid, and is especially recommended in summer and fall. Liquid plant food used at ten-day intervals for a month will also see the new lawn off to a good start.

Water a little more carefully than usual for a few days. In very hot or windy exposed places, additional sprinkling (at least once a day) is needed. But *never* water in the evening or your lawn will be a fungus paradise. Avoid walking on freshly watered areas.

Spot-Patching on Existing Lawns

Damage from winter and traffic often requires patching. Poor or weedy areas caused by light soils, debris in the soil, or too shallow topsoil can also be renovated. Always check to make sure there's sufficient topsoil. Regrade by spading deeply; remove stones, debris, and poor soil. Add at least 3 inches of fresh topsoil. Cut a sharp straight edge along existing good sod so that the new will join it smoothly without ridging. Allow only ¾ inch drop in grade. Make sure the soil is sufficiently compacted, then add fertilizer. Never lay fresh sod directly over old sod: First turn under and chop up an old sod in areas to be patched.

A Baker's Dozen Steps to a Beautiful Lawn

Step 1.   *Dethatching*

Do this in early fall or in early spring, *before* all other lawn chores.

Step 2.   *Mowing*

When the grass begins to appear in early spring, mow it as

low as you can. Then mow it often enough so that you never cut off more than one-third of the grass blade at each time. Always use a sharp blade.

Step 3. *Crabgrass Control*

Use a premerge control every spring before the crabgrass sprouts.

Step 4. *Feeding*

In early spring and early fall, feed a dry lawn food at one-half the recommended rate. In between, feed every three weeks with a liquid or dry food at 20 to 30 percent of the recommended rate.

Step 5. *Watering*

Begin watering daily as soon as you have dethatched. Always water between 11:00 A.M. and 2:00 P.M.—never in the evening.

Step 6. *Spring Tonic*

Use Grandma Putt's tonic recipe in early spring and early July (recipe on page 5).

Step 7. *Broadleaf Control*

Liquid weed killer works best, but it's dangerous to your other plants. "Weed and feed" is safer but it doesn't work as well.

Step 8. *Insect Control*

If—and only if—you have an insect problem, use a product containing Diazinon. Shop for bargains—cheapest is best.

Step 9. *Disease Control*

If your lawn is sick, contact your county extension agent for information on controls. But if you dethatch and use the spring tonic, you may never have to worry about disease.

Step 10. *Spot Seeding*

If you have to spot-seed, trick your seeds into thinking you spread them last fall by soaking them in tea in the refrigerator for 36 to 48 hours and then drying them before spreading.

Step 11. *Aerating*

If your lawn gets compacted from wear or aging, aerate it

each year by walking over it with spiked shoes or using a spiked roller.

Step 12.   *Summer Tonic*

As the hot weather sets in, give your lawn a dose of Grandma Putt's summer tonic (recipe on page 14).

Step 13.   *Soil Conditioning*

Apply lime and gypsum every fall to keep your soil sweet and fertile. Then perk up your old grass with Grandma Putt's fall tonic (recipe on page 16).

CHAPTER 2 Shade and Flowering Trees

If Tree Care Drives You Up a Tree, You're Doing It Wrong!

If ever there was a member of the growing world that is abused, misused, and generally forgotten, it's the shade tree.

When you are looking for a new home to buy, in most cases one of the deciding factors, besides the style and size of the house itself, is the number of trees on the property. Yet little thought is given to how those trees got to be as big as they are or how you keep them healthy and happy. Most people who buy a new home on a treeless plot seldom consider anything more in their tree selection than cost. My impatient friends, that is just plain dumb! In the long run this short-sightedness is going to cost you a lot more in both comfort and insured value of the property itself.

Plan Before You Plant

I have said this so many times that I sound like a broken record. If you don't heed this advice, it is going to cost you money and your trees their lives! Your landscaping can be anything from a simple diagram on a brown paper grocery bag or loose-leaf sheet to a professionally drawn landscape layout by a trained designer or landscape architect. If you draw up your own plan, follow these steps:

Choosing Your Trees

Draw a garden plan before you plant.

Step 1.

Measure the property and draw it to scale or photocopy your abstract plan layout. Draw in the home, walks, and drive.

Step 2.

Take soil samples in every location where you intend to plant trees, shrubs, or evergreens. Dig holes at least 30 inches deep to see what surprises your builder hid from you.

Step 3.

Visit your local library or bookstore and secure a book on the trees, shrubs, and evergreens recommended for your area. Find out what they look like when mature, what conditions they thrive under, and how they're cared for. Make a list of potential candidates for your yard.

Step 4.

Visit both an independent local garden center and a discount or mass merchandiser's garden department in your neighborhood to get an idea of which plants on your list are the most popular and abundant in your area. It will also give you an idea of what price ranges to expect.

Step 5.

Before you draw your tree selections on the plan, make sure you understand how big and how fast your plant choices will grow. Allow for plenty of space for them to grow into.

If you opt for a professionally designed plan, ask that it be designed for phase planting (you plant gradually, as you can afford it). The professionally designed layout will, of course, cost you more—usually about $75 to $125.

Utility Companies Aren't Bullies; They Have the Right-of-Way!

I cringe every time I see the forestry crew trucks in my neighborhood, because I know that for the next few days I'm going to have to watch grown men cry. There are times when I have had a tear or two on my cheek too, when I saw a tree topper (man with a chain saw) go to the top of a beautiful 60-foot spruce, and simply cut 20 feet off the top—because it was interfering with the power lines. Folks, if you plant tall-growing shade, palm, or evergreen trees within 15 feet of utility lines, you are asking for trouble. My advice is, think ahead before you plant. To answer your questions: No, you have no recourse. I might also add that the same thing goes for underground water, sewer, and gas lines. To avoid hard feelings and save money, call your local utility company before you landscape. They will come out free of charge and mark the line or direction of underground pipes and wires.

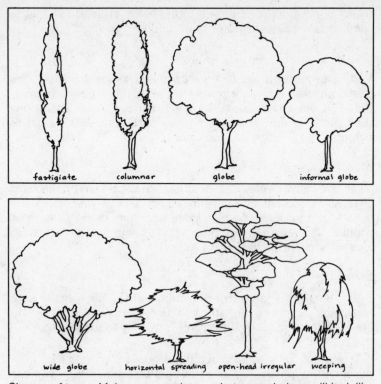

Shapes of trees: Make sure you know what your choices will look like

Let Me Introduce You to a Great Group of Tree Friends

At the end of this chapter you'll find a map of forestry zones and a list of which trees grow well in each zone. The trees are categorized under the following headings: broadleaf evergreens, narrowleaf and scale leaf evergreens, deciduous, palms, and leafless. My list is far from complete, but it should fuel your imagination. To find out what the different trees look like, get a book about trees out of the library; look for one that has many color plates and photographs. Then discuss your ideas with your local nurseryman and your designer, if you have one; they are sure to have helpful suggestions.

I am describing correct planting in some detail here so that later on you can't say, "I didn't know." The success or failure of any plant to prosper is determined by the care and caution you take when planting. A haphazardly dug hole will condemn an otherwise healthy tree to death. To ensure the continued health and beauty of your newly purchased tree, follow the steps outlined below to the letter.

Types of Planting Stock

Bare Root. This stock is generally harvested in the fall and stored in refrigeration in a safe, dormant state until early winter. At this time it is moved into the packing area. Its roots are inspected for damage, and then covered with a thick, rich quantity of wood chips and organic compost, wrapped securely with moisture-proof paper or encased in a plastic container and shipped to your local garden center.

Container Grown. Every type of plant can be container grown, including evergreens, fruit trees, shade and flowering trees, shrubs, and roses. Young seedlings are transplanted into metal or plastic containers and grown in plastic or glass greenhouses for one to three years, depending on the size of plants desired. At this time they are shipped to your area. Container-grown nursery plants are considered the hardiest type of planting stock, because there is little chance of trauma in shipment, storage, or planting.

Balled and Burlap. You generally will find larger evergreens, trees, and shrubs transported and marketed in this form. Professional landscapers often use this type of stock, which usually is sold in bulk. The tree or shrub is dug up

Planting Trees, Shrubs, Evergreens, and Roses

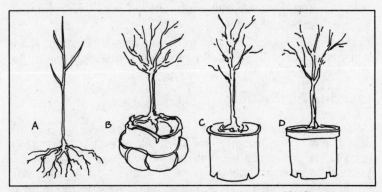

Kinds of stock: (A) Bare root (B) Balled and burlap (C) Container grown (D) Field potted

with a sharp spade, leaving a ball of soil around the roots, and the soil ball is wrapped in burlap. This large root ball is tied with twine to hold the soil and burlap in place, and the plant is transported in this form to its new location. Balled-and-burlap nursery stock must be handled more carefully than container stock to avoid dropping and breaking the soil ball, which could destroy the plant.

Field Potted. Nursery stock is dug in the late spring or early fall, transplanted into plastic, metal, wood, or fiber paper containers and shipped to local markets.

How to Prepare Stock for Planting

Bare-root Stock. Roses, shrubs, and trees should be removed from the packaging material. (Do not reuse this material for mulch or soil conditioner, as it is useless and may contain insects and diseases.) Next, soak the roots in a solution of very warm (80° to 85° F) soapy water with one-half cup of Epsom salts per gallon of water. Soak overnight or for at least four hours. Next, inspect roots. Untangle the fine, hairy basic roots; look for broken support roots (support roots are the thick, long ones), and cut off with a sharp knife or hand pruners. Always cut root stock under water and allow to soak another half hour before planting.

Container-grown Stock. Inspect all branches and foliage for damage 24 hours before planting. Wash foliage with a combination of liquid soap (1 tablespoon per gallon) and K-Gro Fruit Tree Spray at one-half the recommended rate.

Ball-and-Burlap Stock. Treat as container grown. Water the ball well and cover or move into shaded area until planting.

Field-potted Stock. Treat as container grown. Place in shade and cover soil with wadded newspaper until planting.

Planting Instructions

Soil. Most plants do not like heavy, wet soil or clay. A loose, sandy loam or gravelly soil will encourage speedy root growth. If you must plant in heavy soil, mound planting is your plant's only hope, because it allows you to add new, lighter, sandy soil to the existing muck with a minimum of effort. Mound planting involves digging a shallow depression

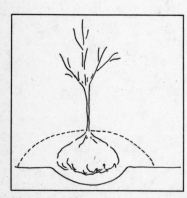

Mound planting

Dig hole twice as wide as the root ball

Improve the soil removed from the planting hole

just below the normal soil level and balancing the soil ball in the depression, then covering the soil ball with new soil in an attractive mound that blends into the surrounding landscape. Most landscape designers use this method in backfilled subdivisions.

Size of Planting Hole. Dig a hole twice as wide as the root ball, to give the roots plenty of room to spread out. But don't dig more than 4 to 6 inches deeper than the ball, container top, or soil mark on bare root stock.

Preparing the Soil. When digging a hole for planting, it is an excellent idea to loosen the earth twice as deep as your final hole will be to encourage deep root growth. Mound the soil removed from the planting hole and add a handful of bone meal, a handful of gypsum, and a small handful of planter mix

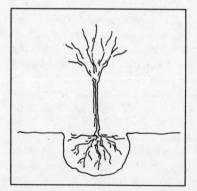

Placing bare root tree in planting hole

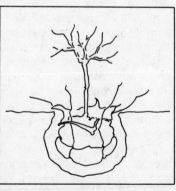

Placing balled and burlap tree in hole

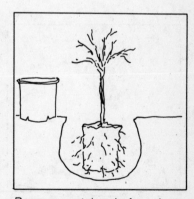

Remove container before planting container-grown tree

Refill the hole halfway, water, and firm soil

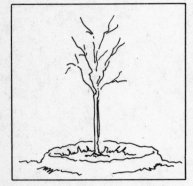

Leave a raised ring around the edge of the hole

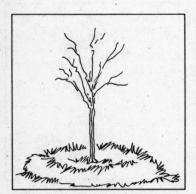

Add a layer of mulch

per bushel of soil and thoroughly blend together. Now, fill the hole up to the desired depth for the plant base and firmly pack down the soil with your foot. Next, fill the hole with water and let it soak in.

Planting. Plants in plastic, metal, or wood containers should be removed carefully before planting. Plants in fiber paper containers should have the container bottom removed. Set plant into position and refill the hole halfway. Again, fill the hole with water and let it soak in. Continue to refill while firming the soil with your foot as you fill. Make at least a 4-inch-high ring around the edge of the hole; fill with water again and let soak. Cover the soil surrounding all trees, evergreens, shrubs, and roses with a 4- to 6-inch layer of fine bark mulch to retain moisture evenly. *Do not feed plants immediately after planting.*

After-planting Care

If you take a moment to read the instructions that accompany your tree or shrub, you will find that you are directed to cut most bare root plants back by one-third. Are you reluctant? Don't be. Ignoring this instruction hurts your plant's chances for survival. Use a sharp pruner and cut back all branches one-third, just above an outside bud at a 45° angle; this will encourage branching. Sterilize all wounds with a mixture of 2 tablespoons of household ammonia, 2 tablespoons of mouthwash, and 2 tablespoons of liquid soap per quart of water. Slosh this mixture on the wounds, let dry, and seal wounds sparingly with tree paint.

Young trees should have their trunks wrapped with tree wrap for the first season (see page 49). All trees over 5 feet tall should be supported for the first season. There are two ways of doing this. One way is to drive three or four tall stakes into the ground around the tree trunk and tie them firmly together with twine. The second way is to drive two or three short stakes into the ground a couple of feet from the trunk. Attach guy wires to the stakes and loop them around the main branches of the tree, or around the crotch between a main branch and the trunk, to pull gently and evenly on the tree from two or three directions. The wire should be wrapped with rubber hose everywhere it touches the tree bark to avoid cutting into the tree.

Newly planted nursery stock should *not* be fed for two weeks. When this time is up, apply K-Gro Liquid Plant Food at half the recommended rate, except after fall plantings in the north where ground freezing occurs. Never feed after August 15.

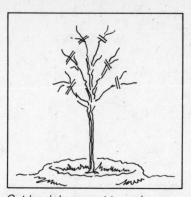

Cut back bare root trees by one-third

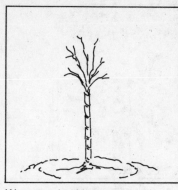

Wrap trunk with tree wrap

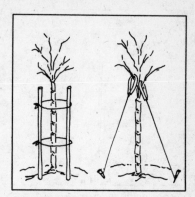

Support tree with stakes

If these few simple steps are followed, your new plant's survival is guaranteed.

Just to Make Sure They're Doing Their Part— Give Them a Smack!

People look at me real funny when I tell them to beat their trees with a bearing switch, but this time-honored practice really works.

A bearing switch is simply a long soft twig used to beat the trunk of fruit, shade, or flowering trees in the early spring (mid-April) to stimulate sap flow. If using a switch makes you feel cruel, use a rolled-up newspaper instead. You will be pleasantly amazed at the results. If you really feel foolish, try this technique late at night. Please, do not sing or chant and dance around the tree; after all, what would your neighbors do with all of that extra rain?

A Hearty Meal for Your Trees

Feed your trees in the early spring with any garden (not lawn) food (5-10-5 or 4-12-4). Or you can use tree spikes, but make sure you use enough to do some good. Purchase a tree auger that fits your electric drill, from your garden center or one of the big catalog houses, and drill a series of holes ½ inch in diameter, 18 inches deep, and 24 inches apart in a full circle out at the weepline (that's the ground directly below the tips of the farthest branches). Now, mix together equal quantities of sharp sand and fertilizer. (Sharp sand is coarser than beach sand; buy it at your garden center.) Fill each hole with this mix. If you are using tree spikes, force them into

Basic Care of Trees

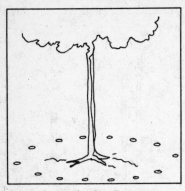

Auger holes for feeding tree

Feeding with root feeder and tree spikes

Spread lawn food on ground under tree

the 18-inch-deep holes. If the tree is in the middle of the lawn, it is a good idea to spread ordinary lawn food at one-half the recommended rate over the whole area from trunk to weepline and a little beyond to avoid ending up with a bunch of green clumps 24 inches apart where the holes were.

Cleanliness Is Next to Godliness (In Most Cases, That's Who It's Left Up to)

Trees get dirty, just like people and pets. Airborne dirt (smog, dust, soot, and other forms of pollution) collects on your trees and weakens them to the point where they can no longer fight off disease and insect invasions. Insects tend to attack the weaker trees because their bark and heartwood are softer and easier to chew into. The solution is simple: Wash your trees once in awhile, and take steps to discourage insects and destroy diseases before they can establish residence in your pet trees.

Here is a bath and preventative care program to ensure health and happiness for your favorite trees.

1. Wash your trees with soap and water. Add 2 cups of cheap liquid dishwashing soap and 2 cups of mouthwash to a hose-end sprayer with at least a 10-gallon capacity. Fill the balance with water and spray every tree in sight. Bathe your trees in this fashion three or four times a year in the northern states (above the Mason-Dixon line), and six or eight times in warmer areas like the South and Southwest. In the North, start your bath program when the temperature stays above freezing and end it at the first frost; in the warmer areas, start any time and keep it up all year round.

2. In the northern states, use a product called dormant spray each spring, as soon as the temperature will stay above freezing for 24 hours. Dormant spray contains a highly re-

Spray tree regularly

fined oil called volk oil or dormant oil. Some formulations also contain lime sulphur. The dormant oil works its way into the protective coverings that insects coat themselves with in the winter and kills them. It is highly effective because it kills the overwintering bugs before they are up and about and chomping on your trees. In areas where gypsy moths, tent caterpillars, and inchworms are a problem, dormant spray is a must. Apply it before the buds on the trees start to swell, however, or you may injure the new growth.

In other parts of the country, spray in early April with a chemical called Methoxychlor. Add 2 tablespoons of hot dog-type mustard and ¼ cup of liquid soap per 10 gallons of spray. This concoction will give unwelcome bugs and diseases a good reason to get lost.

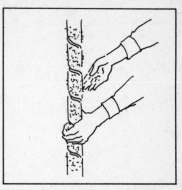

Band trees with Tree Tanglefoot

3. As soon as the temperature stays above freezing in your area, band *all* trees with Tree Tanglefoot, a tacky substance that traps crawling insects that travel up and down the tree trunk each morning and evening to eat or sleep. Follow the directions on the Tanglefoot container. Burn the trapped insects. Keep the trees banded until the temperature goes below freezing again (all year round in southern states).

4. In the month of April, keep your eyes open for the young larvae of the gypsy and tussock moths, tent caterpillar, bagworm, inchworm, and other caterpillars. At the first sign of them (chewed leaves or the caterpillars themselves), spray with a combination of Malathion and liquid or wettable Sevin. Add ¼ cup of liquid soap per 10 to 15 gallons of spray to help it stick to the foliage.

5. In the northern states, apply Paradichlorobenzene (otherwise known as moth crystals) in early May to the soil beneath the trees and shrubs bothered by borers. These include birches, dogwoods, and lilacs. Use 1 cup of moth crystals per 3 feet circumference. Spray the soil beneath trees bothered by caterpillars and leaf miners (birches are again likely victims) with Diazinon, packaged under many brand names.

6. In mid-May, spray the foliage of all small trees with Kelthane to control most mites. In areas where gypsy moths, inchworms, and tent caterpillars are a problem, apply a chemical called *Bacillus thuringiensis*, sold under such brand names as Dipel™ and Thuricide.

7. In the northern states, apply the Methoxychlor and mustard spray described in step 2 in late May.

8. In early June, in all areas, add a can of beer and 2 cups of liquid soap to a 15- to 20-gallon hose-end sprayer and give each tree a 5-gallon shot at the weepline (the area of ground directly below the farthest reaching branches).

9. Well-fed trees are far more resistant to attack by bugs or disease, so feed them. The quickest way is to use the tree spikes that are now available in garden centers. Buy the ones

that are displayed in bulk rather than the individually wrapped ones; they are just as good and cost a lot less. I use the Ross Tree Spikes because they have different formulas for different types of trees, they are available almost anywhere, and they are reasonably priced.

10. If you have trouble with birch borers or other borers, spray with any product containing Lindane in late June or early July.

11. Spray for leaf miners again in June, July, and August with Kelthane. The eggs of the leaf miners are laid at this time by a small, beelike insect called the sawfly. You will see hundreds of them near your birch tree.

12. In late September, finish up the season by applying Paradichlorobenzene moth crystals beneath the trees bothered by borers and spraying the soil with Diazinon. When most of the leaves have fallen from your fruit, flower, and shade trees, and the first frost is imminent, use dormant spray again.

Know Your Plant Medicines

Sometimes, even if you follow the above bath schedule, you may need a little something extra to keep your trees safe and sound. The following rules should suffice to keep most bugs and diseases in check.

If it flies, jumps, or hops, use Methoxychlor, Kelthane, Malathion, or Sevin—any one or a combination.

If it crawls, use a chemical called *Bacillus thuringiensis*, sold under brand names like Dipel™ or Thuricide.

If your tree's problem is diagnosed as a disease (not an insect), use any combination spray containing Captan, Benomyl or Thiram.

Any one of the many fruit-tree sprays will also stop most tree troubles in their tracks. Remember to add a liberal amount of liquid soap to all spray solutions to make them stick better.

Know Your Local Tree Bugs

Here are some more specific guidelines to help you in your fight against the insect world. There is an infinite variety of insects that just might harass your pet shade trees, but in most cases you'll only need to worry about the most common and highly visible.

Insect	Popular Control
Aphids	Diazinon, Dipel™
Bagworms	Diazinon, Sevin

Borers	Lindane
Bud Moths	Diazinon
Canker Worms	Diazinon, Dipel™
Cottony Scale, and most other scales	Diazinon
Grubs	Diazinon, Dursban
Gypsy Moths	Diazinon, Sevin, Methoxychlor, Dipel™
Japanese Beetles	Sevin
Leaf Miners	Diazinon, Lindane
Leafrollers	Diazinon
Mealybugs	Diazinon, Kelthane
Mimosa Webworms	Diazinon
Mites	Diazinon, Kelthane
Root Weevils	Diazinon
Skeletonizers	Diazinon
Tent Caterpillars	Diazinon
Tussock Moths	Diazinon, Dipel™
White Flies	Diazinon

If you see any indications of bug damage, take a few minutes out to try to find one of the culprits. If you can't identify it, take it (dead or alive) down to the garden shop. They will be able to tell you its name and reputation as well as the chemical recommended to stop its aggravation and damage.

Fall Care of Trees

These beauties should have very close attention in early September through mid-November to ensure their health and safety through the winter months.

Dormant spraying in the fall is an absolute must for all trees, shrubs, and bushes. See steps 2 and 12 of the bath schedule for details.

Deer and rabbit repellents will be necessary in areas where these two are problems in the late fall and winter. Commercial deer repellents containing bone tar should do the trick. It also helps to wrap wire fences around large shrub areas. Use tree wrap or plastic tree tubes to help control bark damage from rabbits. A repellent containing Thiram will help to scare off the bunnies.

Windbreakers are advisable in areas where the temperature goes below freezing, to protect young trees and shrubs from the wintery southwest wind. In late fall, wrap their trunks with a special wrap designed for this purpose. Ask for tree wrap at your garden center.

Don't let trees dry out over the winter. After the ground freezes, you can't water your trees and shrubs, so they don't have as much moisture available to them as at other times.

However, they are still losing water to the atmosphere through the process of respiration. You can prevent dehydration by applying a product called Wilt-Pruf, which coats the leaves with a thin layer of a substance that allows them to breathe but slows down the rate of water loss. Wilt-Pruf can be applied with a hose-end sprayer attachment.

Pruning

Pruning should only be attempted for five reasons:

1. To remove or repair damaged or dead wood
2. To redirect growth pattern
3. To restrict uncontrolled growth
4. To influence natural symmetry (shape)
5. To remove nonproducing wood

There is a right time, a right tool, a right way, a right place, and a right angle to prune to ensure the plant's safety.

When to Prune

Do your major pruning of shade trees in the early spring when the buds are swollen and raring to go. All shaping and other cosmetic pruning should be done at this time. If your tree flowers, however, you cannot prune in early spring because you will cut off too many blossoms. Wait until after the tree blooms.

Prepare your shade trees in fall for the winter ahead by removing damaged limbs and dead wood. Do not do any more pruning than necessary for your safety and the plant's survival through the winter at this time. Should damage from an ice or snow storm make pruning necessary in mid-winter, remove the ailing branches immediately and make sure you sterilize and seal the cut thoroughly (see page 52).

Use the Right Tools

Make sure that the tools you use are clean, sharp, and sturdy, and that you use the right size tool for the job. All too often a well-intentioned gardener spots an injured limb, reaches into his hip pocket for the small pair of hand pruners that most of us carry and begins to cut, only to find that the limb is too large for the tool on hand. Rather than walk to the garage or toolshed for the proper tool, he attempts to make the amputation in two cuts, and the result is a ragged tear, exposing the tender layer of tissue beneath the bark that carries the plant's life fluid. You should own and have access to four pruning tools:

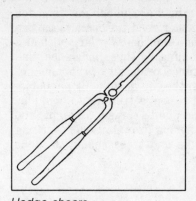
Hedge shears

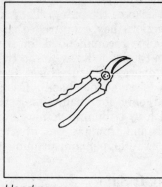
Hand pruners

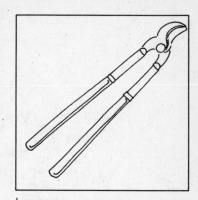
Loppers

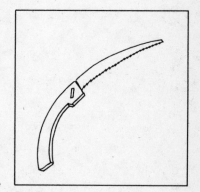
Pruning saw

Hedge shears, for soft growth *only*.

A good size pair of hand pruners, for limbs no bigger than your thumb.

A pair of loppers, for limbs half the size of your wrist.

Pruning saw, for limbs bigger than half your wrist but smaller than your neck.

When in doubt, use a bigger tool rather than a smaller one.

Purchase tools carefully; remember that "cheap" does not necessarily mean "bargain." Make sure the steel is not rough and the blades come together without bending. The handles must be firm and the blades securely anchored; if they twist or hesitate during a cut, they will rip the bark and damage the sensitive layer of tissue underneath.

The gasoline chain saw and electric hedge trimmers may well be two present-day mechanical wonders, but in the hands of an untrained amateur they are power-packed killers of both people and plants.

Use of the chain saw by most home gardeners should be confined to cutting up firewood. The felling of trees and removing of very large limbs that would require this type of equipment should be done by professional tree companies for the safety of both you and your tree. The Yellow Pages will direct you to your local professional. Ask for bids from two or three in the same manner you would pursue collision repair on your auto. Believe me, you will save money in the long run by hiring a pro.

The electric hedge trimmer is also a misused and abused piece of trimming equipment. In a recent personal survey I conducted of 42 owners of electric hedge trimmers, not one had ever had the blade sharpened and most didn't know that was necessary or possible. The average age of the trimmers was five years old.

Most homeowners purchase a hedge trimmer for its speed and ease of trimming. They neither read the manufacturer's directions nor even care that no limb or twig larger than a pencil is recommended for trimming by these machines, and then they wonder why the trimmed branches of their hedges and evergreens turn black from the top down (this phenomenon is called die back). Electric hedge trimmers should be used only for maintaining the plant's present height and width by trimming young new spring growth. Severe cutting back and thinning out of shrubs and trees should be done with the lopper and pruning saw.

Play It Safe

Never attempt to do any pruning alone that you cannot do safely and comfortably by yourself. Never permit children, pets, or neighborhood sidewalk supervisors in the area where any large limbs are to be removed. I highly recommend that you have a lookout to warn unsuspecting passersby of potential danger.

You may wonder why I am wasting valuable space and time on this unnecessary caution. Well, I have been a witness to just such accidents all too many times because these warnings were not heeded. And as foolish as they may make you feel, a hard hat, protective glasses, heavy-duty gloves, and the sound of "timber" at the top of your lungs may save a life!

Clean Your Tools

Clean tools both before and after each use. Wash and scrub the blades of tools with a solution of ½ cup of mouthwash, ½ cup of household ammonia, and a generous quantity of liquid soap per 2 gallons of *hot* water. Dry well and wipe down with alcohol. Wipe or spray the clean, dry blade with Pam, Wesson Oil, or other vegetable oil. Never use mechanical lubricants, gasoline, or turpentine as these can cause severe damage. WD-40 is acceptable because it is highly refined, but don't use more than the tiny bit necessary to ensure smooth movement of the blades.

Never Leave a Tree to Bleed to Death

Any time you hack, whack, saw, chop, or prune a woody caned plant, you *must* sterilize the cut. The same holds true for large gouges made by power equipment bumps, and insect and disease damage to bark or heartwood. Always carry a solution of:

2 tablespoons of household ammonia
2 tablespoons of Listerine mouthwash
2 tablespoons of liquid dish soap
1 quart of water

Spray, paint or douse the disinfectant on the cuts or wounds. Next, seal the wounds with any of the commercial pruning paints or a coat of inexpensive latex paint, shaded to match the bark. Nail polish, lipstick, waxed crayons or candles can be used to seal small cuts.

How to Make the Cut

Where to make your cut has a great deal to do with what you wish to accomplish. If you are going to remove a large branch, it will be necessary to make three cuts.

Cut one will be 10 inches from the main trunk, on the underside, 1 inch deep. This cut prevents the bark from ripping all the way down the tree when the limb falls off.

Cut two will be 12 inches from the main trunk, from the top all the way through. This is your removal cut.

Cut three will be ½ inch from the main trunk, all the way through. This cut finishes your work; it's clean, neat, and just the right distance from the trunk. Make sure you do *not* scrape or cut the bark of the main trunk.

Limbs from 1 inch to 2 inches in diameter should be cut with loppers, making sure that the limb is all the way back in the jaw and the rounded sharp blade is on the bottom. For small branches use a sturdy pair of hand pruners in the same manner as described for the loppers.

The angle of the cut determines the direction of the growth and the quality of new growth. Never cut straight across a dormant bud or the top wood will die back and kill the new buds, but at a 45° angle just above an outside bud.

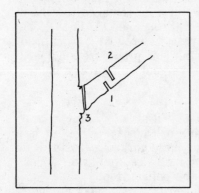

Removing a large limb

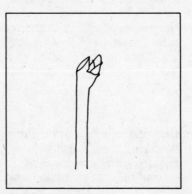

Pruning a branch

Root pruning

Root Pruning

There is one more pruning job that most home gardeners never do but all of them should. It's called root pruning.

Root pruning is the severing of the roots at the weepline (the area of ground directly below the tips of the longest branches) in the early to mid-fall—September through November. Root pruning should be done with a razor-sharp flat spade (sharpen it with a number 10 bastard file). Plunge the spade straight down, about 10 to 12 inches deep at the weepline, all the way around the tree or shrub. This action will force the roots to branch out with more feeder roots and, in many cases, will force a slow bloomer or no bloomer into a mass of blooms.

Always spread three to four cups of bone meal and two cups of Epsom salts per bush over the soil at the cut. Do not feed trees or shrubs in the fall in areas where freeze or frost are imminent.

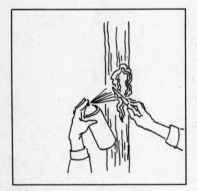

Repairing damaged wood

Hollow Tree Trunks Are Trouble, Trouble, Trouble!

There are a lot of hollow tree trunks in the forest, and that's nature's way, but nature doesn't pay premiums on a homeowner's insurance policy that charges double for acts of God, and a thirty-foot tree coming through your neighbor's room generally loses you a neighbor. If a branch on your tree or the trunk itself has been damaged and begins to decay, drastic action is needed. Take a sharp knife or a hatchet, depending on the extent of the damage, and cut out *all* of the decayed wood until you are down to clean, fresh heartwood. Spray the exposed area with alcohol and let dry, then coat it with pruning paint.

Go to the hardware store and purchase a can of triple-expanding urethane foam. It's used to insulate and stop leaks around windows and cracks. This material is lightweight and easy to handle, and it's ideal for use on damaged trees. Fill the prepared cavity in the tree with the foam. After the foam dries, paint over it with latex paint to prevent it from beading down in the heat of the sun. This procedure may seem like a lot of work, but it will save your ailing tree's life.

Flowering Trees

One of the most beautiful sights a landscape can offer is a flowering tree in full bloom, but these gorgeous creatures do require some special care. If nothing else, you have to clean up the mess they make when the petals drop!

Personally, I can't resist flowering trees, and I'm more than willing to do a little cleaning up after the show.

Most Flowering Trees Grow Fast—Too Fast!

Most flowering trees are planted with one thing in mind—their floral beauty. That's a mistake. The floral beauty generally lasts only 14 to 21 days, and the rest of the season you have a lonesome shade tree. When you are considering a flowering tree, think utility as well. Take into account what the overall shape of the tree without the flowers will be and whether the foliage will be dense enough to provide shade or screen.

Before you plant any of the flowering trees, make sure you give them plenty of room to develop. As a rule, most flowering trees do not exceed a height of 20 to 25 feet, but there can be exceptions. Their mature spread is about 20 feet. They reach mature size relatively quickly, so plan for the adult tree when you plant the baby.

Flowering Trees Like Company

Flowering trees are displayed singly in most home landscape designs. But they can also be used as colorful fences, noise barriers, or driveway and sidewalk liners. Let your imagination be your guide. The chart at the end of the chapter will help you make your selections.

Impatience Kills!

Flowering trees are available in a variety of forms: the low-cost packaged or bare-root plant found in most discount garden departments; the container-grown trees found in the chain garden centers; and the professionally dug and balled field-grown plants purchased directly from the grower. These three types of growing stock vary in cost according to their relative maturity. If you need a large number of plants but have a limited amount of capital, the packaged or bare-root plant may be your choice by necessity. If you will need only one or two plants to accent your landscape, the larger, and as a rule more expensive, container-grown stock will fill the bill. The wealthy and the commercial landscape planners prefer a full-grown, blooming spectacle outside their window on the first day of occupancy. Believe me, folks, they pay plenty for that front-row seat.

Mix and match the size of the plants you select. Buy some larger plants if you can afford it, but don't be afraid to buy smaller, less expensive ones as well. Fast-growing plants can be purchased in bare-root or packaged goods, while the low-growing, bushier trees, like some of the magnolias and dogwoods, are reasonably priced in 5-gallon tin, plastic, or *papier-mâché* containers. When you buy a large, almost fully matured tree, keep in mind that it can go into shock from the move just as easily as a smaller one, and your financial risk is much greater.

Winter Is Safe for These Blooming Beauties

In areas that get below freezing weather, it is a sound practice to plant winter-hardy flowering trees anytime after they have dropped their leaves in the fall until early May—even in the cold, dead of winter. Just make sure you predig the holes when the soil is soft in the fall. Winter-planted flowering trees must be mulched heavily with wood chips instead of filling the hole with soil, because soil won't settle properly at this time. Come spring, remove all the wood chips you can reach and fill the hole with soil as for normal plantings.

In less severe weather areas, fall is an excellent time to plant; and planting just before the rainy season (late fall in the north, early fall in the south), helps to ensure your yard of a season full of blooms.

You Have Got to Be a Cut-up to Make Flowering Trees Grow

All newly planted flowering trees must be cut back to stimulate growth. Take at least one-third off the top. Use sharp tools that have been disinfected with rubbing alcohol. Sterilize all wounds with alcohol, rather than the ammonia solution described for shade trees, as flowering trees are especially fragile. Then seal with pruning paint.

As mentioned earlier, flowering trees should be pruned and shaped in the middle of June, after they have bloomed. Removal of broken, sick or damaged wood must be taken care of as soon as it is noticed. Again, sterilize with alcohol and seal with pruning paint.

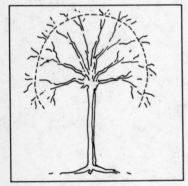

Shaping flowering trees

In Sickness and in Health

These words should be spoken by every home gardener as he or she plants any tree or shrub, but especially a flowering tree; sooner or later they all get sick, although not always seriously. Flowering trees have been bred so intensively that they have lost some of their natural resistance to disease. Fortunately, the care of the flowering tree is a great deal easier than that of its cousin the fruit tree, because you do not have to worry about a crop. Follow the Dormant Spray Program described in this chapter (see page 49) and follow up by applying any fruit tree spray just as the petals drop. Apply again in two weeks, again a month after the first spray, and then just keep your eyes open. This spray program, along with the tree banding (see page 49) I have suggested, should keep you from having to complete that vow when you marry a tree to your yard area—*til death us do part*. There are approximately 66 insects and 14 or more diseases that can threaten this marriage, so be vigilant.

Birth-Control Pills for Your Flowering Trees

Most of us enjoy the early beauty of the flowering trees but we despise the mess we must clean up in the late summer and fall from flowering crabtrees and some of the other fruit and berry trees. You can cut down this mess considerably by spraying the tree with a product called Amid-Thin, available in most professional garden centers, which kills the blossoms. Another way to reduce the number of fruit or berry sets is to take the hose with the nozzle set on hard stream and blow the blossoms off before they have a chance to develop.

Flowering Trees Are Hungry Buggers!

It stands to reason that if you and I worked as hard as flowering trees do, we would be hungry all the time as well. Flowering trees can be fed early each spring (just before they bloom) with the tree spikes designed for fruit trees. I have terrific luck with the Ross Root Feeder and its specially designed cartridges of combined feed and systemic insect control.

Think Before You Cut a Bouquet

Flowering tree buds can be cut early and brought into the house. When placed into water, they burst into bloom and fill the room with fragrance. This is a perfectly acceptable practice, but do take some notice of where and how you cut your bouquet. To start with, use a sharp pair of pruners. If at all possible, cut a limb that needs cutting back anyway. Cut at a 45° angle just above a bud that is facing outward, so that the new shoot will grow out, up and away from the center. To make your bouquet last longer, add four tablespoons of clear corn syrup and three drops of bleach per quart of warm water and set the bouquet in it.

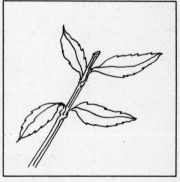

Pruning flower stem

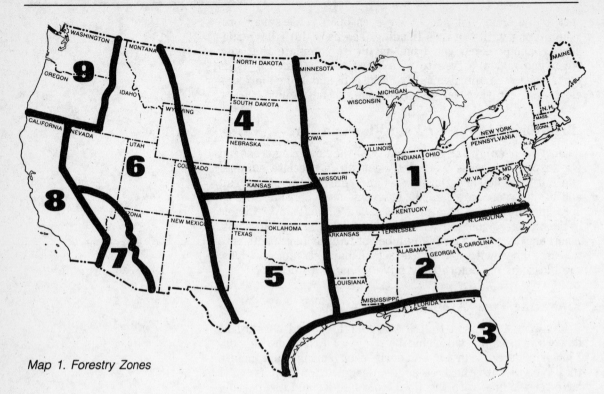

Map 1. Forestry Zones

ZONE LISTS OF TREES

Region 1

Evergreens, broadleaf

Holly, American
Magnolia, Southern

Evergreens, needle leaf and scale leaf

Arborvitae, Eastern
Arborvitae, Japanese
Cedar, Deodar
Cedar, Eastern Red
Cedar of Lebanon
Cryptomeria
Cypress, Lawson False
Fir, White

Hemlock, Canadian
Juniper
Pine, Eastern White
Pine, Red
Spruce, Colorado Blue
Spruce, White

Deciduous

Ash, Green
Ash, White
Aspen, Quaking
Bald Cypress
Beech, American
Beech, European

Birch, Cutleaf European
Birch, Paper
Birch, White
Buckeye
Buckeye, Red
Catalpa, Northern
Catalpa, Southern
Cork Tree, Amur
Cucumber Tree
Elm, American
Elm, English
Elm, European Field
Elm, Scotch
Ginkgo
Goldenrain Tree
Hackberry, Eastern
Hickory, Bitternut
Hickory, Mockernut
Hickory, Pignut
Hickory, Shagbark
Honey Locust, Thornless
Hornbeam, American
Hornbeam, European
Hornbeam, Hop
Horse Chestnut
Horse Chestnut, Red
Horse Chestnut, Ruby
Japanese Pagoda Tree
Kalopanax
Katsura
Kentucky Coffee Tree
Larch, European
Linden, American
Linden, Littleleaf

Linden, Silver
Linden, Black
London Pine
Magnolia, Cucumber
Magnolia, Sweetbay
Maple, Norway
Maple, Red
Maple, Sugar
Maple, Sycamore
Mimosa
Oak, Black
Oak, Bur
Oak, Chestnut
Oak, Northern Red
Oak, Pin
Oak, Scarlet
Oak, Shingle
Oak, Turkey
Oak, White
Oak, Willow
Oak, Yellow
Pear, Bradford
Pignut
Sassafras
Silver Bell
Sourgum
Sweetgum
Sycamore
Tamarack
Tulip Poplar
Willow, Weeping
Yellowwood
Zelkova

Region 2

Evergreens, broadleaf

Camphor Tree
Holly, American
Holly, Chinese

Holly, English
Laurelcherry
Magnolia, Southern
Oak, Laurel

Oak, Live
Wax Myrtle

Evergreens, needle leaf and scale leaf

Arborvitae, Eastern
Arborvitae, Oriental
Cedar, Atlas
Cedar, Deodar
Cedar, Eastern Red
Cedar, Incense
Cedar of Lebanon
Cryptomeria
Hemlock, Caroling
Pine, Eastern White
Pine, Loblolly
Pine, Longleaf
Pine, Shortleaf
Pine, Slash
Spruce, Colorado Blue
Spruce, Red

Deciduous

Ash, White
Bald Cypress
Beech, American
Beech, European
Birch, Cutleaf European
Buckeye
Catalpa, Northern
Catalpa, Southern
Cherry, Black
Chinaberry
Chinese Tallow Tree
Crape Myrtle
Cucumber Tree
Elm, American
Elm, Cedar
Elm, English
Elm, Winged
Ginkgo

Goldenrain Tree
Hackberry, Eastern
Hickory, Bitternut
Hickory, Mockernut
Hickory, Pignut
Hickory, Shagbark
Honey Locust, Thornless
Hornbeam, American
Hornbeam, Hop
Japanese Pagoda Tree
Katsura
Kentucky Coffee Tree
Linden, American
Linden, Littleleaf
London Plane
Magnolia, Cucumber
Magnolia, Sweetbay
Maple, Norway
Maple, Red
Maple, Silver
Maple, Sycamore
Mimosa
Mulberry, Paper
Oak, Black
Oak, Bur
Oak, Chestnut
Oak, Pin
Oak, Post
Oak, Scarlet
Oak, Southern Red
Oak, Water
Oak, White
Oak, Willow
Pear, Bradford
Pecan
Persimmon
Pignut
Redbud, Eastern
Sassafras
Silver Bell
Sourgum
Sourwood

Sweetgum
Sycamore
Tulip Poplar
Umbrella Tree

Yellowwood

Palms

Palmetto, Cabbage

Region 3

Evergreens, broadleaf

African Tulip Tree
Bell Flambeau
Brazilian Pepper
Cajeput
Coco Plum
Fig, Fiddle Leaf
Fig, India Laurel
Fig, Lofty
Geiger Tree
Holly, American
Holly, Chinese
Indian Rubber Tree
Jacaranda
Laurelcherry
Magnolia, Southern
Mahogany, Swamp
Mahogany, West Indies
Oak, Laurel
Oak, Live
Oxhorn Bucida
Pigeon Plum
Silk Oak
Silver Trumpet
Was Myrtle

Evergreens, needle leaf and scale leaf

Pine, Longleaf
Pine, Slash
Pine, Spruce

Deciduous

Bald Cypress

Bo Tree
Crape Myrtle
Cucumber Tree
Fig, Benjamin
Goldenrain Tree
Linden, American
Magnolia, Cucumber
Maple, Red
Mimosa
Mimosa, Lebbek
Oak, Water
Orchid Tree
Pecan
Redbud, Eastern
Royal Poinciana
Sweetgum

Palms

Palm, Coconut
Palm, Cuban Royal
Palm, Fishtail
Palm, Florida Royal
Palm, Manilla
Palm, Mexican Fan
Palm, Washington
Palmetto, Cabbage

Leafless

Beefwood
Beefwood, Cunningham
Beefwood, Horsetail
Beefwood, Scaly Bark
Casuarina

Region 4

Evergreens, broadleaf

None

Evergreens, needle leaf and scale leaf

Arborvitae, Eastern
Arborvitae, Oriental
Cedar, Eastern Red
Cedar, Incense
Douglas Fir
Hemlock, Canadian
Juniper
Juniper, Rocky Mountain
Pine, Austrian
Pine, Ponderosa
Pine, Scotch
Spruce, Colorado Blue
Spruce, White

Deciduous

Ash, Black
Ash, Green
Ash, White

Birch, Cutleaf European
Birch, Paper
Birch, White
Catalpa, Northern
Cherry, Black
Cottonwood, Plains
Elm, American
Elm, Siberian
Hackberry, Eastern
Hackberry, Western
Honey Locust, Thornless
Katsura
Larch, Siberian
Linden, American
Linden, Littleleaf
Maple, Silver
Oak, Bur
Oak, Northern Red
Oak, Pin
Oak, Scarlet
Poplar, Plains
Sugarberry
Zelkova

Region 5

Evergreens, broadleaf

Oak, Live

Evergreens, needle leaf and scale leaf

Arborvitae, Oriental
Cedar, Atlas
Cedar, Eastern Red
Cryptomeria
Cypress, Arizona
Juniper
Juniper, Rocky Mountain

Pine, Austrian
Pine, Loblolly
Pine, Ponderosa
Spruce, Colorado Blue

Deciduous

Ash, Green
Bald Cypress
Beech, European
Buckeye
Catalpa, Northern
Catalpa, Southern

Chinaberry
Desert Willow
Elm, American
Elm, Chinese
Elm, English
Elm, European Field
Elm, Siberian
Goldenrain Tree
Hackberry, Eastern
Hackberry, Western
Honey Locust, Thornless
Huisache
Japanese Pagoda Tree
Katsura
Kentucky Coffee Tree
Maple, Silver
Maple, Sycamore
Mesquite
Mulberry, Paper
Mulberry, Russian
Oak, Bur
Oak, Chestnut

Oak, Pin
Oak, Post
Oak, Scarlet
Oak, Shumard
Oak, Spanish
Oak, Texas
Oak, Yellow
Pecan
Pistache, Chinese
Redbud, Eastern
Retama
Sassafras
Soapberry, Western
Sugarberry
Sycamore
Umbrella Tree
Zelkova

Palms

Palm, Mexican Fan
Palm, Washington

Region 6

Evergreens, broadleaf

Olive, Common
Olive, Russian

Evergreens, needle leaf and scale leaf

Arborvitae, Giant
Arborvitae, Oriental
Cedar, Atlas
Cedar, Eastern Red
Cedar, Incense
Douglas Fir
Fir, White
Juniper
Juniper, Rocky Mountain
Pine, Austrian

Pine, Ponderosa
Spruce, Colorado Blue

Deciduous

Ash, Arizona
Ash, European
Ash, Green
Ash, Modesto
Beech, European
Buckeye
Buckeye, Red
Catalpa, Northern
Cottonwood, Plains
Elm, American
Elm, Chinese
Elm, European Field

Elm, Siberian
Ginkgo
Goldenrain Tree
Hackberry, Eastern
Honey Locust, Thornless
Horse Chestnut
Horse Chestnut, Red
Horse Chestnut, Ruby
Japanese Pagoda Tree
Katsura
Kentucky Coffee Tree
Linden, American
Linden, Littleleaf

London Plane
Maple, Bigleaf
Maple, Norway
Maple, Sugar
Mulberry, Russian
Oak, Bur
Oak, Northern Red
Oak, Pin
Oak, White
Poplar, Plains
Sweetgum
Zelkova

Region 7

Evergreens, broadleaf

Carob
Eucalyptus
Gum
Olive, Common
Olive, Russian
Palo Verde, Blue

Evergreens, needle leaf and scale leaf

Cedar, Atlas
Cedar, Deodar
Cedar, Eastern Red
Cypress, Arizona
Cypress, Italian
Douglas Fir
Fir, Silver
Juniper
Juniper, Rocky Mountain
Pine, Aleppo
Pine, Austrian
Pine, Canary Island

Deciduous

Acacia, Baileys

Ailanthus
Ash, Arizona
Ash, Green
Ash, Modesto
Chinaberry
Cottonwood, Fremont
Cottonwood, Plains
Desert Willow
Elm, Chinese
Elm, Siberian
Ginkgo
Goldenrain Tree
Hackberry, Eastern
Hackberry, Western
Honey Locust, Thornless
Huisache
Linden, Littleleaf
Locust, Black
London Plane
Maple, Silver
Mesquite
Mulberry, Russian
Oak, Pin
Oak, Southern Red
Pecan
Pistache, Chinese

Poplar, Bolleana
Poplar, Caroling
Poplar, Plains
Sugarberry
Sweetgum
Tree of Heaven

Umbrella Tree
Wattle, Baileys
Wattle, Sydney

Palms

Palm, Canary Date

Region 8

Evergreens, broadleaf

Cajeput
Camphor Tree
Carob
Cherry, Australian Brush
Coral Tree
Eucalyptus
Fig, India Laurel
Fig, Moreton Bay
Gum
Jacaranda
Laurel, California
Laurelcherry
Laurel, Grecian
Magnolia, Southern
Oak, Canyon Live
Oak, Coast Live
Oak, Holly
Oak, Live
Palo Verde, Blue
Tanoak

Evergreens, needle leaf and scale leaf

Arborvitae, Oriental
Cedar, Atlas
Cedar, Deodar
Cedar, Incense
Cedar of Lebanon
Cryptomeria
Cypress, Arizona

Cypress, Lawson False
Norfolk Island Pine
Pine, Aleppo
Pine, Canary Island
Spruce, Colorado Blue

Deciduous

Ash, Arizona
Ash, Modesto
Chinaberry
Chinese Lantern Tree
Cottonwood, Fremont
Desert Willow
Elm, American
Elm, Chinese
Elm, Siberian
Ginkgo
Goldenrain Tree
Hackberry, Eastern
Honey Locust, Thornless
Japanese Pagoda Tree
Locust, Black
London Plane
Maple, Bigleaf
Maple, Norway
Maple, Red
Mimosa
Mulberry, Russian
Oak, Bur
Oak, English
Oak, Northern Red

Oak, Pin
Oak, Scarlet
Oak, Valley
Orchid Tree
Pistache, Chinese
Sweetgum
Tulip Poplar
Umbrella Tree

Palms

Palm, Canary Date
Palm, Mexican Fan
Palm, Washington

Leafless

Beefwood
Beefwood, Horsetail
Casuarina

Region 9

Evergreens, broadleaf

Holly, English
Madrone
Magnolia, Southern
Tanoak

Evergreens, needle leaf and scale leaf

Arborvitae, Giant
Arborvitae, Oriental
Cedar, Atlas
Cedar, Deodar
Cedar, Incense
Cryptomeria
Cypress, Lawson False
Pine, Austrian
Pine, Ponderosa
Spruce, Colorado Blue

Deciduous

Ash, European
Ash, Green
Ash, White
Beech, European
Birch, White
Buckeye, Red
Cork Tree, Amur

Dogwood, Pacific
Elm, American
Elm, Chinese
Elm, English
Elm, Scotch
Elm, Siberian
Ginkgo
Golden Chain Tree
Goldenrain Tree
Honey Locust, Thornless
Hornbeam, American
Horse Chestnut
Horse Chestnut, Red
Horse Chestnut, Ruby
Japanese Pagoda Tree
Kentucky Coffee Tree
Linden, American
Linden, Littleleaf
London Plane
Maple, Bigleaf
Maple, Norway
Maple, Red
Maple, Sugar
Mimosa
Oak, Northern Red
Oak, Oregon White
Oak, Pin
Oak, Scarlet

Oak, White   Sweetgum
Silver Bell   Tulip Poplar
Sourwood   Yellowwood

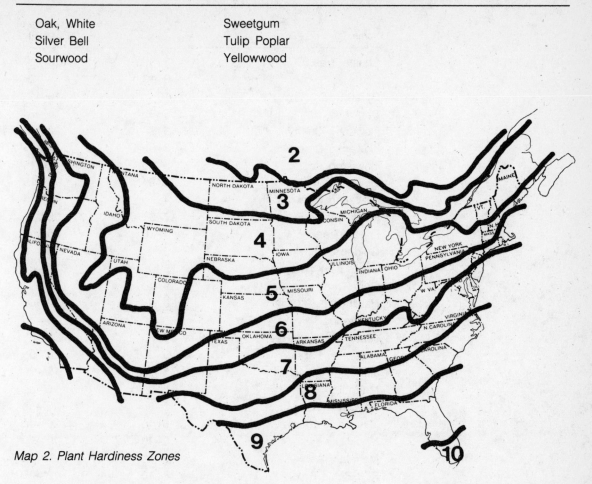

Map 2. Plant Hardiness Zones

POPULAR FLOWERING TREES

Note: The zones indicated in this list refer to plant hardiness zones (map 2) and not forestry zones.

Name	Zone	Height At Maturity
Acacia	9–10	20'–up
Blue Palo Verde	8–10	10'–20'
Buckeye	3–9	30'–40'
Carolina Silver Bell	5–9	20'–30'
Cassia	10	20'–30'
Catalpa	5–9	40'–up

Name	Zone	Height At Maturity
Chaste Tree	5–9	10'–20'
Citrus	9–10	10'–20'
Coral Tree	10	10'–40'
Dogwood	5–9	15'–20'
Flowering Cherry	6–9	20'–30'
Flowering Crab	3–5	12'–15'
Flowering Peach	5–10	12'–15'
Flowering Pear	5–9	12'–15'
Flowering Plum	4–10	12'–15'
Franklin Tree	7–9	30'
Fringe Tree	4–10	15'–up
Golden Chain	5–8	10'–20'
Goldenrain Tree	5–9	20'–up
Gum Tree	9–10	30'–up
Hawthorn	5–9	20'–up
Jacaranda	9–10	20'–up
Japanese Lilac Tree	3–8	8'–10'
Japanese Pagoda Tree	5–9	20'–up
Japanese Snowbell	6–9	15'–20'
Magnolia	5–9	15'–up
Mayday Tree	2–8	25'–up
Mimosa	6–10	20'–up
Mock Orange	5–10	10'–20'
Mountain Ash	3–8	20'–up
Red Bottle Brush	8–10	10'–25'
Redbud	4–10	15'–up
Ruby Horse Chestnut	3–10	20'–up
Service Berry	3–9	15'–18'
Sweet Shade	9–10	20'–up
Yellow Bell	9–10	10'–15'

CHAPTER 3 Fruit Trees and Fruit Bushes

Not All Fruit Trees Have Worms!

As you probably have figured out, I am not one of the crowd when it comes to giving garden advice. So it should come as no surprise when I tell you that for easy care and fast growing, I recommend apple, pear, citrus, avocado, or any one of 40 to 50 other fruit trees. No, you are not reading wrong. I'm suggesting that you seriously consider using fruit trees as normal members of your overall landscape plan. You have only so much land area—so why not get the most production out of it?

With the many new hardy, high-yield dwarf fruit, nut, and berry trees and plants, nearly everybody can have fresh fruit at their fingertips. Even apartment dwellers with a balcony can have peaches, pears, and many other fresh fruit trees growing in planters.

I know what you are thinking. You think fruit, nut, and berry trees and plants take too much care. That's where you're wrong. Fruit- and nut-bearing plants take no more care than your average shade tree—in fact, even less!

Choosing Your Fruit Trees

As with any tree, it's foolish to invest in a fruit tree that isn't adapted to the environment you can provide. Do some research before setting your heart on a certain kind. At the end of this chapter you'll find a list of which fruit trees grow in which regions, and my recommendations for particular varieties. I've made my selections on the basis of taste, easy

69

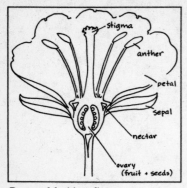

Parts of fruiting flower

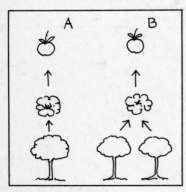

(A) Self-pollinating
(B) Cross-pollinating

care, availability, and affordability. You may have other ideas; discuss them with your nurseryman.

It Takes Two to Tango

Another important consideration in making your choice is the requirements for pollination of the fruit tree or bush you favor. Pollination is the sex act of the plant world. To make a baby fruit, pollen from the anther of one flower has to be transferred to the stigma of another. The pollen is transferred primarily by bees—your fruit tree's best friend. There are two kinds of pollination:

Self-pollination is the transfer of pollen from the anther of one flower to the stigma of another on the same plant or on a second plant of the same variety. One tree can produce plenty of fruit.

Cross-pollination is the transfer of pollen from the anther of a flower on one plant to the stigma of another on a different plant of a different variety. Two trees are needed to produce fruit.

Most trees are no different from people; it takes two to make a baby. These varieties are cross-pollinating; unless you have enough room to provide your lonely tree with a mate, it won't produce any fruit. Some varieties of trees and bushes, however, are self-pollinating; they can fruit without a partner.

Should Your Tree Get Married?

The chart below describes the pollination needs of the major varieties of home fruit trees and bushes. If you're still in doubt as to whether your plant needs a lover, call your county extension agent.

Apples
1. All apples do best when cross-pollinated.
2. Cross-pollination is best accomplished with two very distinct varieties, like Jonathan × Lodi but not Jonathan × Jonalicious.
3. These apple varieties provide good pollen for cross-pollination with most other varieties: Golden Delicious, Red Rones, Red Delicious, McIntosh, Yellow Transparents, Jonathans, and Grimes Golden.
4. These are four varieties that seem to do very well when *not* cross-pollinated: Golden Delicious 5-in-1 and 4-in-1, Starks Jon-A-Red, and Red Rome Beauty.
5. These apples will not pollinate themselves or pollinate any other variety: Baldwin, Gravenstein, Mutsu, Wine-

saps, Winespurs, Double Red Staymen, Spigold, and Sir Prize.
6. These three disease-resistant varieties need special pollination: Sir Prize, Priscilla, and Prima. Cross-pollinate Prima and Priscilla with each other. Use either to pollinate Sir Prize.
7. All crabapples are self-pollinating—one tree does it.
8. Research now indicates that some varieties of crabapple are good pollinators for apple trees. (More info later, we hope!)

Apricots
1. Most varieties are self-pollinating—one tree does it.
2. The Sungold variety should be cross-pollinated with Moongold.

Blackberries
Self-pollinating.

Blueberries
It's best to cross-pollinate with a second variety.

Boysenberries
Self-pollinating.

Cherries
1. All sour cherries (like Montmorency, Meteor, Morello, North Star, etc.) are self-pollinating—one tree does it. Sour cherries will not pollinate sweet varieties.
2. Almost all sweet cherries (Van, Bing, Viva, Black Tartarian and others) need cross-pollination with a different variety of sweet cherry.
   a. Stella is self-pollinating—one tree does it.
   b. Stella is a good pollinator for other sweets.
   c. Van, Stark Gold, and Black Tartarian are especially good pollinators for other varieties.
   d. Cross all Schmidt's with Bind or Napoleon.
   e. Do not cross Gold with Viva, Bind or Napoleon.
   f. Cross Van with Bing or Napoleon.
   g. Black Tartarian seems self-pollinating, but it still produces best when cross-pollinated with a different variety.

Crabapples
Self-pollinating.

Currants
Self-pollinating.

Dewberries
Self-pollinating.

Elderberries
It's best to cross-pollinate with a second variety.

Figs
Self-pollinating.

Gooseberries
Self-pollinating.

Grapes
Self-pollinating.

Nectarines
1. All nectarines are self-pollinating.
2. They can pollinate and be pollinated by all peaches.

Nuts
1. Black walnuts, butternuts, and Persian walnuts are self-pollinating.
2. Chestnuts, English walnuts, and hickories need cross-pollination with a different variety of the same kind of nut (a hickory will not pollinate a chestnut).

Peaches
1. Most varieties are self-pollinating—one tree does it.
2. J.H. Hale and Halberta need cross-pollination with any other peach.
3. Peaches and nectarines will cross-pollinate each other.

Pears
1. It's best to cross-pollinate all pears with a different variety.
2. These varieties are good cross-pollinators: Bartlett, Moonglo, and Starking Delicious.
3. Bartletts are best-pollinated by Anjou or Bosc.
4. Magness needs cross-pollination (Moonglo is good) but it will not pollinate other varieties.
5. These three cannot cross pollinate each other: Stark Jumbo, Bartlett, and Seckel.
6. Duchess is self-pollinating—one tree does it.

Plums and Prunes
1. The three groups of plums are the following:

Japanese	European	American
Abundance	Green Gage*	Superior
Burbank Plum	President	Waneta
Delicious	Stanley Prune	
Methley Plum*	Starks Giant Damson Plum	
Redheart	Starks Blufre Plum*	
Santa Rosa*	Starks Fellenburg	
Satsuma (pollinate	Stanley German Prune*	
with Santa Rosa)	Valor	
	Yellow Egg*	

2. Those marked with an asterisk (*) are often considered self-pollinating.
3. It's best to cross-pollinate all plums; they must be pollinated by a variety from the same group. Example: Cross Abundance with any other variety from the Japanese group.

Quince
Self-pollinating.

Raspberries
Self-pollinating.

Strawberries
Self-pollinating.

No Surprises!

For the life of me, I can never understand why the average home gardener acts so surprised four or five summers after he or she has planted a tree or shrub (especially a fruit-bearing one) to find it growing over the drive or sidewalk or growing into the branches of another tree. That's why you planted it—to grow.

The truth of the matter is that most of us have little confidence in our ability as a green thumber and take it for granted that most of what we plant will not survive and will need continuous replacement. So, I guess it's no wonder we are surprised to find a tree we planted beat the odds and live.

If I only accomplish one goal from your reading this book, I will go on to the Big Orchard in the Sky happy. That goal is to help you gain confidence in your ability to plant and harvest, thanks to your own green thumb! The only acceptable surprise is when one of your plant friends doesn't make it.

The way to avoid having your tree run out of room to grow is to give your fruity and nutty friends plenty of space to begin with, keeping in mind their mature size.

Planting and Basic Care

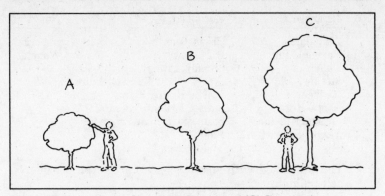

Sizes of fruit trees: (A) Dwarf (B) Semidwarf (C) Standard

1. Standard size trees will grow to 20 feet wide.
2. Semidwarf trees will grow to 15 feet wide.
3. Dwarf size trees will grow to 10 feet wide.

If you plant with these sizes in mind, you and the trees will have a growing head start. The mature height of these trees need not be of any great concern, because you will keep them topped off to a convenient height for spraying (15 to 20 feet for mature standards, 10 to 15 feet for semidwarfs, and 5 to 10 feet for dwarf size).

For the average patio, porch, or balcony, container-grown fruit trees should be dwarf size. Semidwarf trees will need to be in much larger containers and heavier equipment will be needed to move them around.

Spring Fever Is Well Timed

For most of the plants' sake, I am glad that you folks only get turned on to gardening once a year, or the mortality rate for outdoor plantings would be out of sight.

In all parts of the country that get snow and hard freezes, early spring is the best time to plant fruit- and nut-bearing plants.

In areas where the temperature will get below 40° for periods of more than 14 days, spring is again the best time to plant.

Where there is no chance of freezing weather, fall is the best planting time, despite the recommendations you'll hear to the contrary. I have given the eulogy at many a tree funeral, simply because an over-rambunctious home gardener couldn't wait until fall to plant.

No matter what your region, follow the planting instructions given in Chapter 2, pages 40 to 45.

No Hanky-panky—No Baby Fruit!

Some folks call it pollination, but you know what they mean! If there is no hanky-panky going on among your fruit trees, there won't be any fruit. To give Mother Nature a helping hand, here's what you should do:

Hang a bouquet from another tree in yours to help the bees

1. Maintain good soil fertility—don't overfertilize with nitrogen and be sure plenty of phosphorus is available from bonemeal or superphosphate.
2. Hope for proper climatic conditions—warm and dry.
3. Don't sprinkle water on blooms; cover blooming tree with cheesecloth when frost is predicted.
4. For cross-pollination, provide two trees of different varieties:
   a. The partner trees should be planted in the same vicinity—about 50 feet apart.
   b. The two trees should bloom at the same time.
   c. The two different varieties must be the correct ones (see pages 70 to 73).
5. Bees are absolutely needed for pollination!
   a. Bees work in the early, cooler part of the day—do not disturb them or they'll get mean.
   b. Bees are killed by insecticides—no spraying during bloom time!
   c. Bees tend to visit only two trees per trip from the hive—plant trees for cross-pollinating close together.
   d. Bees are distracted from fruit trees by weedy flowers—keep area weed free! But be careful that none of the weed controls touch the foliage or flowers on your trees—or it's good-bye fruit!

If your tree is a cross-pollinating variety but you can't plant a partner tree for it, try this trick. Gather a large bouquet of fruit tree blossoms from another tree of the appropriate variety. Place them in a bucket filled with warm water (not hot) and one cup of clear corn syrup and hang them high in the tree on the sunny side. Change the bouquet when necessary.

Prune Not . . . Grow Not!

You would think that after thirty years of beating my head against the trunk of a tree, I would consider it useless to try to convince most of you that you can do more good than harm by pruning, sawing, shearing, hacking, chopping, or otherwise removing branches or twigs from woody caned plants. Fruit-bearing plants are pruned for one of four reasons:

Shaping fruit trees

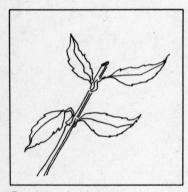

Pruning a fruiting stem

1. To reduce the number of fruiting buds, enabling the plant to produce fewer but bigger fruit. In the case of dwarf or semidwarf trees, this is necessary to prevent overloading.
2. To shape it, opening the center for full light and easier picking.
3. To remove weak, damaged, and diseased wood.
4. To force formation of fruit-bearing buds.

When you pick up a pruning tool, ask yourself what you wish to accomplish before you start to cut. That way you and your fruit trees will remain friends.

I like to think of proper pruning as being in the right place at the right time with the right tool! Simple, eh? It can be, if you know *why* you're pruning and *when* that goal is best achieved:

1. Repair or removal of damaged wood, thinning out buds, and shaping are best done in late winter, before the buds swell up.
2. Repairing and removing sick and injured wood must be taken care of as soon as it is discovered.
3. To force fruiting spurs, the best time to prune is just after the tree has blossomed.
4. Any transplanted tree or shrub must have one-third of its top growth removed (cut straight off the top) after planting. This is to stimulate root vigor.
5. Grapes can only be pruned in the winter; if grapes are pruned after the sap begins to flow, they will bleed to death.

As you learned in the previous chapter, you can't prune safely without the right tool. It's always better to use too big a tool than too small a one. Clean and lubricate the blades before each use. Remember that all cuts bigger than your finger must be sterilized and sealed.

Fruit Trees Can't Grow on an Empty Stomach

If ever there is a tree in your care that can't make it on handouts from the grass beneath it, it is the fruit tree. Feed your fruit trees in the early spring, when they are growing their best, with any garden food (5-10-5 or 4-12-4) or tree spikes (only the low-nitrogen ones). Follow the instructions in Chapter 2. Water your fruit trees well after feeding and continue watering right through blossom time.

Container-grown dwarf fruit trees should be fed with a light application of fish emulsion two or three times early in the season. Light application means 25 percent of the rate recommended by the manufacturer.

Guess Who You Don't Want to Come to Dinner?

You guessed! Our mutual friend: the worm. And folks, they really don't have to be a problem. You can't just wish them away, you have got to put a little time into their elimination. Here's the plan of action:

Fruit Tree Spray Program

1. Very early in the spring, just as soon as the temperature stays above freezing for 24 hours, spray your trees with a solution of soap and mouthwash as described in Chapter 2.
2. Ten days later, apply a dormant spray (volk oil and lime sulphur).
3. Before the buds begin to swell, spray the entire tree with liquid fruit tree spray. Look for one that contains both insect and fungus control. K Mart and Ortho both sell a good product.
4. Use same material *after* blooming, as soon as the petals have fallen. (Never spray during blooming or you'll kill the bees!)
5. Repeat in 14 days.
6. Repeat in 7 days.
7. Repeat in 21 days.
8. Dormant spray again late in fall.

Spray fruit trees regularly

Band all trees (as described in Chapter 2) with tree wrap bands and Tree Tanglefoot.

If any signs of caterpillars appear, spray the foliage with a chemical called *Bacillus Thuringiensis*, often sold under the name Dipel™. Spray the soil below the trees with Diazinon, adding 1 cup of tobacco juice per 10 gallons of spray.

To control borers, sprinkle Paradichlorobenzene crystals (mothballs) on the soil near the trunk in mid-September and again in early April.

All of the home orchard sprays can be applied with either a tank-type sprayer or a hose-end jar sprayer attached to your hose.

Bird Damage in the Fruit Garden Can Drive You Nuts!

Birds are tremendously valuable for the hordes of insects they consume. A few birds also include tender young sprouts and ripening fruits in the diet, much to the annoyance of the

Feed your fruit trees in early spring

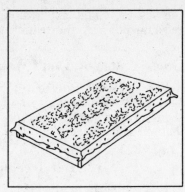

Protecting strawberries with netting

gardener; robins, catbirds, and brown thrashers are the prime offenders in most regions. These birds seem to know that a good place for nesting is near a future food supply, or right in it! Sweet cherry branches provide sturdy crotches for the robin; blueberry and larger ornamental shrubs are preferred by thrashers and catbirds. But, Annie, don't get your gun . . . yet.

At the risk of infuriating our bird-loving friends, I suggest that to discourage robins, catbirds, and brown thrashers from taking residence on the premises, you learn to recognize their nests and remove them—persistently, until the birds move elsewhere; although it be only to the neighbors. Feeding sunflower seeds and grain mixtures will *not* deter birds from our fruits. Flickering reflections of sunlight from spangles, bangles, and baubles made from tin can covers and aluminum foil plates are sometimes successful for a day.

A long-term practical approach for diverting fruit snitchers is to plant ornamental shrubs that produce berries at the same time. Two really good ones for early crops are Nanking (bush) cherry, and shadblow (serviceberry or Juneberry), both suitable for sandy soils. Mulberry is a great favorite, fruiting later and for much of the summer; try to keep these at a little distance from the garden, and dig out (don't cut off) any seedlings that may appear in the shrubbery. Late-fruiting shrubs are more numerous, few being more palatable to the birds than mountain ash.

Whether you decide to scare the birds off with baubles or distract them with ornamental shrubs, there are specific measures you should take to protect your share of the fruit crop.

Strawberries. Ah, strawberries! "Plant enough for thee and me," the robin may be heard to say. Cover beds before berries begin to color; once the wise robin has a taste, he is persistent, even to squeezing berries through a net! Do not drape regular bird netting loosely over or along edges of the patch. It's better to use an 8-inch-high board frame around the planting, stretching the netting over the top, looped over nails for quick removal at picking time. You can make more efficient use of netting if you use manufacturer's sizes without cutting; they range from 6½×21 feet, to 13×13 feet, 13×45 feet, and up to 75 feet long. Netting should last for up to six years with care; put it under cover when the need for it is over. The same netting can be used to protect your vegetable garden. Tougher tobacco cloth can be draped over strawberries as well.

Blueberries. When these berries are ready, insects seem to be forgotten, as we find all our bird friends flocking to the feast. Blueberries may be somewhat relieved by cherries early in their season, and raspberries later. Since the bushes grow to 6 feet, the best way to protect them is with light wood frame sections, erected in a few minutes, covered and secured around the base with netting. Such frames should be stored out of the weather at other seasons. It may be quicker in the long run to wire staple pieces of netting to each frame than to wrap the frames with netting each time. In fact, these permanently netted frames (which can be bought prebuilt) can also be used over vegetables and strawberries earlier in the season, to make them more worthwhile.

Cherries. Dwarf tart cherries are fairly easy to cover with large squares of netting. Sweets become too large for covering economically. A simple trick works wonders: Use a large spool of No. 40 black thread, unreeling it over the tree, back and forth, distributing it all around. Once they discover the

Protecting blueberries

Protecting cherries with black thread

Protecting raspberries and blackberries

Protecting grapes

thread, birds seem to fear getting entangled and will avoid the tree.

Raspberries and Blackberries. Due to the prickles and spines on these bushes and frequent removal or shifting for pickings, plastic netting hardly lasts a season unless it can be supported well above the foliage on tall stakes. Cheesecloth or tobacco cloth may be used.

Grapes. These bring the season near the end. Draping large sections of netting over the vines and securing them to the ground with rocks or stakes is the only way to protect them.

Dwarf Fruit Trees Are Just Shorter

Dwarf forms of favorite fruiting trees find wide acceptance in gardens both large and small. They create splendid landscape effects all year, as either patio planters or garden dividers and partial screens; they train readily as espaliers, for interesting architectural effects against blank sunny walls and fences, and they even help in cooling a hot south wall. The peach's pink blossoms are unsurpassed in beauty, and the cherry billows in great clouds of white each spring.

Dwarf trees are usually composed of more than one type of stock. The understock, or root stock, consists of the roots and lower part of the trunk. The understock is usually a dwarf variety of the kind of fruit tree you've chosen to grow or a closely related kind (for example, pear trees grow on quince understock). The top growth of the tree, which actually bears the fruit (the variety stock), is grafted onto this understock. In this way many varieties of the given fruit can be grown on one or two types of dwarf understock; for example, almost any type of sour cherry can be grown on Nanking cherry understock. Sometimes the understock and the chosen variety stock are incompatible, and it becomes necessary to sandwich an interstock of a third variety between the understock and the variety stock. Because they are really two or more varieties of tree coexisting on the same trunk, and the variety stock is only "dwarfed" by virtue of being supported on the dwarf stock, dwarf fruit trees are more fragile than ordinary fruit trees and need close attention.

Intensive care must be given if the dwarf is to produce superior fruit. Pay close attention to preparing a suitable site and soil, pruning, early fruit thinning (except for the cherry), insect and disease prevention, fertilizers, mulches, and protection in season against birds, rabbits, and mice. All these considerations fall easily into line for the practiced gardener who schedules his or her annual maintenance program logically, although it takes more time than the few minutes each weekend you may be used to giving your trees.

Apples

An apple a day keeps the doctor away, so the old saying goes. But in most cases when you need an apple the only ones in sight are out of reach at the top of the tree. Dwarf apple trees are the answer. They grow 8 to 10 feet tall and only occupy about 10 square feet of ground. With a little bit of your time and good cultural practices, each dwarf apple tree should favor you with a yield of one to two bushels of fruit.

March and April are the best months to plant dwarf trees. Choose a location that gets full sun, and where there is no interference from surrounding shade-tree roots. The soil should be light and fast-draining year round. Standing water will kill your trees.

Since dwarf stock has shallow roots, you must make sure that the top 12 to 18 inches of soil are abundant with organic matter. Prepare the soil by spading 10 to 12 inches of well-rotted leaves, straw, compost, poultry manure, and peat moss into the soil in the 10-foot-square planting area. This preparation will ensure a good foundation for root development.

As soon as you plant your new dwarf tree, cut the branches back by one-third, seal the cuts with lipstick or pruning paint, and wrap the trunk with tree wrap.

Dormant spray the first fall, and begin a normal fruit tree spray program the following spring. Feed dwarf apples in the early spring, as soon as the soil softens up enough for you to drill the feeding holes or drive the fruit tree stakes into the ground.

Pears

The French have produced top-quality market pears for centuries on 6-foot dwarf condons and espaliers, grown very close together on taut wires. The understock was and still is a form of dwarf quince now known as Angers. Our modern horticulturists have not progressed far as yet in their search for greater range in dwarfing understocks. Trained as round-topped trees, dwarfed pears develop to 8 to 10 feet tall and require a ten- to twelve-foot spacing. Some varieties, such as Bartlett, are not compatible with quince and require an inter-stock of other pear, making them more costly.

Find a sunny space with loose but moisture-retentive loam of three to four feet deep. For all varieties except Seckel and Bosc, a companion with good pollen is needed. Dwarf pears appear less susceptible to serious fire blight disease than other pears, but are best grown in tight sod without cultivation nonetheless, to prevent the fire blight virus from taking hold in the soil. Nitrogen further induces blight; give it sparingly and not later than May.

Prune as for dwarf apples. Encourage spur branch development and reduce long, soft growth.

Peaches

The numerous varieties of dwarf peach grow to approximately half normal height, about 6 to 8 feet. New types that look more like bushes than trees are appearing on the market; Com-Pact Red Haven is the leading variety at this size. There are very tiny varieties such as Bonanza, suggested for patio planters, but these are warm climate strains and need careful winter protection in many parts of the country. If the cold is a problem in your region, you must move the planter to safe cool storage in winter or set the tree in deep cold frames protected by glass and rush matting.

Peach trees should be planted in early April in soft, well-drained clay loam. They need full sun, but they do best on a slope that faces north. Newly planted trees should be cut back by one-third. Keep trunks of new trees wrapped for two years for protection against sun scald, bark split, and rabbits. Keep well watered for two seasons.

Considering the cost of dwarfing (almost double that of regular peach trees), the naturally small size of the latter, and the frequent need for replacement in the colder states, it often makes more sense to plant standard-size trees. Either type begins to fruit in only two or three years.

Apricots

Like peaches, these are sun lovers, yet hardiest on a north facing slope. As with peaches, you will have to replant when low winter temperatures damage the trees severely. Moorpark and Early Golden are naturally small trees; on certain plum root stocks an even shorter 6 or 7 feet will result. Set two or more trees 10 to 12 feet apart; stake and tie securely for life.

For the most part, peaches and apricots do not develop new fruiting shoots. Prune long leaders (the longest shoot on a branch) to encourage vigorous shorter ones to fruit the next year. Remove twiggy unproductive growth, and open the center of the tree to allow sunlight in.

Cherries

Dwarf sweet cherries have not yet been developed. Standard tart (sour) cherries are naturally short but spread widely. Decidedly dwarfed cherries grown on understock of Nanking and other species of cherry become low-branched, bushy trees 5 or 6 feet tall. North Star is quite dwarf as is. Space any of these about 12 feet apart, in full sun; sandy, well-drained loams are ideal. Companions are not needed. Prune to encourage spur branch development.

Selected forms of Nanking cherry produce great quantities of half-inch, mildly acid, delicious fruits and are attractive landscape shrubs as well. All cherries are most in need of protection by bird netting at June fruiting time.

Plums

Plums are small or bushy trees in their standard form; most fruit can be picked without a ladder. The multipurpose beach plum and others double as landscape shrubs.

Special Note

Fertilize dwarf fruit trees only in spring, never after mid-May or very early June at the latest. Except for pear as noted, all thrive under 6 inches of mulch or other organic matter, which helps to fertilize and maintain even soil moisture. Prune heavily to start—reduce the 3- to 4-foot tree you buy to 30 inches, and side branches accordingly to compensate for heavy loss of roots in transplanting. Wrap trunks at once. Stone fruits, such as cherry, plum, peach, and apricot, must be closely guarded against wood borer insects at all times. Trees are ready for you in early April as packaged stock, and later in container-grown form.

There's Nothing Nutty About Growing Nut Trees!

The large, well-furnished garden ought to include a grove of nut trees. These trees are, however, space takers, many being forest giants, and for good crops there must be several of each species for efficient pollination. So, you had best have the room.

Nut trees prefer deep, rich, loamy soil, with good drainage. Only chestnuts require an acid soil. For the early-flowering and late-maturing species, avoid frost pockets (high spots of ground that are unprotected by surrounding trees). Trees in almost any location will make good shade, but flower buds are easily lost to frost in unusually cold springs.

Early flowering trees are pollinated by wind, not bees, and the pollen will shed after the nut flowers have gone. To ensure cross-pollination, different varieties of one early-flowering species are essential. Good crops require good feeding, and some nut trees, like the walnut, do have insect problems.

Transplanting

Walnuts, hickories, and pecans are taprooted—the main root goes straight down. All transplanting must be done in spring, within the first two years for best results. Later on it will be impossible to dig up that taproot. Transplanting techniques are the same as for shade trees. Cutting back the top will greatly aid in establishing new roots in the first season.

Distribution

The Northern Nut Growers' Association, together with other nut growers' organizations, has worked for years to hybridize and select hardier, improved forms to extend commercial production beyond the old limits—pecans in the South, Persian (English) walnuts and almonds in California, and filberts in Oregon.

Now the limits are expanding, as new varieties are being introduced. Almonds can be grown wherever peaches are grown; Persian (English) walnuts will bear, if not every year, even here in southern Michigan. The European filbert can even be grown along the Great Lakes and in large cities; cold and pollution killed the old varieties.

Walnuts

Ever give up in desperation, trying to crack a black walnut? Now we have thinner-shelled, larger-meated varieties such as Thomas and Schwartz. These newer ones are grafted; never try to plant them from seed as they will not develop the new, desirable characteristics. Space trees 60 feet apart.

The Persian (English) walnut grows up to 40 feet tall and

makes a beautiful shade tree. New strains from colder sections of Poland are especially promising for our cooler states, but nut production will not occur every year, since around 150 growing days are needed. Six weeks of dry weather are also helpful at harvest time, as nuts will sometimes mold in northern climes. Plant 45 feet apart.

Chestnuts

With the demise of our handsome American chestnut, newer hybrids of blight-free strains are being tested, based on the Chinese chestnut. Fruiting is not as yet consistent in the northern states. Only seedlings of the Chinese varieties are available. Plant 35 feet apart. This is a beautiful, summer-blooming, little dooryard tree.

Filberts

Our native American filbert is a very hardy bush growing up to 8 feet tall, with tasty, small nutlets. In frost-free regions, European filbert hybrids Reed, Bixby, and some others are fruitful. Use several of either American or European varieties in hedgerow plantings, 4 and 10 feet apart respectively.

Hickories

Amazing improvements of the hickory tree give larger, thin-shelled nuts in Wilcox, Glover, and Stanley. Near the Great Lakes, the very hardiest pecans should be tried; nuts will be small but thin-shelled, and require a dry season at harvest time.

Once a crop is underway, keep the squirrels out. (I know this is easier said than done—see Chapter 7 for some advice.) A good crop, harvested and in dry, cool ventilated storage, will keep for several years if necessary.

Bush Fruits Are Not Bush League

Bush fruits are a large clan. They include raspberries, blackberries, dewberries, and a few hybrids. Our cultivated types were developed and widely used in bygone days when virgin soils were plentiful and stocks were free of disease. But over the past 50 years or so, culture of some berries became difficult due to virus diseases. Life in the garden was short and production relatively poor.

Through the magic of science, we can plant these delicious fruits once again. A controlled method has been found to produce virus-free plants of our old favorites. If we practice good, clean garden culture, there should be little difficulty.

Soils and Sites

The best soil for bush fruits is sandy loam, deeply enriched with organic matter, as the roots descend 2 feet or more. Annual applications of rich compost or manure really help. Soil must retain moisture through the summer, yet have rapid drainage above and below for excess water. A pH of 6.0, slightly on the acid side, is correct. Open, sunny places where strong winds will not buffet long canes are preferred.

Bad Neighbors

Keep red raspberries apart from black raspberries by several hundred feet; likewise keep them from wild brambles of any sort. Try to avoid using soil that has grown potatoes, tomatoes, eggplants and melons in several years, or any brambles in 20 years (including roses).

Tender but Tough!

Aside from brittle, breakable canes, the berry bushes have exceedingly thin bark or skin that is easy to injure. Airborne disease spores enter bruised and torn spots with ease. Nature goofed in providing spines and prickles; tough tissues should have reinforced the skin instead. Wind can tangle the canes, causing the thorns on one cane to cut the thin skin on another, which may then bleed to death.

Build Up Hardiness

Berry bushes are the least winter-hardy of all bush fruits in the north. Beginning with red raspberry, in increasing tenderness are black, purple, amber and white raspberries, blackberries, dewberries, and hybrid boysenberries and loganberries. Winter hardiness can be increased by withdrawing nitrogen from the soil in late summer by planting cover crops of rye or oats over all open soil. Areas with winter mulch and frost-free soil are ideal. Most organic mulches of summer should be removed from plants before cold weather because they retain frost too long in open winters.

Good and Bad Habits of Growth

There are two main types of growth pattern among the bush fruits. The first type reproduces itself by spreading out suckers in ever-expanding circles; red raspberries, blackber-

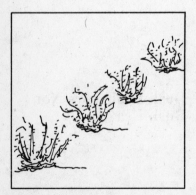

Set red raspberries in rows

Set black and purple raspberries in clumps

ries, and dewberries fall into this category. The second type, which includes purple and black raspberries, forms tight clumps for life and reproduces by branching. In the first group, plants are set 2 to 4 feet apart in each row, with rows 10 to 12 feet apart. By maintaining a cultivated strip or path between rows, suckering is limited to form a solid bed of no more than 5 feet in width for ease in picking. In the second group, plants are set 6 to 8 feet apart in the row, with cultivation possible from all sides for several years.

When to Plant

Plants are retailed only in the early spring, packed in bare-root form; freshly dug home-grown plants can be moved in October as well.

Pruning

Even if new plants are guaranteed disease-free, they may carry harmful spores, so you can't let the foliage stay around. Use the tops as handles for planting, then cut the plants to the ground at once and burn the cuttings. If markers are needed, use temporary wood stakes.

The canes of these plants are biennial. They grow for one year. The next year they flower and bear fruit. Then those canes are done; they will never again produce. After they have borne fruit, cut them to the ground.

The only other reason for pruning bush berries is to stimulate new growth.

Red Raspberries, Blackberries, Dewberries. In late May, cut the new growth back to 4 feet, except for blackberries, which must be left long. Cut out any runts or broken branches. Now go through the bushes and cut out all but four canes per foot of growth in the row.

Black and Purple Raspberries. In the early spring before the plants show any new growth, cut the laterial (side) branches back to 1 foot in length. This year's fruit will bear on these 12-inch side shoots. Early in summer, probably before the fourth of July, when the new shoots out of the ground are 3 feet high, pinch off the tops of the plant to force more lateral branching for more fruit next spring.

Seal cuts with Tanglefoot to keep stem borers out, and burn all prunings.

Spraying Makes It or Breaks It

Dormant spray is very important. Use Orthorix lime sulphur (not volk oil) in early April, after pruning, to clean up scale, spider mite and aphid eggs, and disease spores resting

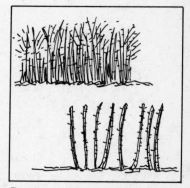

Pruning red raspberries

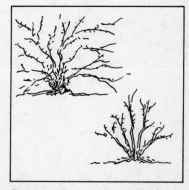

Pruning black and purple raspberries

on the skin. Keep foliage in good health all summer to build in hardiness. If mottled foliage appears, dig up and burn the whole plant. Weak stems can indicate crown and root galls; dig and burn.

Home Blueberries Make the Best Pies

The blueberry is the all-American fruit; we should thank the many U.S. horticulturists who have brought this native berry to such national prominence, amazing size, sweet flavor, and ease of growing. The natural habitat of the blueberry is marshy land; now it thrives on higher ground when attention is given to its special needs.

The blueberry shrub is ornamental in the landscape, producing shapely, pleasing flowers in spring, and red, orange, and purple foliage in autumn. Few insects bother it; sprays are seldom needed. It can double as a hedge; or it can be sheared into a design. All it asks is a place in full sun, well away from trees for good fruiting.

Special Care Is Necessary

Two special requirements in the culture of the blueberry shrub can be mastered easily these days: strong acid soil and constant moisture. It does not stand drought well. Gardeners who have a low, damp area are in luck, although water must not stand there. On higher ground we overcome this problem by working copious quantities of organic matter into loose, porous soil to act as a sponge. Clay soils are not suitable. Fresh or rotted sawdust is best, peat is excellent; partially composted oak leaves or pine needles work as well. All these are especially beneficial, as they help acidify the soil. A pH of 4.0 to 5.1 must be maintained; 4.4 is ideal.

Other organic matter may be used but with some types acidifying chemicals may have to be added, sometimes detracting from the berry flavor. Use of organic materials rather than chemical additives is now becoming common practice in the small garden. There is further use for acid mulches in helping retain soil moisture; a loose blanket of 4- to 5-inch depth, spread to well beyond branch tips, should be maintained regularly. It settles slowly into the soil, nourishing the plants; add to it as needed. Fresh sawdust will make a good mulch even without fertilizer.

Bed Preparation Should Be Rich

Try to make the planting space ready before the bushes arrive in very early spring. Dig and mix the organic matter well to a depth of 12 inches or more.

Buying Plants

The best blueberry plants are three to four years old; these move quite easily. Bearing age plants are older, and can take another two years to recover and show signs of fruiting. Look for bare-root and packaged plants in March and April for economy. Later, plants growing in tin containers are available in limited selection. Blueberries are rated as early, mid-season, and late. Popular varieties are, from earliest to latest: Earliblue, Berkeley, Rubel, and Coville. Have several bushes (of one or several varieties) for good cross-pollination.

Planting blueberry bushes in rows

Planting Is More than Jamming Them in the Ground

Space plants for fruiting 5 to 6 feet apart in the row, with rows 8 feet apart. Dig the hole 12 inches deep and about 15 inches wide. Mix acid peat into the bottom of the hole with a digging fork, and construct a cone-shaped mound in the center, building it halfway up the hole. Remove plant from wraps and spread roots over the cone. Fill the hole with water and allow to settle. Pull more soil mix in around the plant to finish, and tamp the spongy soil firmly, leaving a shallow basin around the bush for periodic waterings.

Prune back heavy canes by one-third, and remove small twigs, especially those with fat flower buds. Fruiting should not be expected the first year.

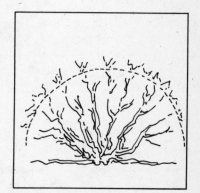

Pruning blueberry bushes

Fertilizers and Maintenance

If you mulch shortly after planting, you probably won't need to use fertilizers. If the foliage appears pale and yellowish, use superphosphate or a complete fertilizer in early spring as the buds start to appear. Drought calls for some irrigation, even with deep mulches. Test soil for pH once a year and make corrections while the problem is still slight.

The largest fruit is produced on vigorous wood from the previous season. After the third season, remove thin, twiggy growth in late winter annually to encourage vigorous new branching.

Always be prepared to protect bushes against frost by covering with cheesecloth or newspaper. Early spring frosts and freezes often occur during or after the early flowering. Most gardeners also find a wooden framework covered with bird netting absolutely essential before the fruit begins to ripen. A wire enclosure for winter is desirable, or the rabbits will do a thorough pruning job when you least want it.

Strawberries Can Be Called the Best of the Bunch

Strawberries are the most popular fruit crop for home planting. Plants are hardy and easy to grow and produce good crops in less time than other fruit bushes—about a year after planting. A 100-foot long row should produce plenty of berries for a family of four—and additional fruit for the freezer. For successful planting follow these easy instructions.

Site and Soil

Strawberries need drainage, so select a site with sufficient slope. Make sure the site gets direct sunlight; avoid shade. Sandy to gravelly soils are ideal for strawberries. The soil should be well supplied with organic matter. Cattle manure is helpful in building up the organic matter content of the soil. Use up to 10 pounds per square yard of soil surface.

Strawberry bushes stop producing after five or six years, so you will need to replace them every few years or so. For bonus strawberry production, rotate your plantings from one spot to another in your garden each time you make a new planting. For the best results, choose an area that has been cultivated for at least a year and that is free of weeds and grass. This will reduce the number of grubs and weevils in the soil that could badly damage your berries. Avoid planting strawberry bushes where they have grown in the past four years. And try not to plant them where tomatoes, peppers, eggplants, and potatoes have been grown for at least three years. This practice prevents diseases from spreading to your berries.

Time of Planting Is the Key to Success

Plant as soon as the soil can be properly prepared in the spring. Before planting, plow or spade deeply as early in spring as the soil can be worked. Cultivate several times until the soil is thoroughly pulverized.

In regions that get cold winters, fall is the best time to plant. For best results, make a new planting each year. That way you will always have berries, and you can rotate your locations to give them adequate rest between plantings.

Everbearing varieties give the best crops in the year they're planted. June bearers produce best crops the following year.

Buy the Best

Purchase only inspected and certified plants. All plants should have medium to large crowns and large, light-colored, healthy roots. (The crown is the thick fleshy part from which the leaves and roots originate.) Unpack the plants upon arrival and plant at once or cover the roots with soil, straw, wood chips, or leaves to keep them moist until planting.

Basic Training Should Be Tough

The matted row system of planting is popular in home gardens for June-bearing strawberries. Set plants 22 to 24 inches apart in the row, with rows spaced 3 to 4 feet apart. Allow runners to form a mat 15 to 18 inches wide, with runner plants spaced 4 to 6 inches apart. Maintain at least 18 inches between matted rows. This system is easiest to maintain.

The Hill system is best for everbearing varieties of strawberries. It also produces a greater yield. Set plants 12 to 15 inches apart in double or triple rows. Use sharp scissors or a knife to remove runners as they appear.

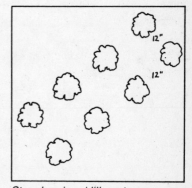

Strawberries: Matted row system

Planting and Cultivation Hints

Strawberries are tough and will probably prosper no matter what you do to them, but these hints will ensure your success.

Hint 1. The crown must be level with the soil surface.

Hint 2. Roots should extend vertically into the soil and spread out like a fan. Pack the soil firmly about the roots.

Hint 3. Apply fertilizer during the first growing season for best results. Cattle manure is good. Sidedress 10 days after setting with 2 to 3 pounds complete garden fertilizer per 100 feet of row. Do not allow fertilizer to come in contact with damp foliage and do keep it at least 4 inches from the plant crowns. Do not fertilize in the spring prior to harvest.

Hint 4. Remove all flower clusters as they appear up to July.

Hint 5. Water liberally during and immediately following bloom.

Hint 6. Shallow cultivation and hand hoeing are needed for weed control.

Hint 7. Water during dry spells—apply sufficient water to wet the soil 6 to 8 inches deep, but only when needed.

Hint 8. Thin or space plants grown in matted rows 4 to 6 inches apart. Allow early runners to root and remove those developing later in the season.

Hint 9. Mulch when the temperature falls to about 20°, to protect plants from winter injury, to suppress weeds, and to conserve moisture. Straw is good.

Strawberries: Hill system

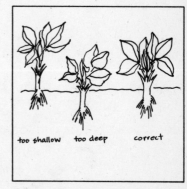

Correct planting depth for strawberries

Grapevines
The popularity of grapevines seems to go up and down like the thermometer. When one person in the neighborhood has success with growing grapes, there is sure to be a run on them at the local garden center the following spring. Grapevines will grow in just about any kind of soil, weather, and location. They need little attention and in some cases do better when neglected.

You should not expect to produce an award-winning wine from your home vineyard for a while, but you can grow some good grapes for eating, wines, and jellies and have a lot of fun in the process. Furthermore, grapevines are great living fences and patio shade roofs.

Planting

Grapevines grow best in soil that has a loose texture—light gravel to sandy loam topsoil. It is essential to provide good drainage. Open space and sunlight are necessary, because they stimulate the air movement that helps control grape diseases.

Plant your new vines right away—preferably in spring. Dig the planting hole at least 12 inches deep and 12 inches wide. Mix the soil with an equal quantity of peat. Add some sheep manure and 1 cup of bonemeal per bushel. Use this mix for planting the vine. Plant it to the same depth in the ground as it was at the nursery. Water well weekly the first summer.

Watering

Established grapevines are deep-rooted and consequently are not affected by minor droughts. In prolonged dry spells, soak the ground near the base of the plant every 2 weeks with 6 to 8 hours of sprinkling (3 to 4 inches of water); try to keep the foliage dry. Withhold water from mid-September on to allow the fruit to ripen and finish.

Fertilizing

Feed each vine ½ cup ammonium sulphate in late May the first season. Apply it evenly, using a watering can to make a circle with a 2-foot radius around the vine. The second year use 1 cup in a circle with a 3-foot radius. The third year use 2 cups of 12-12-12 fertilizer in a circle with a 4-foot radius. From the fourth year onward use 3 cups of 12-12-12 each May. Instead of chemical fertilizer, you can use sheep manure at the rate of 25 pounds per vine annually. If you use manure, the fruit will be less acid and tastier.

Spraying

Insect pests and fungus diseases can easily be kept under control by spraying grapevines four times a season according to the following schedule, starting in the spring:

1. Spray when the new shoots are 6 to 10 inches long.
2. Spray two weeks after time 1, just before the vines bloom.
3. Spray two weeks after time 2, after the blooming is done.
4. Spray two weeks after time 3.

Use a combination fungicide and insecticide suitable for food crops or mix your own spray using Captan and Diazinon. If you garden organically, use sulphur and rotenone.

Pruning

If your grapevine serves as fencing, shade, or decoration, and you do not expect it to bear fruit, no pruning is required. If you want to grow grapes, however, severe pruning is required every year. The vines bear fruit on one-year-old stems. After their second year, the stems will no longer bear, and simply burden the plant. In late winter, when the vines are dormant, cut out all but four long stems per vine, two on each side. Each of the four stems should be about as thick as a pencil and have at least eight buds; ten or twelve is better. At or near the trunk of the vine also leave four short stubbly stems with two or three buds on them. Next year's fruiting canes will grow from these stubs. All other canes must be removed.

Properly pruned, a grapevine should produce for 35 to 40 years.

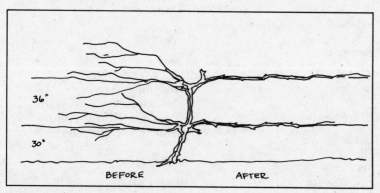

Pruning grapes

ZONE HARDINESS FOR FRUIT AND NUT TREES

(Refer to Plant Hardiness Zones, Map 2, page 67)

Fruit Trees	Zone
Apples	4–8
Apricots	5–10
Avocados	10
Blackberries	4–5
Blueberries	5–10
Boysenberries	4–5
Cherries	4–7
Citrus	9–10
Currants	4–6
Elderberries	4–6
Gooseberries	4–6
Grapes	5–6
Nectarines	5–8
Papaws	5–9

	Zone
Peaches	5–10
Pears	5–8
Plums	5–10
Raspberries	3–6
Rhubarb	4–6
Strawberries	5–6

Nut Trees	Zone
Black Walnut	5–8
Butternuts	3–5
Chestnut	5–8
English Walnut	7–8
Filberts	6 only
Hickory	6–9
Pecan	6–9

The Pick of the Crop

Apples

Double Red Delicious
Ida Red
Lodi
Red McIntosh
Red Rome
Solid Red Jonathan
Yellow Delicious
   (Use Yellow Delicious to
   pollinate all apples.)

Apricots

Curtis
Goldcat

Blackberries

Black Satin
Darrow

Blueberries

Blue Crop

Blue Ray
Burlington
Earliblue
Jersey
Rancocas
Rubel

Boysenberries

Thornless

Cherries

Bing
Black Tartarian
Hedelfinge
Montmorency
Napoleon (Royal Ann)
Schmidt's Bigarreau

Currants

Red Lake

Elderberries

Adams
Johns
Nova
York

Gooseberries

Pixwell

Grapes

Catawba (best of the reds)
Concord (big crop, blue)
Fredonia (earliest to ripen)
Foch (black, super for
  Burgundy-type wine)
Golden Muscat (golden
  yellow)
Interlaker (yellow seedless)
Interlocken (yellow seedless)
Lakemont (yellow)
Niagara (big crop, white)
Seibel Aurora (white)
Seibel De Chaunac (super
  for homemade red wine)
Suffolk (red seedless)

Nectarines

Nectared

Papaws

Michigan Banana (need two
  for pollinating)

Peaches

Cresthaven
Glohaven
Harmony
Newhaven
Redhaven
Redskin

Pears

Bartlett
Bosc
Clapp's Favorite
Red Bartlett

Plums

Blue Damson
Blue Fre
Eureka Plum
Green Gage
Red Grant
Stanley Prune

Raspberries (Black)

Black Hawk
Jewel

Raspberries (Gold)

Fallgold (Blavin spring and
  fall)

Raspberries (Red)

Canby
Heritage
Hilton
Latham

Rhubarb

Strawberry Red
Valentine

Strawberries

Aurown
Brilliant
Earliglow
Guardian (best for jam)
Jumbo (biggest)
Midway
New Scott
Ozark Beauty
Raritan (best dessert berry)
Redchief
Robinson (best late berry)
Surecrop (mid-season, heavy
  bearer, trouble-free)

Dwarf Fruit Trees (These
  can all be grown in
  containers on the patio.)

Dwarf North Star Cherry
Dwarf 4-1 Apple

Dwarf Curtis Apricot
Dwarf Goldencot Apricot
Dwarf Bonanza Peach
Dwarf Yellow Delicious
Dwarf Red Rome Beauty
  (Use Yellow Delicious for
  pollination.)
Dwarf Empire (Use Yellow
  Delicious for pollination.)

Dwarf Bartlett Pear
Dwarf Clapp's Favorite
  Pear
Dwarf Duchess Pear
Dwarf Collette
Dwarf Sapa Plum
Dwarf Texas Everbearing
  Fig

Nut Trees for the Home Garden

Black Walnut

Juglans Nigra Black
Thomas

Butternut

American

Chestnut

Chinese (blight resistant)

English Walnut

Manriglan
Paper-shell Carpathian

Filbert

American
Barcelona
Royal

Hickory

Skellbark

Pecan

Grafted Stuart

CHAPTER 4
Shrubs, Evergreens, Ground Covers, and Vines

There's a Shrub for Everyone's Taste— and Pocketbook!

If I had to pick one class of plants that gives you the most for your money, I would have a hard time choosing between the evergreens and the flowering shrubs. A well-balanced, attractively arranged group of evergreens just can't be beat— and they take up very little of your time, effort, or money after they are properly planted. But it's also true that you can fill up more space faster, cheaper, and with a greater variety of color with shrubs than you can with evergreens. So, how about some of each?

Actually these two groups have a lot more in common than most folks realize. In fact, some of the plants that you may think of as shrubs—rhododendrons, azaleas, and boxwood, for example—are actually broadleaf evergreens. The familiar needle-type evergreens are known as the narrowleaf evergreens, and have somewhat different requirements from their shrublike cousins. In this chapter we'll discuss both types of evergreens as well as the many deciduous shrubs, vines, and ground covers that can dress up your garden.

Look All Gift Shrubs in the Stem before You Buy

Basic Shrub Care

When you plant a shrub in the wrong spot, you don't have to wait years to find out. You will know it by the end of the

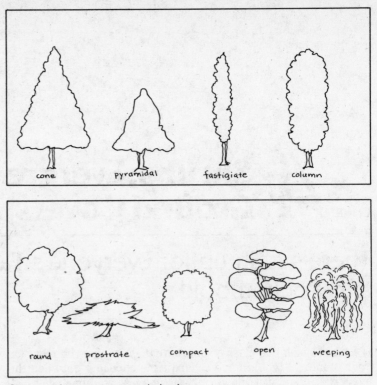

Shapes of evergreens and shrubs

first growing season. Shrubs, both foliage and flowering, grow fast, and double or triple their size in one or two years. Make sure you read the instruction tags before you buy and plant. Most reputable garden product retailers, mail-order houses, garden centers, and nurserymen will make sure that growing instruction tags are attached, and they should be more than willing to answer your questions.

Recognize a Bargain—or a Bust!

I get so mad when I go to a retailer who advertises top-quality nursery stock at rock-bottom prices, only to find that he has rock-bottom quality at top prices. If you purchase a poor-quality, sick plant for pennies, you've paid too much. Here are some of the tricks to beware of:

- Oversized plants in undersized containers or balls. These are often sold to inexperienced buyers who think that more top growth means more tree. The grower has to get these big plants out of his fields to make room for more merchandise, and he keeps the size of the soil ball down to keep the weight low so he pays less for freight. The problem is that there isn't enough root stock left to support a plant this large.

- Bare-root plants that have been transplanted into containers and placed on sale before they have developed enough root stock.
- Infected nursery stock that has been shipped to the retailer instead of being treated or destroyed.
- Undersized plants in oversized containers that are sold by pot size, not plant size.

Enrich soil in planting hole

If you think you are being ripped off, call your local branch of the Department of Agriculture, Plant Inspection Division, and alert them to your suspicions. They will come down so quick and hard that the unscrupulous merchant won't know what hit him. The fines are big, real big.

Make sure that all plants you buy look green and healthy. Look for clean, bright, fresh-looking foliage, with signs of new growth. The plant should have a root ball that looks adequate for the plant—ideally, it should be half as wide as the spread of the branches. If you see any signs of insects, move on.

Don't Let Anyone Say, "I Told You So"

The planting instruction tags that come with your new shrubs will, as a rule, give you a good idea of the soil, water, and light conditions that will ensure health, prosperity, and carefree growth. Don't get too cocky and figure that you will play the odds and get a shrub that prefers light, well-drained soil to grow in heavy, dry clay. You and the plant will both lose.

Full Sun Means 360°

When you read a planting instruction tag that calls for "full sun," I know what most of you have on your mind. You wonder what difference a little shade makes. Answer: The difference between beautiful and ugly. Here is a very simple explanation that an old forester I worked for once gave me:

Full-sun-loving plants in the shade will grow tall, thin and ugly.

Shade lovers in the sun will be short and dumpy.

Do your shrubs a favor; respect their preferences and they will repay you tenfold with performance. The second part of this chapter, "Choosing Your Shrubs," will help you determine which varieties of shrubs would thrive in your garden.

Proper Planting Is More than a Hole in the Ground

The trouble with most of you is that you try to do too much planting in too short a time. Oh, I know! You're anxious for the end result. You put in a lot of physical effort and then in a few weeks you wonder why the plant isn't performing the way it was billed.

Properly preparing soil can be more enjoyable and require less effort than you would believe. As a matter of fact, I have a friend, Arnold Smith (Smitty), who takes at least four months to plant a tree or shrub; six months is more like it. "Pokey," you say. Smitty refers to it as *careful*. What Smitty does is prepare the soil area long, long before he buys any plants. He starts by dumping his leaves, grass clippings and table scraps on the planting area and turning it into the soil. A few weeks later he adds more and turns it again. Another friend of mine digs a hole 3 feet deep and 3 feet wide—the full width of his shrub bed—and throws his kitchen and garden refuse into it all summer, covering each layer with an inch or so of soil. By the time summer is over, the hole is full. Next season he digs a hole 3 feet wide and 3 feet deep just behind it and begins all over again. In this way he prepares a plot for a new shrub each season.

You might want to speed up the schedule a little, but make sure you work plenty of peat moss, compost, and other organic matter into your soil before you even think about planting your shrubs.

Planting It Right Does Not Mean 6 Feet Under

Mound planting is the best way to plant shrubs, especially in heavy clay soil or areas with a high water table, where the plants might be in danger of drowning. The roots will be primarily above the waterline and excess water will run off the mounds. Chapter 2 explains how to mound-plant.

Even if you don't mound-plant, remember my advice: When you plant any bare-root, balled-and-burlap, or container-grown stock, never plant it more than 3 inches deeper than it was in the nursery. Shrubs as a rule do not need support poles or wires like trees; however, I find it helpful with some of the very large shrubs to place a concrete block on the soil at the base of the trunk on the opposite side from a prevailing wind for about a month or so.

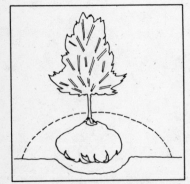

Mound planting: The best way to plant shrubs

No Food, No Action!

I have found that a few handfuls of bonemeal and two handfuls of a starter food benefit most trees and shrubs right after planting. There are several plant starters on the market, like Ortho's Upstart. Scott's has a dry plant starter, as do others. Please read the directions *first;* not after all else fails.

If your shrubs have flowers, feed them in the early spring with any dry garden food or any liquid plant or rose food; better yet, use the safe and easy root feeder that attaches to your garden hose (along with the proper cartridges). The easiest method is to drive a tree or shrub spike into the ground. However you do it, *feed the poor things every year.* Nonflowering shrubs, hedges, and ground covers can be fed with dry or liquid lawn food instead of garden food or the root feeder or spikes. The difference is that garden food is low in nitrogen and high in phosphorous and potash, so it stimulates the growth of flowers and roots, whereas lawn food is high in nitrogen and low in the other two substances, so it stimulates foliage growth.

Feed shrubs in the early spring

Cool Their Heels

A plant's roots are its feet. If it is properly planted in light and rich soil and its roots are covered with a decorative mulch, you should have very little trouble with the growing. Weed control can be accomplished with the systemic (or, more properly, osmetic) grass and weed controls. The control is misted onto any unwanted grass or weeds growing under your shrubs. It is absorbed through the weed's foliage down to the roots and destroys the unwanted grass or weed, but won't hurt the shrubs or trees. K Mart's Super K-Gro line has a good inexpensive one; Ortho also has one. If weeds are controlled, stone is an attractive choice for covering the area around the shrub.

Sunscreens and Snowsuits

In every part of the country, heat, wind, or cold affects the growth of plants; too much or too little of any of them can stunt or destroy a treasured plant.

Don't plant a shrub in full sun unless you're sure it's meant to be there; full sun in summer, and especially in winter, has killed many an otherwise healthy plant. Water generously during the summer months (good drainage is a must) to compensate for the heat.

If strong winds are a problem on your property, try to protect your plants by creating some kind of windbreak. A wooded area, such as a group of pines, is ideal if it does not block out too much light. Of the common shrubs, the narrow-leaf evergreens tend to be the most wind-resistant.

All shrubs should be protected from dehydration during the winter if the temperature goes below freezing in your area. After the soil freezes, you can't water your plant, so you should make sure it has an ample supply of moisture for the winter months by watering it frequently all fall. In late fall, spray the foliage with a product called Wilt-Pruf. This substance is an antidesiccant, which means that it slows down the rate at which the plant loses water to the atmosphere through respiration. It also prevents dehydration during hot, dry periods, when the plant may lose water faster than you can replace it.

Where Does It Say Butcher a Bush?

When I watch some folks prune or trim hedges, shrubs, and evergreens, I have to shake my head in bewilderment. These people are brutal! Easy does it, please. You are trying to improve the plant's looks, not ruin them.

Shrubs that produce flowers should be pruned or shaped only after they have bloomed or very early in the spring—*never* in the fall, because they produce next season's flowers on this year's wood. Nonflowering shrubs or hedges can be cut nearly anytime you have the time and energy. The same is true of evergreens, but the ideal time in areas where the weather goes below freezing is early June. If you have to cut back large limbs from your evergreen, the safest time is late winter.

Here is a checklist of the most popular shrubs and when to prune them:

Pruning deciduous shrub branches

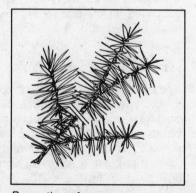

Prune tips of evergreen branches to thicken

While Dormant

Abebia
Barberry
Beauty Berry
Butterfly Bush
Caryopteris
Crape Myrtle
Indigo Bush
Lespedeza
Ligstrum

Rose of Sharon
St. Johnswort
Smoke Tree
Spirea (except Bridal Wreath)
Sumac
Sweet Pepper Bush
Tree Lilac
Willow
Witch Hazel

After Flowering

Abelia
Azalea
Beauty Bush
Bittersweet
Daphne
Deutzia
English Hawthorn
Flowering Almond
Flowering Cherry
Flowering Plum
Flowering Quince
Forsythia
Fringe Tree
Honeysuckle

Hydrangea
Laurel
Magnolia
Mock Orange
Pearl Bush
Pieris
Potentilla
Red Bud
Rhododendron
Shadblow
Spirea (Bridal Wreath)
Strawberry Shrub
Viburnum
Weigela

Don't forget, all canes bigger than your little finger should be sterilized and sealed. You may use pruning paint, lipstick, nail polish, candle wax or crayon. If you must cut into heavy wood, cut on a 45° angle (see Chapter 2, page 53), and make sure the exposed stub will be covered by overhanging foliage.

I'm Rooting for Mister McGregor

I don't want to sound mean, but rabbits just raise Cain with shrubs and trees in the winter. To save these plants, spray them with a rabbit repellent containing Thiram; a good one manufactured by Plantabbs is found in most garden shops. To ward off hungry deer, use a repellent containing a foul-smelling substance called bone tar; Plantabbs also makes one of these. It stinks, but it works.

Insects that Bug Your Shrubs and Vines

The following table lists the most common insect trouble-makers on your shrubs and vines, along with the applicable control.

Shrub or Vine	Insect	Damage	Time	Control
1. Arborvitae	Bagworms	Defoliation	Mid-June	Pick and burn; Sevin spray
	Black vine weevils	Leaves, roots	Late June	Diazinon to leaves and soil, spray
	Juniper scale	Foliage	Summer	Dormant oil; Malathion in mid-May to July
	Juniper webworms	Tip foliage	May, August	Sevin spray, with Miticide
	Lecanium (scales)	Twigs	Late summer	Dormant oil; Miticide in summer
	Mites	Foliage	Early spring and early fall	Kelthane
2. Azalea	Lace bugs	Foliage	When hot	Sevin or Malathion, under leaves
	Leaf miners	Foliage	May on	Sevin or Lindane, before serious
	Thrips	Foliage	When hot	Lindane, repeat at 10-day intervals
3. Bayberry	Aphids	New growth	Summer	Malathion, repeat at 10-day intervals
	Webworms	New growth	Summer	Sevin or Malathion
4. Bittersweet	Euonymus scale	Twigs, foliage	From May on	Dormant oil; Malathion in summer, repeated; cut and burn the worst
	Aphids	New growth	Summer	Malathion, repeat at 10-day intervals
5. Boxwood	Leaf miners	Foliage	Summer	Malathion in May, before adults
	Mites	Foliage	Early spring and early fall	Kelthane
	Nematodes	Roots	Summer	When serious, dig and burn
	Psyllad	Foliage	Summer	Spray nicotine, in June
	Oystershell scale	Twigs, leaves	Summer	Dormant oil
6. Cherry, peach, plum, flowering almond	Scale	Twigs, foliage	From May on	Dormant oil; Malathion in summer, repeated; cut and burn the worst
	Pear slugs	Foliage	Spring	Sevin, as bud opens; repeat
	Borers	Heavy stems	Summer	Coat with Methoxychlor June 1 and at monthly intervals 3 times
7. Clematis	Nematodes	Roots	Summer	When serious, dig and burn

Shrub or Vine	Insect	Damage	Time	Control
	Borers	Roots	Summer	Treat soil, Diazinon in spring
	Blister beetles	Flowers, leaves	Summer	Sevin, as needed
8. Cotoneaster	Scale	Twigs, foliage	From May on	Dormant oil; Malathion in summer, repeated; cut and burn the worst
	Lace bugs	Foliage	When hot	Sevin or Malathion, under leaves
	Pear slugs	Foliage	Spring	Sevin, as bud opens; repeat
	Webworms	New growth	Summer	Sevin or Malathion
9. Currant	Aphids	Foliage	Late spring	Malathion under leaves, early
	Borers	Heavy stems	Summer	Coat with Methoxychlor June 1 and at monthly intervals 3 times
	Stem girdlers	Heavy stems	Early summer	Cut and burn or coat with Methoxychlor June 1 and at monthly intervals 3 times
10. Euonymus	Euonymus scale (on both evergreen and deciduous)	Twigs, foliage	From May on	Dormant oil; Malathion in summer, repeated; cut and burn the worst
11. Forsythia	4-lined plant bugs	New leaves	Late spring	Sevin, used early, repeated
12. Hydrangea	Aphids	New growth	Summer	Malathion, repeat at 10-day intervals
	Leaf tiers	Leaf tips	Summer	Sevin, used early, repeated
13. Japanese quince, other flowering quinces	Scale	Twigs, foliage	From May on	Dormant oil; Malathion in summer, repeated; cut and burn the worst
	Aphids	New growth	Summer	Malathion, repeat at 10-day intervals
	Tent caterpillars	Branches	Mid-spring	Dipel™ or Malathion, before tent enlarges
14. Juniper	Bagworms	Defoliation	Mid-June	Pick and burn; Sevin spray
	Scale	Twigs	Late summer	Dormant oil; Miticide in summer
	Mites	Foliage	Early spring and early fall	Kelthane
	Webworms	Tip foliage	May, August	Sevin spray, with Miticide

Shrub or Vine	Insect	Damage	Time	Control
15. Lilac	Borers	Twigs	From May on	Dormant oil; Lindane at 10-day intervals, repeated 3 times; cut and burn the worst
	Scale	Heavy stems	Summer	Cut and burn before May 1; after coat best remaining with Methoxychlor
16. Pachysandra	Scale	Twigs, leaves	Summer	Dormant oil
	Nematodes	Roots	Summer	When serious, dig and burn
	Leaf-chewing caterpillars	Foliage	Spring	Sevin
17. Privet	Thrips	Foliage	When hot	Lindane, repeat at 10-day intervals
	Borers	Twigs	From May on	Dormant oil; Lindane, repeat at 10-day intervals, 3 times; cut and burn the worst
	Scale	Twigs	From May on	Dormant oil; Malathion in summer, repeated; cut and burn the worst
18. Pyracantha	Scale	Twigs, foliage	From May on	Dormant oil; Malathion in summer, repeated; cut and burn the worst
	Mites	Foliage	Early spring, early fall	Kelthane
	Pear slugs	Foliage	Spring	Sevin, as bud opens; repeat
19. Rhododendron	Lace bugs	Foliage	When hot	Sevin or Malathion, under leaves
	Borers	Twigs	From May on	Dormant oil; Lindane, repeat at 10-day intervals 3 times; cut and burn the worst
	Black vine weevils	Leaves, roots	Late June	Diazinon to leaves and soil, spray
20. Rose of Sharon	Aphids	New growth	Summer	Malathion, repeated at 10-day intervals
21. Spirea	Aphids	New growth	Summer	Malathion; repeat at 10-day intervals; thin to control mosquitoes
22. Viburnum	Mealybugs	Twigs, leaves	Summer	Dormant oil; Malathion in late May

Shrub or Vine	Insect	Damage	Time	Control
	Scale	Twigs, foliage	From May on	Dormant oil; Malathion in summer, repeated; cut and burn the worst
	Aphids (on Old-Fashioned Snowball)	Foliage	Late spring	Malathion under leaves, early; or destroy
23. Yew (Taxus)	Black vine and strawberry root weevils	Leaves, roots	Late June	Diazinon to leaves and soil, spray
	Mealybugs	Twigs, leaves	Summer	Dormant oil; Malathion in late May
	Lecanium	Twigs	Late summer	Dormant oil; Miticide in summer

An Ounce of Prevention . . .

A little preventive action on a comfortable fall day and again on a balmy spring Saturday morning will save you a lot of trouble with your shrubs and evergreens. Dormant spray your evergreens, fruit, flowering and shade trees, your berry bushes, roses, grapevines, and shrubs with a dormant oil (volk oil—don't use lime sulphur) packaged under many brand names. This highly refined oil controls overwintering insects like scales, mites, leaf rollers, red spiders; case bearers like the gypsy moth and tent caterpillar; and the mealybug. It is also a deterrent against the ugly spruce gall. Dormant spraying must be done on a day late in the fall and again early in the spring when the temperature will stay above freezing for at least 24 hours. Dormant spraying is the single most important garden chore that you can do to reduce time, effort, money, and damage to woody caned plants. *Do it!*

Scale Insects—Your Shrub's Little Itches

The scale insects deserve some special attention because they are so prevalent and unattractive. They are small, sucking, waxy insects that spend their entire lives motionless, feeding on the twigs, branches, and leaves of their favorite plants. They create a white or gray scale on the plant, which looks like a coating of tiny oystershells. The scale insects have a penchant for evergreens, but some will go for other trees and shrubs as detailed below.

These are the most common scale insects found on trees, shrubs, evergreens, and vines:

Euonymus scale is the most difficult to control because it multiplies so quickly. This scale not only likes your euonymus but will have a go at your pachysandra as well. In many cases, the entire plant becomes covered with the white bodies of this tough scale. Leaves will generally fall off from the heavy feeding and, in many cases, the plants will have to be removed. The eggs hatch in late May and early June. The young crawl for a short period and then begin to feed. A second generation develops in mid-July.

Oystershell scale looks, as the name implies, like miniature oystershells. Oystershell scale has a hankering for ash, lilac, maple, birch, dogwood, poplar, pachysandra, and many other plants. These insects overwinter in the form of eggs under the protective scale on open branches. The eggs hatch in late May to early June. The good news is that there is only one generation a year of this scale, and the bad news is that it can get so thick that it forms a crust over the branches, often killing the smaller ones.

Juniper scale is a real fooler, and, in most cases, red spider mites get the blame when the foliage begins to die. It attacks arborvitae and cypress as well as juniper. When attacked by this scale, the plants lose their green color and look sick. This scale overwinters as immature insects. In the spring the scale begins to eat again and matures in May. New crawlers appear in June. They start all over again in July.

Pine needle scale. Wow! These guys go after darn near anything with a needle—Scotch, white, mugho, red, and Austrian pine; Douglas fir; most of the spruce family; and even cedars. Their small white bodies cover the needles, sucking out the sap, causing them to turn yellow and then brown. This scale also overwinters as half-grown insects in reddish eggs, which hatch in mid-May, crawl for a week or so, then cover themselves with a shell until early July. By mid-July they hatch and begin to crawl again.

Pine tortoise scale. These insects only produce one generation a year and reach maturity in June. The females then lay eggs that hatch into crawlers in late June or early July. The pine tortoise scale usually develops in the lower limbs of narrowleaf evergreens, sucking the juice from the needles to make a honeydew (sweet fluid), which results in a black, sooty mold on branches and needles. This stunts the growth of these needles and turns them yellow.

Now, let's fight them, folks. Spray all plants attacked by any of these scales in the spring, before plant growth begins, with a dormant spray like Ortho volk oil. Read all directions before you begin; you don't want to cure one plant and kill another. Then spray as follows to fight these scales:

Euonymus scale is sprayed in early June and mid-July with Malathion or Sevin.

Oystershell scale is sprayed in late May and early June with Malathion, Sevin, or Spectracide.

Juniper scale is sprayed in early June and mid- to late June with Malathion or Sevin.

Pine needle scale is sprayed in late May and mid-July with Diazinon, Sevin, Malathion, or Spectracide.

Pine tortoise scale is sprayed in mid-June and early July with Sevin, Spectracide, Diazinon, or Malathion.

I have found that the Burgess Redi-Mix #7 or #12 tank sprayers give me the best coverage and better control with less wasted material.

When it comes to purchasing garden chemicals, it really is the price that counts. Don't be fooled; buy the cheapest. Read *all* directions before using and don't buy or mix more than you need; it doesn't keep.

Finding the Right Shrub for You

Choosing Your Shrubs

The basic care of shrubs and evergreens as described previously could hardly be easier. The real trick to successful growing of this diverse group of plants is choosing the varieties that thrive under the conditions your yard can provide, and attending to the particular needs of each plant. In the pages that follow, I describe in more detail the types that are best suited to certain conditions, such as partial or full shade and sandy soil, as well as the special characteristics and uses of shrub-related plants, such as hedges, vines, and ground covers.

Here Are Some Shady Shrub Characters

Shade is not nearly as serious a problem as poor, sandy soils, unless the shade is caused by too many trees in too small an area. There are happy solutions, even to this problem.

The first consideration is the degree of shade and how it is created. *Full shade*, which means the area gets *no* sunlight, is not healthy for any plant except a few very hardy ground covers. *Open shade* and *medium shade* refer to clear north light against walls of buildings, or sun only in morning or late afternoon. *Bright shade* means sunlight filtered through high, thin foliage all day. Plants respond much the same in open or half shade as they do in bright shade. Full sun is not always desirable; for example, it may burn the foliage of broadleaf evergreens in winter.

Sandy soils are not as great a problem in bright shade as they are in less sunny locations. On the other hand, sandy soils in full sun will dry out quickly and must be enriched with organic matter and heavily mulched. Deeply prepared, heavy soils in bright shade can support a virtual garden paradise, not to be outdone by full sun. As shade decreases, more kinds of shrubs can do very well. Pines and oaks provide desirable acid soil in their shade, but pines may be too densely shading for many shrubs.

For deep or full shade, myrtle and lily of the valley are the only long-term solution, even if you add improved beds to the existing surfaces; wintercreepers, pachysandra, Baltic ivy and pachistima may also last several years, with annual spring feedings. For extra summer color, fill planter boxes, raised slightly off the ground to avoid tree roots, with begonias, impatiens, Browallia, fancy caladiums, and coleus, and place them in the shady area. Decorative architectural features, such as stone and brick in walls, walks, and sitting areas, contribute to year-round interest.

The following table describes some common shade-preferring shrubs and ground covers according to their average mature size, light requirements, and ordinary use. They all like moist soil, except where noted.

EVERGREENS

Fl Flowering
* Acid

Arborvitae	Up to 20'; brightest shade; hedges, screens, accent, foundations
Boxwood, English	4–6'; brightest shade; hedges, foundations
Boxwood, Korean	1–4'; medium shade; low edgings, clipped formal work
Hemlock	As understory to 25'; medium shade; clipped hedges, backgrounds, mixed borders
Holly, Shrubby*	4–6'; bright shade; deep humus; hedges, foundation
Leucothoe*	3–4'; medium shade; Fl; foundations, banks, along steps, with rhododendron
Mountain Laurel*	5–8'; medium shade, deep mulch; Fl; background, mixed borders
Oregon Grape	3–8'; medium shade; Fl; fruits, bird sanctuary, foundations, slopes
Pachistima	10"; deep shade; carpets, ground cover, low foundations, edging
Pachysandra	8"; deep shade; carpets, ground cover, low foundations, edging

Pieris*   4–6'; medium shade, deep mulch; Fl;
                      foundations, rhododendron borders,
                      accent

Rhododendron*   6–10'; medium shade, deep mulch; Fl;
                      hedges, flowering borders, accent

Wintercreepers   Groundcover to 10", or climbers to 15';
(Euonymus)   many forms; edging

Yews:

  Densiform   4–5'; bright shade, heavy soil; best for
                      foundations

  Hicksi   Columnar to 12'; bright shade, heavy
                      soil; accent, screens

  Japanese Spreading   5–6'; deep shade, heavy soil, keep
                      moist; background, sheared hedge

Yucca   2–2½', Fl to 6'; bright shade, sandy,
                      heavy soil; accent in clumps,
                      foundations, borders

DECIDUOUS SHRUBS AND SMALL TREES

Aronias   5–8'; bright shade; Fl, fruiting; fall color,
                      birds, mixed borders, background

Azaleas*   3–8'; medium shade, deep mulch; Fl;
                      foundations, borders, accent, with
                      rhododendrons

Barberry, Japanese   3–4'; medium shade; fall color
                      foundations, barriers, hedges, borders

Bayberry   6–8'; bright shade, sandy soil; gray
                      frond screens, background

Bladder-senna (Colutea) 6–8'; bright shade; Fl; background,
                      mixed borders, specimens

Buckthorns   8–12'; medium shade; sharp thorns;
                      screens, background

Coralberry   3–4'; medium shade, sandy soil; fall
                      color, foundations, mixed borders, birds

Cotoneasters, various 2–8'; bright shade; showy fruits; all-
                      purpose group

Daphne, Winter   3–4'; bright shade, sandy soil; early Fl;
                      small groups near walks

Dogwood, Flowering*   12–20'; bright shade, deep mulch; Fl;
                      accent, mixed backgrounds

Dogwood, Shrubby   6–8'; bright shade; small Fls, showy
species   fruits; winter color, mixed backgrounds

Five-leaf Aralia	6–8'; deep shade; barrier, slopes, backgrounds
Forsythia	6–9'; bright shade, moist clay loam; mixed borders, background, early Fl
Fothergillas	3–8'; bright shade, sandy soil; Fl; foundations, background, specimens
Fringetree	to 20'; bright shade, sandy soil; Fl; specimen, mixed backgrounds
Globeflower (Japanese Double Kerria)	4–5'; medium shade; Fl; foundations, flowering borders
Honeysuckles, various	8–12'; medium shade, sandy soil; Fl; backgrounds, screens, hedges, birds
Hydrangea AG and Oakleaf	4–6'; deep shade; Fl; foundations, groups, borders
Hypericums	2–4'; bright shade; Fl; foundations, flowering borders
Jetbread	4–6'; medium shade, moist clay loam; Fl; mixed borders and backgrounds
Mock Oranges, various	3–15' up; medium shade; Fl; foundations to backgrounds
Potentilla	2–4'; medium shade; Fl; foundations, flowering borders, low hedges
Privets, various	4–8'; bright shade; sheared hedge to mixed backgrounds, screens
Redbud	As understory, to 20'; bright shade; Fl; specimen, mixed backgrounds
Shadblow*	As understory, to 20'; bright shade, sandy soil; Fl; specimen, mixed backgrounds, accent
Spireas, various	3–6"; bright shade; Fl; foundations, borders, backgrounds, hedges
Summersweet (Clethra)*	4–6'; bright shade, sandy soil; Fl late; mixed acid borders, fragrance
Viburnums, many varieties	Bright shade, mulch; backgrounds, fences, borders
Viburnums, Arrowwood	5–8'; sandy soil; autumn color, backgrounds
Viburnums, Cranberry Bush	6–8'; damp soil; Fl, fruits
Viburnums, Doublefile	6–8'; clay loam; Fl; specimen
Viburnums, Wayfaring Tree	6–10'; late foliage, fruits

VINES

Honeysuckle, Halls Japanese	to 12'; bright shade; Fl. all summer; fragrant, for light trellises
Baltic Ivy	to 20'; protect from heavy snow and ice; ground cover
Lycium	to 15'; bright shade; small blue flowers with spines; good barrier on fence, screen

You Can Kick Sand in These Shrubs' Faces

He who gardens on clay wishes for sand. He who gardens on sand wishes for clay. Each type of soil provides an ideal environment for some plants—and a deadly one for others. It is far simpler and saner to choose plants known to thrive in your particular soil, and set about a program of slow but sure reconditioning over the years, than to alter radically the basic content of the soil. Fortunately for gardeners with sandy soil, shrubs and trees can get by on quite limited soil preparation immediately around their roots if you have at least 4 inches of sandy loam. With good watering and normal revival from transplant shock, it will be a year or two before new roots extend outward in search of wider feeding ground, so you have ample time for gradual soil reconditioning. Where some tree roots occur, it is best to build a new bed 18 inches to 24 inches deep above them for shrub planting.

Sandy soil loses moisture rapidly, so organic matter must be worked in by fork or tiller. Peat is the best choice, but you can use whatever comes to hand—composted leaves, grass clippings, or manure (not horse, dog, or cat).

Surface mulches further help to conserve moisture and suppress weeds. Here again fresh grass clippings, straw, wood chips, and leaves to a depth of three or four inches are ideal. Each year the old mulch can be turned into the soil ahead of outward root development (2 to 3 feet beyond the weepline), leaving the soil nearer the plants undisturbed. Sandy soils will go through periods of drought, for which mulches can spell the difference between success and failure.

The following table lists basic shrubs for sandy loam. Shade tolerance (indicated by "S or S"—Sun or Shade) is for light, filtered shade only, not the full shade found under dense trees such as maple. Good drainage is required for all.

Name of Shrub	Height	Light Requirements	Flowers	Comments and Landscape Use
Barberry, Japanese	3–4'	S or S		Reliable, but needs some care; hedges, barriers, fall color from fruit and foliage
Beach Plum	4–6'	Sun	White May	Open, windy dune areas and thin, sandy lakeshores; fruits for jelly
Bladder-senna	8–10'	S or S	Yellow July until frost	Background, mixed shrub border, and as single specimens
Coralberry	3–4'	S or S		Low borders, near house; long, arching branches with red fruits into winter
Five-leaf-aritila	to 9'	S or S		Backgrounds, steep slopes; good barriers due to spines
Glossy Buckhorn cv. Tallhedge	8–12'	Sun		Dense in full sun, ideal narrow screening without shearing; set 2' apart in row
Gray Dogwood	4–8"	S or S	White June	Can spread into colonies; flowers small, berries white; screens, birds
Honeysuckle: Tartarian, Zabel, others	6–8"	S or S	Pink May	Fragrant flowers; backgrounds, screens, slopes, erosion control, birds
Junipers, all kinds	Creepers to trees	Sun		Indispensable evergreens for foundation plantings, rockeries, background, screens
Pea Tree, Siberian	12–20'	Sun	Yellow May	Soft gray-green foliage, green twigs; screens, mixed backgrounds, accent
Potentilla, Shrubby Cinquefoil	2–3'	S or S	Yellow Summer	Ideal near house, keep moist for continued bloom; low hedges, borders
Privets; Amur, border Regel, Vicary	4–8'	Sun best		Sturdy, but not drought-resistant; hedges sheared for natural screens
Rose Daphne	8" mat	Sun	Rose pink, fragrant	Darling evergreen for sand only; edging, rockeries, patio (avoid excess heat)
Russian Olive	to 20'	Sun	Tiny, fragrant	Leaves have silvery underside; foliage accent, singly in backgrounds, borders, screens
Sand Cherry, Red-leaved Hybrids	to 7'	Sun		Unusual color accent, use sparingly for best effect; mixed borders, specimens
Smokebush	to 10'	Sun	Purplish haze	Use newer purple-leaf sorts; fine lawn specimen, singly in mixed borders

Name of Shrub	Height	Light Requirements	Flowers	Comments and Landscape Use
Sumac, Fragrant (and others)	3–4'	S or S		Good autumn color; oakwoods, slopes and erosion control; general landscaping
Wayfaring Tree	6–9'	S or S	White June	Densely bushy, foliage til late; berries red to black; hedges, screens

Suggest also:
Trees—Koelreuteria and Sophora
Bushy trees—Amur Maple, Shadblow
Vines—American Bittersweet, Trumpet Creeper, Virginia Creeper, Japanese Honeysuckle (with restraint), and old-fashioned Rambler Roses
Other native shrubs—Groundsel Bush, Wafer Ash, Sweet Fern, and Jersey Tea

Flowering Shrubs That Know It

Flowering shrubs can be the glory of your garden. Unfortunately, lots of people choose the wrong variety and then fret because their shrub won't flower. There's no reason for that to happen if you use the preceding charts to help you decide which kinds of plant and follow the directions on the planting instructions tag to the letter. In most cases, you have so many types to choose from that you can be sure of enjoying blossoms in every color of the rainbow each spring and summer. The following list of space-filling, easy-care shrubs will help you pick your color scheme:

Home Garden Name	Zone	Flower Color
Andromeda	5	White
Azalea	5	Many colors
Barberry, standard and dwarf	3	Yellow
Beach Plum	4	White
Beauty Bush	5	Pink
Blue Spirea	5	Blue
Blueberry	4	White
Bottlebrush Buckeye	5	White
Broom	6	Yellow, Red, Blue
Butterfly Bush	6	Lavender
California Lilac	4	Blue
Camellia	7	Pink, Red, White
Cherry Laurel	6	White
Chinese Redbud	6	Lavender

Home Garden Name	Zone	Flower Color
Cotoneaster	4	Pink
Crape Myrtle	7	Pink, Red, Lavender, White
Daphne	5	Red, Pink, Lavender, White
Deutzia	5	White, Pink
Firethorn	6	White
Flowering Almond	5	Pink, White
Flowering Plum	6	Pink
Flowering Quince	5	Red
Forsythia	5	Yellow
Gardenia	8	White
Genista	2	Yellow
Glossy Abelia	5	Pink
Hardy Orange	6	White
Heath	6	Red, White, Lavender
Heather	5	Red, Lilac, White
Holly Olive	7	Green
Honeysuckle	3	Pink
Hydrangea	3	White, Pink, Blue
Japanese Snowbell	6	White
Jetbread	6	White
Kerria	6	Yellow
Konsa Dogwood	5	White
Korean Abelia-leaf	5	White
Leatherwood	6	White
Leucothoe	5	White
Lilac	3	Pink, Lavender, White, Red
Mahonia	5	Yellow
Mock Orange	4	White
Mountain Laurel	4	Pink, White
Ocean Spray	5	White
Parrotia	6	Red
Pearl Bush	5	White
Photinia	7	White
Privet	4	White
Pussy Willow	5	Gray
Rhododendron	5	Red, Lavender, Pink, Yellow, White

Home Garden Name	Zone	Flower Color
Rockrose	8	Pink
Rose	5	Yellow, White, Pink, Red
Rose Acacia	6	Purple
St. Johnswort	6	Yellow
Sand Myrtle	6	White
Sapphireberry	6	White
Shadblow	4	White
Skimmia	7	Yellow, White
Smoke Tree	5	Green
Snow Wreath	6	White, Green
Spicebush	4	Yellow
Spike Heath	6	Pink, White
Spiraea	4	White, Pink, Red
Star Magnolia	5	White
Stewartia	7	White
Strawberry Shrub	5	Yellow
Summer Sweet	4	White
Sunrose	6	Yellow, Red, White
Sweet Spire	6	White
Tamarisk	5	Pink, Red
Trailing Arbutus	3	White, Pink
Tree Peony	5	White, Pink, Yellow
Viburnum	5	White, Pink
Vitex	5	Lavender
Weigela	4	Pink, Red, White
Winter Hazel	6	Yellow

Rhododendrons, the Iron-Willed Pussy Cats!

Congratulations! You have discovered rhododendrons! And welcome to the growing circle of admirers who find the "King of Flowering Shrubs" so exciting and rewarding. The "rhodies" differ in many ways from the usual garden shrubs and evergreens. However, once their few and exacting requirements are met, aristocratic beauty without equal can be yours to enjoy for years to come.

Never Use Lime

Rhododendrons, azaleas, blueberries, mountain laurel,

sourwood, hollies, Pieris, drooping Leucothoe and wintergreen are closely related. All demand porous, very acid soil, of not less than two-thirds organic matter. Plentiful moisture must be assured all year long, partly retained under a deep mulch of rotting oak leaves or pine needles. Standing water will kill rhododendrons in a matter of days; there must be rapid drainage of excess water above and below the surface at all times.

Exposure and Ideal Site

Select a planting site where strong winds or intense sunshine will not strike the shrubs in winter. The full heat of the sun in summer can harm the foliage, so rule out the south wall foundation planting and most west sides too. ("Foundation planting" means planting the shrub right next to a wall or building.) The north wall foundation planting remains the ideal location in most instances, with east walls a close second. Natural woodlands of pine work well as a planting site if the shade is very bright. A windbreak-screen of tall evergreens will help reduce wind damage, if they are some distance away.

Soil Preparation

The planting bed is best built above the surface, not into it, especially with clay soils. Planting holes are inadequate. Mound plant as described in Chapter 2. Planting bed depth should be at least 12 inches. The planting bed soil mixture properly consists of one-third sandy loam enriched with rotted grass chippings, two-thirds oak-leaf mold, compost, or acid peat. Test the soil before planting to make sure a pH of 4.5 to 5.5 is reached. Use agricultural sulphur or iron sulphate, thoroughly mixed through the soil, to adjust acid (pH) levels. Aluminum sulphate is not recommended.

Test soil often after planting and adjust accordingly. If foliage shows yellowing, a symptom of chlorosis, soil pH is rising much too high; flower buds will form poorly, if at all, and general hardiness will decrease rapidly. Keep the roots from neighboring trees out of the bed.

Yearly Fertilizing

Before the first of June each year, apply an acid fertilizer (the label will say it's for azaleas, camellias, and evergreens) as recommended by the manufacturer. A handful of cottonseed meal is helpful too. Work fertilizers in lightly with fingertips only; never cultivate because the fine roots are right at the surface.

Watering

Follow up fertilizing at once with a good drenching, then apply a mulch of oak leaf or pine needle compost 2 to 3 inches deep. At all other times water only when foliage appears withered and fails to revive overnight; this will occur often. Use hard water very sparingly; rainwater is the very best for rhododendrons.

Recommend Hardiest Varieties for Survival

I strongly suggest planting only the hardiest varieties, which are listed as H-1 by the American Rhododendron Society and often referred to as "iron-clads." H-1 indicates that the flower buds are hardy to −25° F. The only winter protection required for these plants under normal circumstances is a blanket of new oak leaves over the soil, up to 10 inches deep; remove early in spring to make way for fertilizer and composted mulch.

Wilt-Pruf, sprayed in November after frosts have begun and again in early March, prevents moisture loss from the foliage as well as "winter burn" (scalding of the leaves from the dry, cold southwest wind).

Evergreens Don't Have to Be Every Color but

I am a great fan of evergreens; they have a bit more class than your everyday shrub. If you plant them properly and give them the minimal care they need, they'll be the least of your worries and give year-round enjoyment. But if you try to grow them in the wrong location on the wrong kind of soil, you'll probably end up with sort-of-greens or sometime greens or even everbrowns.

Evergreens Are Two-Faced

As I mentioned earlier, evergreens come in two types: the narrowleaf (with needles) and the broadleaf (with flat, wide leaves). Both types retain their foliage year round.

The narrowleaf evergreens will, as a rule, tolerate drier air, more wind, and colder temperatures than their broadleaf cousins. They like light, well-drained soil. The five classes of narrowleaf evergreens are:

1. Arborvitae—fern type, flat foliage
2. False Cypress—scalelike foliage
3. Yews—dark, dense, soft needles
4. Junipers—combination needle and scale foliage
5. Pine—various needle lengths

The broadleafed evergreens are mostly shade to semishade lovers, and like medium, well-drained soil. They do well on the east and north sides of a building. The most common varieties are:

1. Azalea
2. Boxwood
3. Cotoneaster
4. Holly
5. Mountain Laurel
6. Pieris Japonica
7. Rhododendron

These are among the most popular, but there are 100 or more to select from. Your local nurseryman can guide you to the ones most appropriate for your climate.

Easy Does It Doesn't Mean Lazy!

Evergreen nursery stock should be planted the day you purchase it, and not left in the hot, dry sun for several days nor on the hot drive or walkway. If it is impossible to plant immediately, place the plant in a cool, shady spot and water well. If it must rest out of soil for several days, then cover the ball or container with leaves, bark, or a thick layer of burlap.

Don't Invite Trouble

When you bring a new evergreen into your yard to live, make sure it is not bringing trouble with it in the form of unwanted insects or disease. Before planting, spray it with a mixture of:

4 tablespoons of liquid soap
4 tablespoons of rose dust, available at your garden center (make into a paste by stirring in a little warm water)
1 cup of tobacco juice
1 gallon of water

The Worst Soil Is Best for Evergreens

I cringe every time I see a few bags of topsoil in the same car with a new evergreen because I know that the evergreen is in for one tough pull just to survive. Evergreens love sandy, gravelly soil, where roots can run and ramble. Heavy soil, muck, and clay are killers. If the developer who built your home was as thoughtless as most, who sell off or remove good topsoil and refill with thick heavy clay or free backfill, then here is a remedy:

Dig all planting holes twice as wide as they need be. Next, dig a narrower hole, called a post hole or French well, in the bottom of your planting hole 30 inches or deeper with a post hole digger. Fill the post hole with 60/40 gravel (60 percent stone, 40 percent sand), as well as the bottom 4 inches of the planting hole. Set the new plant into the hole and backfill with a mixture of 50 percent 60/40 gravel and 50 percent sandy loam (average topsoil). Press the soil down firmly with your foot. When the hole is refilled, cover the area around the plant with a shredded pine-bark mulch.

You should end up with a contented evergreen.

A Fish Dinner and a Beer Will Prove Your Friendship

No, not for you; for the evergreens. I mix a half can of beer and a shot glass of fish emulsion per 2 gallons of water for each of my evergreens in early May. A week later I sprinkle a cup of cheap Epsom salts on the soil around each evergreen.

In late May I feed with an inexpensive, lightweight lawn food at the rate of ¼ pound per foot of height (6 feet gets 1½ pounds, 8 feet gets 2 pounds and so on). Use garden food instead on your flowering evergreens. Repeat again in late June. Never feed evergreens after the first of August in areas where the winter temperatures go below freezing, because the food will stimulate soft new growth that will be killed by the first frost.

Basic Care for Your Evergreens

The basic maintenance procedures for shrubs described earlier in this chapter apply to evergreens as well. Make sure you prune as appropriate. Apply Wilt-Pruf in the late fall to prevent dehydration over the winter when the soil freezes. Protect against invasions by hungry rabbits and deer. Most important of all, dormant spray each year to prevent infestations of the many evergreen pests and diseases.

Plant a Living Christmas Tree

It makes good sense to buy a Christmas tree that can be planted when Christmas is past and enjoyed for years afterward. Some folks do this year after year and now have a nice plantation of living Christmas trees to show for it. If you are to have success, you must remember a few basic instructions:

1. Before you purchase, look for nursery-grown trees with

a root ball or container at least half the width of the weepline.

2. After purchase, keep it outdoors in a shady spot until you move the tree inside. Give the tree a pail of water every two to three days. Smart gardeners beat the bad weather by digging the hole at this time and storing some topsoil inside for planting use after Christmas. Be sure to cover the hole with a sheet of plywood to prevent accidents.

3. When moving a tree indoors, choose the coolest spot available in the house, away from warm air registers if possible. Place the tree on a large saucer; a garbage can lid placed upside down and blocked with pieces of wood works nicely. Water the tree daily, directly on the soil ball. Use miniature lights only for decoration, since the larger bulbs create too much heat. It is best if you keep the tree inside no longer than seven to ten days. If it is kept in the warm indoor climate longer, the tree may start to grow, which would jeopardize its health when it's moved back outdoors.

4. When moving the tree back outdoors, follow these guidelines: If temperatures are mild and expected to remain above freezing for a day or two, just take the tree directly outdoors, plant it and water it heavily. In freezing weather, acclimate the tree for 48 hours in the cold garage before planting. In late March, continue watering as with any newly planted tree.

Hedges Are Shrubs With a Purpose

Hedges perform many useful services, often being the only feasible planting for the very narrow area. Hedges give privacy on the patio; they act as sound, heat, and dust barriers, windbreaks, living fences, and coverings for high foundation walls. Only the formal architectural hedge is sheared; flowering hedges are pruned very little, if at all.

When considering a new hedge, be very sure there will be space and light enough for it to grow properly, and that you will have the time, at the right times, to care for it properly. When close to a lot line, make certain there will be room to walk in back for shearing, or that your neighbor will allow you to do so on his or her property; in fact, it's a good idea to make the hedge a joint effort. Hedges can promote neighborhood trouble, however, so make sure you and your neighbor see eye to eye on type, cost, and maintenance before you try to share a hedge. Hedge plantings do require more maintenance than the same plants used elsewhere. Never pinch pennies in buying the right size and quantity; above all, prepare soil adequately before planting.

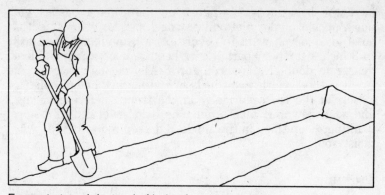

Excavate trench instead of holes for planting hedge

Soil Preparation

A good hedge is uniform in growth throughout its entire length, with branches full to the ground. Good light and good soil preparation are absolutely essential.

Instead of preparing individual holes for each plant, excavate a trench the entire length, 4 feet wide for single rows, 5 feet for double; dig 30 inches deep. If drainage is poor, lay clay tiles end to end the length of the trench. Backfill the trench with good topsoil, to which you've added one-third rotted manure or compost, and settle well with water. Peat may be added after planting in the area around the plants.

Planting

Plan to plant in early spring, using bare-root stock for economy; buy the heaviest bushes available, as these should

Setting hedge plants in trench

have the best roots. To figure out how many bushes you need, measure your plot and buy one bush for every 2 feet or so of ground you want to cover; extra heavy plants can go 6 to 8 inches farther apart. Some hedges, such as privet, look denser in double, staggered rows. Allow open space for an eventual bed width two-thirds of the mature hedge height.

Spread the roots normally in the trench before covering, and soak down. If plants must be held several days before planting, keep them in the shade and keep roots covered with moist soil.

Training

Slender-twig deciduous hedge plants are cut back to 6 inches from the soil at time of planting, no matter how tall they are; this forces thicker branching from the base. Others are trimmed at the ends to reduce slightly and even up the edges. *Note:* Do not cut evergreens back hard at any time.

Allow a maximum of 6 inches yearly growth until the hedge nears two-thirds desired height. Then reduce to 4 inches annually, and finally to only 1 inch on the sides and very little more on top. The best hedges are trained wider at the bottom than the top, with the object of forcing branches solidly to the ground in better light. Never cut the hedge back to its previous size or attempt to keep it at the same size, as balding and dieout will occur, ruining years of work. For the purely architectural or box hedge, use a good electric shear—carefully—whenever new growth reaches 4 inches.

When deciduous hedges become too large or unsightly, they may be rejuvenated by cutting down to 6 inches from the soil in very early spring; feed heavily.

Nip the ends on broadleaf evergreens to smooth up in the summer.

Shear or prune needle-type evergreens in early July only; stick to the same growth limits as for deciduous plants.

The following are suggested uses for hedges, with fine plants to fill them. There are many besides the familiar privet to beautify any neighborhood, and many take far less work.

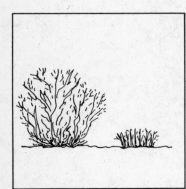

Cut hedge back to 6 inches after planting

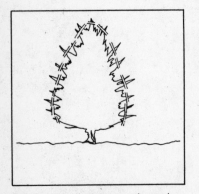

Prune tips of new growth each year

Symbols	Suggested Uses
A	Low hedge for edging under 2 feet. Use along garden walks; slow-growing
B	Hedges 2 to 4 feet; mainly box shape or architectural
C	Hedges 4 to 6 feet; box shape only
D	Screening hedges 6 to 10 feet; box shape or oval; may require stepladder
E	Hedges for drier soils
F	Hedges for pedestrian barriers
G	Auto-traffic barriers when mature

Arborvitae, American D
Arborvitae, Globe B, C
Barberry, Crimson Pygmy A
Barberry, Japanese B, F
Box(wood), Dwarf Edging A
Box(wood), Korean A
Buckthorn, Tallhedge D, F
Burningbush, Dwarf B
Caragana, Pea Tree D, E
Cotoneaster, Cranberry A
Cotoneaster, Peking C, D
Cranberry Bush, Dwarf A
Currant, Alpine B, C
Dogwood, Cornelian Cherry C, D
Elaeagnus, Autumn C, D, E, F
Elm, Chinese C, D, E
Euonymus, Big-leaf B, C
Euonymus, Saracoxie A
Euonymus, Sarcoxie B, C
Five-leaf Aralia C, E, F
Hawthorn, Washington C, D, E, F
Hemlock, Canada C, D
Holly, American C, D

Holly, Japanese B
Holly, Japanese Dwarf A
Honeysuckle, Clavey Dwarf B
Honeysuckle, Tatarian C, D, E, F
Juniper, Red Cedar varieties D, E
Maple, Ginnala D, E, G
Mulberry, White D, F
Osage orange D, E, F
Pachistima A
Prinsepia C, F
Privet, Amur C
Privet, Border C, D
Pyracantha C, F
Quince, Flowering B, C, F
Sand Cherry, Purple B, E
Rose, Japanese (Multiflora) C, F, G
Teucrium A
Viburnum, Lantana C, D
Yew, Capitana C
Yew, Densiform A, B
Yew, Hatfield, Hicks C, D

Many kinds of trees, shrubs, evergreens, vines, grasses, and weeds move in quickly to fill barren spaces in nature as ground covers. For landscaping our homes, however, we think of ground covers as a group of low, carpeting plants that present a neat, finished appearance. The attractiveness of the foliage is all-important; if the plants also flower, we are the richer for it.

Groundcovers Go Where Others Fear to Tread

Requirements for ground covers in modern garden design usually fall into a few well-defined categories:

Symbols	Suggested Uses
A	Shade, where lawn grasses do poorly or refuse to grow (where A is shown in the following lists, B, D, E, F, Ga, and Gb are assumed to be in some shade also)
B	Slopes and banks too difficult to mow; erosion problems
C	Hot, sunny exposures on poor, often dry soils; grasses fail
D	Special permanent pattern beds for design effects
E	Unifying or drawing together of shrub and tree groups
F	Very low foundation plantings
Ga	Rock garden
Gb	Wild borders and roadsides
M	Most satisfactory in large masses
S	Best used in smaller colonies or borders, as near walks

Ground covers are sold as (1) rooted cuttings, (2) one- and two-year pots, (3) three- to four-year grown plants, balled and burlap. Herbaceous types may also be had as (4) divisions. Center to center spacings for good cover effect in three years are shown in inches or feet; plant in a triangular arrangement for best appearance.

WOODY EVERGREENS

Baltic Ivy (Hedera helix)
  A, B, D, F; (1) 8″; (2) 12″; M; S (variegated)

Japanese Spurge (Pachysandra terminalis)
  A, D, E, F; (1) 5″; (2) 8″; M or S

Junipers, low-spreading types such as Bar Harbor, Waukegan, Andorra
  B, C, D, F, Ga; (2) 24″; (3) 3′; M

Myrtle (Vinca minor)
  A, B; (4) 10″; M

Pachistima (P. canbyi)
  A, B, E, F; (1) 6″; (2) 8″; (3) 12″; S (or M)

Wintercreepers (Euonymus fortunei vars.)
  E. fort. radicans (acuta)
    A, B, D, E, F, Ga; (1) 8″; (2) 10″; (3) 10-24″; M; best for shade

E. fort. coloratus
  A, B, Sunny but not dry places, D, E, F; (1) 10″; (2) 15″; (3) 2 to
  3′; M
E. fort. kewensis
  A, Ga; (2) 6″; (3) 10″; S; dainty, tiny foliage
E. fort. Silver Queen
  A, D, F, Ga; (1) 6″; (2) 10″; (3) 16″; S

HERBACEOUS EVERGREENS

Christmas Fern (Polystichum acrostichoides)
  A, Ga, Gb; (3) 15″; S

Christmas Rose (Helleborus niger)
  A, Ga; (3) 18″; (4) 12″; S

Leatherleaf groundcover (Bergenia cordifolia)
  A, D, F, Ga; (2) or (4) 18″; S; handsome accent

WOODY NONEVERGREENS

Hall's Japanese Honeysuckle (Lonicera japonica Halliana)
  A (light), B; (1) 10″; (2) 15-18″; M; fragrant flowering, rampant

Thymes (Thymus serpyllum and others)
  A (light), C (if moist), D, F, Ga; (2) or (4) 9″; S; also as substitute
  for moss in Japanese gardens

Virginia Creeper (Parthenocissus quinquefolia)
  A, B, Gb; (2) 3′; M; rampant

HERBACEOUS NONEVERGREENS

Barrenwort (Epimedium in var.)
  A (light), D, F, Ga, Gb; (2) or (4) 10″; S; tough, beautiful

Bishopswort, Variegated (Aegopodium)
  A, Ga; (2) or (4) 10″; S; restrict

Bronzeleaf (A. metallica)
  A (as above) and in full sun; excellent

Buglewort (Ajugas in var.)
  A (light), F, Ga; (2) or (4) 10″; S; spring flowering

Crown Vetch (Coronilla)
  A (light), F, Gb; (2) 24″; M; rampant, needs shearing

Day Lily, Tawny (Hemerocallis fulva)
  A, B, Gb; (4) 18″; M; mid-summer flowering

Lily of the Valley (Convallaria majalis)
  A, B, F, Ga, Gb; (2) or (4) 10″; M and S

Sedums, in var.
    B, C, Ga; (2) or (4) 10″; S; creeping sorts best for most places

Spotted Dead Nettle (Lamium maculatum)
    A (if light), D, F, Ga; (2) or (4) 10″; S

Sweet Woodruff (Asperula odorata)
    A (light), B, E, F, Ga, Gb; (2) or (4) 10″; M; keep moist

Hardy Flowering Vines Are Garden Window Peepers!

The well-chosen flowering vine will add vastly to garden enjoyment, not only for its weeks of summer color, but also for excellent sound and heat screening. Some work neatly into spaces too narrow for shrubs; happily, a few do well in bright shade. In addition to good soil preparation before planting, all vines should have composted manure and bonemeal worked into the soil each spring before growth begins. Light vines take up to half a bushel, heavier vines up to two bushels. Use a spading fork to work it in, being careful to avoid large roots.

Clematis, Large-Flowered Hybrids

These are slender vines, 8 to 12 feet tall, often used on narrow chain-link trellises, for porches and arbors, or on rose poles. Huge 8-inch blooms of red, pink, lavender, purple, or white, depending on the variety, smother the plants in June and July; some may bloom in May from old stems. Purple Jackmani is the most abundantly flowered of all.

Soil and Situation. These plants are best used where the base will be shaded, the top in sun; an eastern exposure is good. The soil must be well enriched to a 20-inch depth and a four-foot width; make certain it is "sweet" by adding lime if needed. The foliage will yellow if the soil is acid. Perfect drainage is required.

Pruning. Cut the vines to the soil in fall, as they are not reliably top hardy. Or you can wait until spring and cut out the dead wood only. Add a foot deep mulch of leaves or straw to keep the soil from freezing. Allow all growth in spring, and keep the stems 6 inches apart on the trellis to prevent bunching.

Clematis, Paniculata

This variety, also called Sweet autumn or Virgin's bower, grows to 10 feet or more. Masses of small, fragrant white flowers appear in September. The vines are hardy only at the base. The foliage stays green until late fall. Since growth is heavy, this variety requires a sturdy trellis of wire or wood. It makes a good foliage screen on porches, arbors, and fences.

Soil and Situation. Plant as for large-flowered hybrids. Water generously all summer. Any exposure will do, in sun or partial shade, but it's best to keep it out of the wind.

Pruning. Wait until growth starts in spring, and cut back last year's growth, leaving only strong, new, growing shoots. Spread the shoots widely over trellis until the vine reaches a height of ten feet.

Honeysuckle, Hall's Japanese

This honeysuckle grows to ten feet. It is a slender vine with very fragrant white or yellow flowers in abundant clusters from late June to September. It can be grown on light wire or wood trellises, or on fences, and is often used for porch screens and arbors.

Soil and Situation. Any well-drained soil will do; the better and more deeply prepared the soil, the finer the flowering in hot weather. It's best to provide sun in morning and shade in afternoon. Soak soil frequently in summer.

Pruning. Cut back each spring to live, green, pencil-size stems, no longer than 8 feet. If you have to cut them shorter because they've died farther back over the winter, don't worry; the stems will grow out quickly. Keep only six to eight of the most vigorous stems, spaced 6 inches apart; cut out the extras. Don't allow the branches to touch the ground as they take root and run in all directions.

Hydrangea Vine

This vine grows to thirty feet, blooming in large, flat, white clusters in June. It is a heavy grower and clings only to rough surfaces, such as brick or rough-barked trees.

Soil and Situation. Hydrangea vine must have very rich and always moist soil, and prefers cool, light shade. If it is grown on a tree, there should be no limbs within at least 20 feet of the soil, to provide free growing space for the vine to show off well. Older trees are best.

Pruning. Do not prune except to remove dead branches. Forced training is impractical and often useless. Mulch well in winter.

Trumpet Vine

This vine grows to thirty feet, with large clusters of orange-red flowers from July to September. It will climb on any rough surface, or it can be trained by tying to pipe supports (pieces of metal pipe driven into the ground).

Soil and Situation. Plant in full sun only, in any well-drained soil; sandy, unimproved soils are best.

Pruning. Cut back heavily each spring to keep in check. Flowers occur on new growth, so pruning can be vigorous, reducing the vine to 10 feet, or any convenient working height, each year. Allow one stem or trunk only.

Wisteria, Chinese

This wisteria grows to twenty-five feet, with abundant, fragrantly sentimental clusters of blue-violet or white flowers in late May. A very heavy vine, attaining great age, it requires sturdy and permanent supports; pipe is often used. It is ideal for screening a large porch or the bare walls of a two-story house. The flowers are best seen from beneath an arbor.

Soil and Situation. Wisteria needs deeply and widely prepared soil with heavy loam and some lime; add enrichment sparingly each spring, to promote flowering. Keep away from trees.

Pruning. Prune as needed to restrict growth. Laterals (branches) should be cut back to encourage flower bud formation. Three stems from the ground are enough, spread 2 feet or more apart on rack.

CHAPTER 5 Rose Care

Roses *Can* Be a Girl's Best Friend— If You Grow Your Own!

"Diamonds are a girl's best friend," so the song goes; but roses have to come in a close second. Besides, as a rule you get only one diamond in your life, but roses are an on-going symbol of lasting love.

I know, ladies, it all sounds good. Most of you can count on one hand the number of times you have gotten roses after the courtship.

It could be that the cost of long-stem, cut roses has put a damper on your man's sense of romance. It's not unusual to pay $30 to $36 per dozen. So unless he happens to be a millionaire, the best way around the problem is to grow your own.

Wait a minute! You have heard that roses are a pain to grow, and you don't have the time or patience to add a spoiled-brat plant to your garden, right?

Roses are hardly more trouble for you to grow than the average flowering tree, fruit tree, or flowering shrub.

No, I'm not trying to feed you a lot of bull. Roses require a little extra care, but the end results will be well worth it for beauty, fragrance, and ego. After all, you can admire them, smell them, eat them, brew them, wear them, press them, and dry them. What more do you want?

Choosing and Planting Your Roses

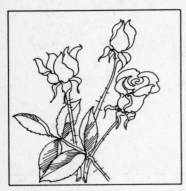

Hybrid tea rose

Grandiflora rose

Let's Take It from the Top!

There are rose bushes, rose hedges, rose trees, and rose vines; so, suit yourself, your space, and your climate.

Hybrid Teas. These are those long-stem, expensive beauties we talked about in the beginning of this chapter. With one flower per stem, these roses grow 3 to 5 feet tall and are year-rounders in the South; however, in Zone 5 and north on the climate map, they need winter protection.

Grandifloras. These are sisters to the teas, and differ in that there are several blooms per stem. Care is the same.

Floribundas. These have large clusters of small flowers and are great in a group or mass planting. In Zone 5 and north they need a comfort cap (Styrofoam rose cap or paper bag over leaf mulch) in winter. Rose hedges are inexpensive, hardy floribundas allowed to grow 3 to 5 feet tall. This style of display generally works best in the South and West.

Shrub Roses. These are wild, old-fashioned varieties used as background for a showy turf area or for crowd control.

Tree Roses. A tree rose is a popular variety of tea, floribunda, or grandiflora grafted on to a hardy variety of understock. Tree roses need a lot of TLC. I highly suggest that you look before you leap with these beauties in Zone 6 and north.

You Get What You Pay For!

I have seen roses priced from .69¢ to $30 each and all

Floribunda rose

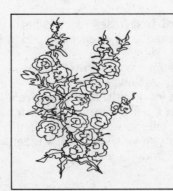

Shrub rose

Tree rose

prices in between. Each one was worth the price advertised. Are you wondering what you could get for .69¢? The answer is junk; unless you know how to make silk purses out of sows' ears. What dummy would pay $30 for a rose bush? Watch your tongue! *I am the dummy.* It was a tree rose, and I love it.

You can buy roses with *bare roots*—I mean naked, without a stitch of root cover—in piles, in crates, and intact. Some communities have sales that include shrubs and trees in the same state of undress. Great bargains!

Mail-order houses, mass merchandisers, and grocery stores sell *packaged roses*. A water-holding material covers the roots, which are sealed in a plastic bag; there is no foliage.

Boxed, or preplanted, roses are sold both by mail and at retail stores. They are usually a more established plant than the bare-root and packaged varieties and consequently are more expensive.

Potted roses are seldom sold by mail, but are a big favorite with large nurseries and garden centers. They are priced higher than the other kinds but generally are in full foliage and blooming—an excellent way to get into the rose game.

When you purchase a new rose bush, look for plants with three canes or more about as big around as your index finger, and with most of the canes 12 to 18 inches long. If they are bare-root or packaged, you want no new growth (plump buds are okay), and no black or dry brown wood.

Boxed plants should be 10 to 12 inches tall with healthy-looking, small, red foliage.

Potted roses should be green and strong with bright, shiny foliage. Avoid sick-looking plants at all costs; they are never a bargain.

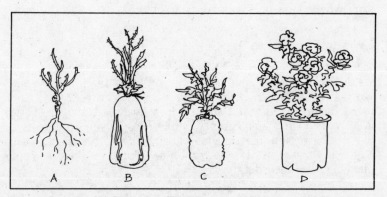

Kinds of stock: (A) Bare root (B) Packaged (C) Boxed (D) Potted

What Plants to Buy

Beginners can test gardening skill with inexpensive packaged roses, available in March and April. From May on, potted roses in full growth and later in bloom are very appealing; that's when the connoisseur finds all the latest award winners.

The kind of store you buy your roses from does not ensure their quality but the store's reputation does. I buy roses from K Mart, Jackson Perkins, Emlongs Nurseries, Inc. catalogs, and the Fruit Basket, Flowerland—all with excellent results.

Whatever roses you buy, be prepared to plant them right away.

Planting Time Confuses the Best of Them

I have worked for some of the world's greatest park superintendents and gardeners and their preferences for timing the planting of new roses differ as much as their personalities. My advice is to plant after April 1 in Zones 6 and 7; after April 15 in Zone 5; after May 15 in Zone 4; and in Zone 3 anytime after you take off your long johns. South of Zone 7, you can plant safely in February or March.

I have also planted rose bushes in early September in Zones 5 and 6 and they grew fine, but you might be taking a chance if a hard winter hits in Zone 5 and north. Don't turn down a bargain or freebie though.

Give Them Room to Breathe

Roses need fresh air just as much as you and me. Plant them in a bed that gets unobstructed air flow, but not a knocking wind. Avoid dead air and high, unprotected spots that are prone to frost, and don't plant in a hollow. Roses also need space for their roots to ramble, so don't plant them in an area where tree or shrub roots are likely to invade the bed.

Let the Sun Shine in!

Roses need six to eight hours of bright sun a day. It is ideal if the sun begins at dawn, to burn the dew off the bushes first thing in the morning. (Disease grows quickly on moist foliage.) In the hot and dry Southwest, afternoon shade is a godsend for man, animal, and roses. Even if you don't live in this region, a little shade during the hottest part of the day will preserve the flowers much longer. Choose your planting site accordingly.

Making Up the Soil Bed

Make certain there will be perfect subdrainage as well as surface runoff at all times. The soil must be porous to a depth of at least 3 feet; heavy clay and compacted soil will not do. In hard clay it may be preferable to build a raised bed, rather than to tile out the bottom.

Roses prefer clay loams, but above all, a high organic content in the soil. If soil is sandy, excavate the entire bed at least 18 inches deep and refill with two-thirds clay loam topsoil from formerly cultivated cornfields or other rich topsoil, thoroughly mixed with one-third organic matter in the form of rotted manure or compost.

If, on the other hand, you have clay soil, you must ensure that roses have at least 3 feet of rich, light, but firm organic soil. Work in copious quantities of compost, humus, sandy loam and peat moss, which may mean a little heavy breathing during the initial bed building.

Test soil early in the spring for pH level, and fertilize it to maintain a pH of 6 or 7. Use an inexpensive soil test kit.

Roses Don't Like to Rub Elbows

Give roses room to bloom and you will have little trouble with damage, insects, or diseases. The reason is fairly simple. If the rosebush has room around it, its stems will grow out, up, and away instead of being cramped and tangled together. This allows sunshine to reach the entire bush, lets air circulate freely around the bush, discourages disease, and permits you to see insect problems easily.

In Zones 2 through 5, tea roses are spaced fairly close together, from 18 to 24 inches apart. In Zone 6, plant roses 2 feet apart. In Zones 7 and south, plant them 3 feet apart; rosebushes grow bigger in the South and West. If you plan to have several rosebushes in a bed, try not to make the bed any wider than 3 feet for a single bed and 6 feet for double beds. A 4-foot wide bed will hold two rows, using a staggered arrangement. If planted near buildings, keep roses well outside roof drip lines. Although shrubs make nice backgrounds for roses, a 6-foot wide grass walk should separate them from the rose bed to prevent the roots and foliage from tangling; nearer than this, use a plastic lawn edging as a shield along the shrub side of the bed.

You Can't Hide the Ugly Knob

Most popular roses are grafted onto a hardy root stock. The graft ends up looking like a small ball or knot, and although it must be protected, it can't be buried. Simply plant it at ground level; however, in Zone 5 and north you must cover it up in the winter with a good mulch.

Each type of rose stock is planted differently, so follow the directions below.

Planting Packaged Roses

Plan to plant packaged roses before growth begins, if at all possible.

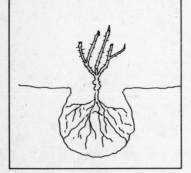

Planting packaged rose: Spread roots over cone in hole

1. Unwrap, shake out packing material; immerse to soak overnight, including tops if not waxed, in one gallon of warm water to which you've added ½ cup of Epsom salts and 1 tablespoon of household ammonia. Plant the next day.
2. In the prepared bed, dig a hole deep enough to bring the graft bulge just below ground level when the hole is filled with soil and firmed.
3. Make a cone of topsoil mix in the bottom and spread roots normally on it.
4. Fill the hole halfway with topsoil mix, flood with water and let stand until it drains away. Continue filling soil and compact with the feet.

With packaged roses it is wise to mound the soil up an extra 10 inches about the branches when you plant to prevent the bed from drying out. As growth shows above the mound, pull the earth down and level the bed.

Planting Potted Roses

Fiber pots decay slowly, eventually adding humus to the soil. Set these plants, pot and all, in holes deep enough to

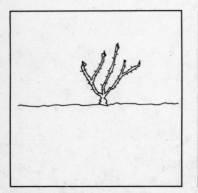

Prune newly planted packaged roses to leave three branches

Planting potted rose

The graft should be just below the soil level

bring the graft just below bed level. Slit or puncture the pot sides so the roots may come through immediately; don't remove growing rose plants from their pots. Soak and fill as described on the planting instructions tag.

Pruning Roses

Prune newly planted packaged roses only; don't cut the roots, but trim back the tops to allow three stout branches. Wait until the 10-inch mound of extra soil is removed to do any pruning. On floribundas leave four or five canes.

Mulching

To conserve moisture and greatly reduce watering and weeding in summer, use organic mulches over the entire bed up to 2 inches deep. Rotted manure or compost are the best bets.

Don't Get Caught with Your Roses Uncovered

Winter protection in Zone 3 and south through Zone 6 is a must. Start by shutting the pantry door August 10: No more food for the roses. This is to prevent the growth of soft new shoots that will freeze. Now, tie the tops of tall bushes together with pieces of nylon stocking (no wire) after the leaves are almost all gone, or cut tops back and place a Styrofoam cone over them. Before the soil freezes, get some new soil with plenty of organic matter and mound it 18 inches up the canes. Tree roses must be dug up, placed in a trench 2 feet

Basic Rose Care

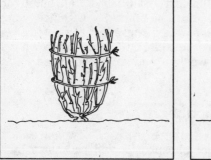

Tie bushes for winter

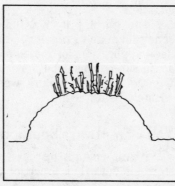

Mound soil over the canes

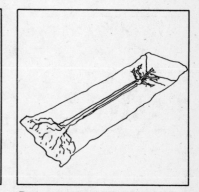

Bury tree rose in trench

Wrap climbers

deep, and buried. Climbing roses can be wrapped in burlap or simply screened from the wind.

Starting Over Every Spring Isn't So Bad

Good preparation in the early spring ensures that you get your share of roses each season. Early in the season, when the plants are dormant, before the weather warms up (in November–December in Zones 8, 9, 10; early April in Zones 5, 6, 7; early May in Zones 3, 4) thin out the damaged canes. Cut back dead wood and extra canes, leaving only four to five of the sturdiest, firmest canes. Now, cover them back up with the soil you used to mound around them and leave covered until new growth begins. As the new growth begins, pull the soil away and spray the new plants with a mixture of 1 ounce of chewing tobacco juice and 2 ounces of liquid dish soap in a quart of water. Sprinkle ½ cup of Epsom salt crystals on the soil beneath each rosebush but don't feed just yet.

Mulch

If you don't mind putting a little extra work into your roses to ensure their health and happiness, add an organic mulch to the soil each spring after you have completed all of the starting-over steps above. The following spring, fork this mulch into the soil before you start over and cover the bed with fresh mulch after you are done with the starting-over steps. This mulching is optional, but it guarantees rich, soft soil for your roses.

Maintain Good Soil

Abundant use of organic matter is recommended for long rosebush life and vigor; do not rely on synthetic fertilizers to produce a wealth of strong, healthy flowers summer after summer.

Although clay loam is preferred as a base, all but light, sandy loam and gravelly soil can be upgraded with heavy and deep applications of rotted stable manure and compost. Even so, in sandy areas one must be constantly alert for crown gall infections; these tumors weaken and kill good roses, often without being seen.

You Can Always Spot a Hungry Rose

Without enough nitrogen, the growth of new leaves and stems is retarded. Lack of phosphorus will be shown by a small number of very small blooms. Not enough potassium means that neither nitrogen nor phosphorus will be utilized

How rose bush looks in winter

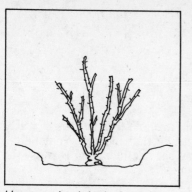

How rose bush looks in spring

Spray when new growth begins

Feed according to schedule

by the plant. So if you want lots of roses, feed the darn things!

When you feed them is simple enough. Follow this schedule:

Feeding Schedule

Zone 6 and North

1. As soon as new growth is 6 inches long
2. Right after they bloom
3. Middle of July
4. August 10

Zone 7 and South or West

1. As soon as new growth is 6 inches long
2. Right after they bloom
3. Middle of July
4. August 10
5. November
6. January
7. March

What you feed your roses is a matter of choice, as long as it's designed for roses. I use K Mart's Systemic Rose and Flower Care; 8-12-4 is the formula. This food also controls many insect pests, and because it is systemic, it goes up through the roots of the plant so you don't have to spray as much. It's also inexpensive. Every other feeding, I use my Ross Root Feeder, with the rose cartridge and the systemic cartridge. Both the K Mart systemic food and the Ross Root Feeder can be used on most other shrubs and flowers.

Blossom Tonic

Here is another one of Grandma Putt's garden tonics, this one for use on roses, flowering shrubs, and perennials. Into a gallon container pour:

1 cup of household ammonia
½ cup of baking powder
½ cup of saltpeter
2 quarts of water
3 cups of dry red wine
¼ teaspoon of active dry yeast
Fill the balance with warm tea

Once a month add 1 cup of this formula to 2 gallons of water and feed a pint or so to everything that blooms. Your neighbors may laugh, but when they see the blooming results, the last laugh will be yours.

When You Eat, You Get Thirsty

When plants eat (even liquid food) they get thirsty, so water well when necessary—at least once a week in hot weather. Use the type of sprinkler that soaks the soil without wetting the foliage. Keep the soil around the plant covered with a decorative or practical mulch like wood chips, buckwheat hulls, or cocoa shells to retain moisture. Think twice before you use rock or stone; it looks nice, but you must remove all the stone each fall before you mound up soil around the plant. When the hot weather comes on, pour nongreasy dishwater under the roses to soften up the dry soil. The soap in the dishwater will help the moisture penetrate the soil better.

Keep Those Roses Coming, Folks!

I don't mean send me bouquets. I mean keep the flowers blooming on the rose bushes. It's simple. Always cut off the spent blooms before they begin to fade. Cut just above a five-leaf cluster, which is where your next flowering spur will come from. Make sure it is an outside five-leaf cluster, so that the new foliage grows up and out.

Pruning Program   Hybrid Tea Roses

As hybrid tea roses continue to grow and flower until hard frosts, pruning is an all-season rule. Little need be done in fall, except to reduce height to accommodate rose cone covers when used. In mid-April, all winter coverings are removed. Rosebushes are then given their most important pruning of the year:

1. Determine extent of winter-kill or dieback, and cut this

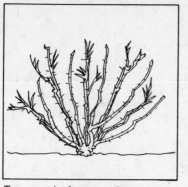

Tea rose before pruning

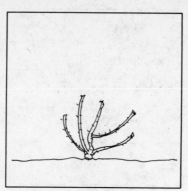

Tea rose after pruning

away. (The dead wood is black or very dark brown; the live wood is green.)

2. Remove all branches narrower than a lead pencil.
3. Prune for shape; an even distribution in all directions of the heaviest branches: three for the second year, four, five, or six as the bush gains in vigor over the years. More than six will cause crowding.
4. Cut back ends to ¼ inch above the first vigorous outside bud, making a sloping cut inward and downward. Dab all cuts with pruning compound, and burn all trimmings at once.

Cut all the hybrid tea blooms you like for gifts and arrangements. Take long stems, as they are usually weak and too small to promote more strong bud development. Likewise remove spent or faded flowers before the petals fall, including their stems. Look for any other twiggy or weak growth that isn't budding and remove it.

IMPORTANT: Watch for any shoots or suckers from below the graft. Pull away enough soil to trim these suckers off flush with the understock root; peel close with a sharp knife. Seal with wound dressing and replace soil.

Florabundas

These are pruned similarly to hybrid teas, except that you should save up to ten of the heaviest canes. Old flower clusters and some of their weaker stems are removed as the petals fall.

Climbers

For June bloomers, pruning begins as flowers fade. A few

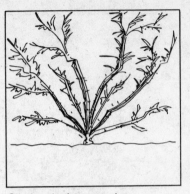

Climber before pruning

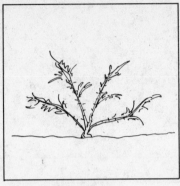

Climber after pruning

of the thriftiest two-year canes may be saved if there are fewer than four or five new canes. Older, weak, and crooked canes are cut to the base. For all summer flowering climbers, remove older canes as they flower out, leaving only five strong, new canes by autumn.

Keep climbers tied to a trellis support all summer, and do not cut new canes back at any time. After removing covers in spring, determine winter injury for pruning out. Hopefully, the five canes you saved will be plump and green for up to 8 feet or the height of the trellis when they are tied up again. Prune to the top of the support only and secure with soft twine or cloth strips.

First Aid for Roses

Roses, given poor care anywhere in the neighborhood, easily become a source of disease for new, clean bushes. Wind carries spores of black spot a long distance. Mildew is everywhere, especially noticeable where air flow is slow. Sandy soils breed almost all kinds of root-feeding grubs, as well as destructive nematodes (microscopic worms that attack roots). Root and crown galls (tumors), once introduced into light soil, will spread by cultivation, on the feet of birds, cats, or man, or by wind and movement of soil water. Attention to bed location and soil cannot be overemphasized in preparing for roses.

Preventatives versus Controls

Resolve to prevent pests from becoming established by a regular program of dusting or spraying. Once infestation sets in, it may prove stubborn to control or eradicate. Don't wait until damage can be seen!

How to Dust and When

Prepared rose dust contains protection against insects and airborne diseases. Plan to dust roses first when leaves are coming out in spring, and continue until growth stops in fall. The best time of day for dusting is late evening, when the air is still and fresh dew on the foliage catches and holds the precious powder. Hold the duster low and shoot up under the bushes without actually walking among them. Allow the protective cloud to settle gently over the whole bed.

The second best time to dust is predawn. When it rains, repeat the dusting immediately thereafter. In times of heavy dews, twice a week dusting is recommended; with light dews and the hotter, drier weather of summer, once a week is enough. Diseases can begin to grow in a droplet of water or dew in less than four hours on unprotected bushes. Excessive use of rose dusts in temperatures above 85° F can burn the foliage, so apply it sparingly when the temperature goes above 75° F.

Further Preventative Measures

For additional protection against insects and disease, make sure you feed periodically with one of the systemic combination rose foods and insect controls, like K Mart's Systemic Rose and Flower Care (see page 139). Also spray as soon as you suspect trouble with K Mart's Garden and Fruit Tree Spray, which controls both insects and disease and will do your whole garden a world of good.

Rose Pests

Here's how to recognize and control the most common troublemakers:

Aphids. Green aphids are common, and are most noticeable on tender, growing tips and new flower buds, sucking sap by the hundreds. They are easily controlled with systemics.

Black spot. This is a very serious problem. Leaves turn pale and drop; black spots appear and enlarge. This disease spreads rapidly. Pick and burn all yellowing foliage. In spring, disinfect beds with lime sulphur. Black spot is best solved by prevention. Use all-purpose rose dust regularly.

Borers. Stem borers enter pruning cuts or damaged bark; be sure to seal such spots with pruning paint. Stem girdlers enter the side of a branch and tunnel spirally around to form a swelling; cut and burn the branch—usually a large one.

Chewing insects. Foliage-feeding caterpillars and thrips are checked with dusts. The presence of slugs indicates overly damp conditions; correct the dampness and use special slug poisons. Carpenter wasps cut circular holes in leaves; there is no control against them. Rose chafers and Japanese beetles are especially attracted to pink and white flowers, and somewhat less to red. They are difficult to control except by area-wide soil treatments with Diazinon to kill the grubs; or if there are only a few, hand pick the beetles.

Galls. Both crown and root galls are prevalent on Euonymus wintercreeper, raspberry, flowering quince, Cotoneaster, firethorn, mountain ash and other rose relatives as well as roses. They cause ugly, gnarled bumps and lumps on the wood. Burn all infected parts. If these galls invade the rose bed seriously, dig up the bed 2 feet deep and have the soil removed from your property. Then prepare the bed for replanting with new, clean soil.

Mildew. This appears as whitish patches on tender new growth; control with Acti-Dione.

Nematodes. These microscopic worms attack the roots of roses and other plants. They frequently crop up in sandy soil and are a real pain in the neck to get rid of. Symptoms are bumps and swellings on the roots. Grandma Putt's remedy works like a charm: sprinkle ¼ cup of beet sugar on the soil under the roses at the weepline. Or you can dissolve ½ cup of clear corn syrup in a gallon of water and sprinkle it on the soil.

Red spiders (spider mites). Watch for these pests after several weeks of hot, dry weather. They are minute and found among their webs and on undersides of leaves. They turn the foliage sickly grayish green. They are easily controlled with special miticides applied at ten-day intervals.

Virus. Foliage will appear mottled and streaked with yellow; flowers appear streaked with green and deformed. There is no control; dig and burn all infected plants before the virus spreads to healthy bushes.

CHAPTER 6 Annuals, Biennials, Perennials, Bulbs, and Wild Flowers

Home-Grown Flowers Are a Real Touch of Class

Give me five bucks, a shovel, a hoe, and a rake and I will turn a sow's ear of a yard into a silk purse of a garden. Likely as not, I will do it all with flower seeds. Make it ten dollars and I might win you first prize in the neighborhood beautification contest.

There is nothing that tees me off quicker than to hear people say they can't have an attractive yard because they can't afford it. Some of the prettiest gardens I have seen have been grown by welfare recipients in ghetto areas or by folks on fixed incomes who used a little imagination to develop a showplace.

Plenty to Pick from

The first step to a beautiful garden is choosing the types of flowers you want. Here are the categories you can choose from:

Annuals:	Here and gone in one year.
Biennials:	Have a two-year life cycle.
Perennials:	Revisit you year after year.
Bulbs:	Earn their keep for years. Corms and tubers fall into this category.
Wild Flowers:	Can change the beast into a beauty with little effort; grow in shade, on slopes, and in fields where grass won't grow.

Annuals   Annuals cost the least and do the most—you can get more beautiful blossoms from a cheap little packet of seeds than you can from an 8-foot flowering shrub. In most cases, this beauty will last all summer long with very little help.

The Choice Is Yours

Here are the more popular annuals to pick from and their recommended uses:

For Sunny Borders

Under 12″ (Edgings)

Ageratum
Alyssum
Celosia, Jewel Box
Dianthus, Wee Willie
Marigold, Petite and Dwarf French
Petunia, Multiflora
Phlox drummondi, and Twinkle
Portulaca
Salvia, Scarlet Pygmy
Snapdragon, Carpet
Verbena
Zinnia, Thumbelina

12″ to 18″

Calendula
Celosia, Floradale
Coreopsis
Cornflower
Dahlia, Dwarf
Geranium, Carefree
Salvia (intermediates)
Snapdragon (bedding)
Zinnia, Pompon

18″ to 36″+ (Backgrounds)

Amaranthus
Celosia, Golden Triumph
Cleome
Dahlia, Flowered
Four O'Clock
Gloriosa Daisy
Larkspur
Marigolds, Tall African, Jubilee, Crackerjack
Nicotiana
Salvia Splendens
Snapdragon, Rocket
Tithonia
Zinnia, Giant Cactus

For Light Shade

Ageratum
Balsam
Begonia
Browallia
Carnation
Forget-Me-Not
Impatiens
Matricaria
Pansy
Periwinkle
Snapdragon
Torenia

For Poor (light) Soil

Alyssum
Calliopsis
Cleome
Coreopsis
Cornflower
Four O'Clock

Gaillardia
Gomphrena
Nasturtium
Poppy
Portulaca
Sand Verbena

For Cut Flowers

Aster (tall branching)
Bells of Ireland
Calendula
Carnation
Gloriosa Daisy
Marigold (all types)

Nicotiana
Scabiosa
Snapdragon (Rockets)
Stock
Strawflower
Zinnia (all types)

For Window Boxes

Begonia (Fibrous)
Coleus
Dusty Miller
Geranium
Impatiens
Lantana

Pandanus (spike)
Periwinkle
Petunia (cascade and
    grandiflora)
Vinca Vine

For Fragrance

Alyssum
Carnation
Heliotrope
Lantana and Marigold
    (foliage)
Migonette

Nasturtium
Nicotiana
Scabiosa
Stock (evening-scented and
    trisomic)
Sweet Pea

Starting from Scratch Can Be Fun

Annual plants for the summer garden can be started easily indoors, to gain time in making them ready to flower or to produce fine vegetables well ahead of those sown out-of-doors. Such a project is entertaining for all ages, and economical too.

Selecting a safe, normally frost-free target date for setting tender plants in the open garden (e.g., Memorial Day in Zone 5), you must plan a certain number of weeks ahead to develop young plants from seed to just the right size—not too small and not too tall and leggy or crowded. It's like preparing a good dinner, having everything ready and just right at serving time. Some seeds must be sown as early as February in Zone 5, being slow to show growth; others need not be sown until early April, as they grow rapidly. The following schedule for planting in Zone 5 allows for one transplanting indoors, to space seedlings in boxes or in small, convenient peat pots for maximum top growth and better roots.

FEBRUARY

1 to 15	16 to 28
Begonias	Carnations
Carefree	Coleus
Geraniums	Double
Lantanas	Petunias
Vincas	Snapdragons
Periwinkles	

MARCH

1 to 15	16 to 31
Cosmos	Ageratum
Dwarf Dahlias	Alyssum
Gloriosa Daisy	Asters
Impatiens	Balsam
Larkspur	Celosia
Single	Morning
Petunias	glories
	Phlox

APRIL

1 to 15	16 to 30
Calendula	Best for hot-
Marigolds	bed plantings
Portulaca	and quantity
Zinnias	sowings of
	early April
	items; plants
	will be smaller

To use this schedule, plant two weeks later for each zone north of Zone 5 (e.g., if you live in Zone 3, plant four weeks later than the schedule indicates). For each zone south of Zone 5, plant two weeks earlier.

Equipment Needed for Starting Plants from Seeds Indoors

You will need a bright sunny windowsill, Gro-Lux lamps, or a home greenhouse for controlled results. For starting containers use sterilized flower pots, peat pots, shallow pans, wooden flats, or plastic trays with good drainage; provide clear glass or close-fitting plastic covers.

Soil Requirements

Use prepared sterilized soil mix only. Or mix your own from two-thirds screened sandy loam and one-third chopped sphagnum moss (sold by the bale at garden centers). To sterilize soil at home, place it in shallow pan in the oven at 250° F and bake with a potato; when the potato is done, take the soil out and allow to cool before using.

Perlite or fine vermiculite may also be used for starting seeds, with liquid feeding after germination.

Procedure for Planting Seeds

Level and firm the soil in the container to 1 inch from the top. Sow the seeds thinly over the surface, or in rows; cover lightly with ⅛ inch of finely chopped sphagnum and moisten soil well with a fine spray. Cover tightly with glass or plastic and place in the windowsill. Shade with one thickness of newspaper when the sun is strong. As seedlings appear, raise glass or plastic slightly to ventilate, a little longer each day; after ten days remove glass and newspaper. Keep moist but not wet at all times (watch this carefully). Liquid feed every ten days after plants appear, with Miracle-Gro or Nurish. When the second set of leaves (the first "true" leaves) forms, lift the plantlets out with the point of a knife and space them in wooden flats or plastic trays 2 inches apart, or plant individually in small peat pots for growing on to ideal size. Always transplant into a good topsoil mixture and liquid feed.

Sow seeds thinly over surface soil

If You Don't Have the Time—but Have the Money

Plant your annuals from seedlings purchased at a garden center. There is a wide range of bedding plants to choose from for almost any garden effect. Most varieties thrive in full sun and also tolerate some shade. Other plants are best suited for a shady location. Consider flower colors and final height of the plants in planning your flower beds: tall (18

Cover pots or trays with glass or plastic

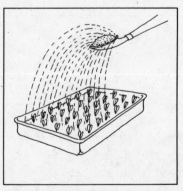

Water to keep moist but not wet

When first "true" leaves appear, transplant

Dig the flower bed 6 to 12 inches deep

Enrich the soil with fertilizer and organic matter

Work in fertilizer with rototiller

inches and up) for backgrounds and cutting; medium height (9 to 16 inches) for the center of the beds; dwarf plants (4 to 8 inches) for foreground or edging. Set out annuals in the spring after the danger of frost is past.

If you are unable to set out your bedding plants immediately after purchase, keep them in a semishaded spot, protected from drying winds. Never let the plants dry out.

Prepare Your Flower Beds for Planting

Prepare the soil as carefully as you would for a vegetable garden; loose, light soil will produce fat, thick, fluffy blossoms by the carload. Spread a 1-inch layer of well-rotted manure, compost, leaf mold or peat moss on the flower beds. Add garden fertilizer, following the directions on the container. Then dig the beds with a spade at least 6 inches deep, or better, 8 to 12 inches deep, and mix in the organic matter

Rake and smooth the flower bed before planting

Don't remove peat pots before planting

Scoop seedlings out of flat to plant

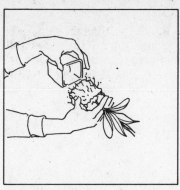

Remove plants from nonpeat pots before planting

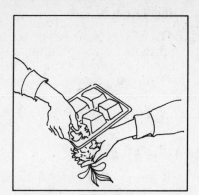

Turn over 6-pack trays to remove seedlings for planting

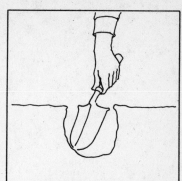

Dig planting hole with trowel

and fertilizer. A rototiller does this job well. You will get bonus results using a rooting hormone such as Transplantone or Upstart. Follow the directions on the container.

Do It Right

Bedding plants are grown either in individual pots or several plants in a tray. Plants in peat pots should be set out, pot and all, deep enough to completely cover the top rim with at least ¼ inch of soil. Plants grown in trays, usually eight to twelve plants per tray, should be carefully removed from their containers while the soil is moist. Cut or break apart as evenly as possible, so you have a good root and soil ball for each plant. With a trowel, dig a hole in the garden bed large enough for the pot or soil ball. Set the plant in the hole at the same height it stood in the tray, and press soil firmly against the roots. Do not cover the lower stems and leaves.

Place seedling in hole and press soil against roots

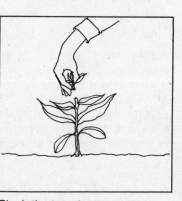

Pinch the tops to encourage branching and flowering

Side-dress with fertilizer in mid-season

Give Them Room

Dwarf plants for foreground and edging should be spaced 6 to 8 inches apart. Medium-tall plants, up to 15 inches tall, should be spaced 12 to 14 inches apart, and tall plants for background planting and cut flowers should be spaced 16 to 18 inches apart. Consult the labels of your plant tray for more specific recommendations.

Water, Water

If the weather is hot, sunny, or windy, water the plants at least once a day; twice a day is better. Do this for a week or until the leaves do not wilt anymore. Thereafter, water thoroughly to a depth of 6 to 8 inches, once a week in cool weather, every three to four days during the hot summer months. Don't let your plants wilt; it will seriously weaken them. A mulch of peat moss, bark mulch or cocoa mulch is excellent to conserve moisture and keep down weeds.

Something a Little Extra

When they are about 6 inches tall, pinch out the tops of young plants of the tall growing varieties, to encourage better branching and production of more flowers. Dwarf varieties seldom need this pinching.

It is also a good practice, especially on varieties that bloom for a long time, such as snapdragons, to remove unsightly old flower stalks. Cut them off before seeds have a chance to form, and the plants will reward you with a longer blooming time. An additional fertilizing is needed about mid-season. Any complete fertilizer will do, but be sure to follow instructions on how to apply to avoid damage to the plants.

You Can Get Away from Them

Bugs were here before you and I, and probably will be a long time after. Insect control is administered as needed. If it's a worm use Dipel ™; if it's fungus, Benomyl. If in doubt, catch one and carry the little critter on down to your local garden shop. I have also found that a fruit tree spray with a garden fungicide does wonders as a preventative; spray every fourteen days all season.

Biennials Are Never Out of Date

Few flowers recall the sweetly fragrant garden of grandmother's day as evocatively as the biennials.

Biennial means "two-year." These plants sprout from seed one spring and grow into a fine rosette of foliage by fall. They flower in their second year, make seed and disappear. In gardens of old, biennials seeded themselves in drifts, with some coming up each year to flower continuously all summer. Most seemed to grow best in partly shaded, moist borders, undisturbed by cultivation, and often in company with native ferns. A few preferred the open garden row, and others sandy places.

Nowadays, space may be limited to only a few plants, for cut flowers and for filling out perennial borders. Instead of growing biennials from seed, you can buy second-year, ready-to-bloom plants; these are available in early spring. For those who wish to grow biennials in abundance from seed, row space in a cultivated garden is the best place for producing sturdy first-year plants. Follow the same procedures as for annuals, except that you plant the biennial seeds in the fall. The following spring dig them up, leaving a large ball of soil attached to the root of each plant, and transplant to the desired location in the flower bed.

Fond Recollections from Grandma's Biennial Collections

All need well-draining soil and bright shade to full sun. Months of fullest flowering are indicated.

Anchusa (A. italica). Bears long spikes of purest deep blue. Wonderful for cutting. Three feet. June.

Canterbury Bells (Campanula medium and C. calycanthema). Single and cup-and-saucer. Spikes of huge bells in pink, soft blue, and white on 30-inch plants. Wonderful for cutting. June.

Dianthus (D. barbatus). Loveable Sweet William, in both tall and dwarf plants. Deep red and white, blue and white, and pink and white blossoms. A glorious old favorite to rediscover. June–July.

Digitalis (D. purpurea). Foxglove. Some know this plant only as a heart remedy. To others, foxglove was the wonderflower of childhood. Graceful spikes up to 6 feet tall, with soft drooping bells in rose, pink, yellow, or white, all gaily spotted within. Hybrid Shirley is a standard variety. June.

Herperis (H. matronalis). Sweet rocket, or dame's rocket. Enchantingly perfumed, lavender or white. This plant now is found wild on moist roadsides and near old gardens in partial shade. June–July.

Biennials

Hollyhock (Althaea rosea). A favorite in colonial times, with its single flowers. Now showier than ever in double powder puffs. Soft colors in a wide range. Handsome 6- to 8-foot accents, or in backgrounds. And don't forget to teach your children how to make hollyhock dolls: Use a bud for the head, two flowers on top of each other for the blouse and skirt, and a toothpick to hold the pieces together. June–July.

Lunaria (L. annua). Handsome silvery membranes in the pods are used for dry arrangements. The live flowers are quite showy too. July.

Lychnis (L. coronaria). Agrostemma, rose campion. Soft, gray foliage with dazzling rosy-purple flowers, to 30 inches tall. An old-time favorite. July–August.

Myosotis (M. alpestris). Forget-me-not. For pure turn-of-the-century sentimentality. Nice combined with yellow or white cottage or Darwins tulips. For cutting and mixed arrangements. July.

Verbascum (V. olympicum). Moth mullein. Thirty-inch spikes in rose, yellow or white. For sandy, sunny places. June–July.

The familiar *pansy* is best started in late August, in frames that can be covered for the winter; plants may begin to bloom in mid-fall and hold the flowers until spring. Similarly treated are the hybrid *English daisy* and *Siberian wallflower*. *Silence* is now widespread near sandy gardens. Wild flowers are biennials, brought here from Europe by colonists as garden flowers.

Perennials

Perennials are a great investment in the home garden because they come up year after year without the need for replanting every spring, as for annual flowers. With proper care they can last a generation or more. One must enjoy learning about them, however, to succeed and be happy with them. Their care is no less than for the same area of lawn, perhaps more; but having an abundance of cut flowers for the home is worth the trouble.

Perennials need not be expensive to make up a pleasing border. Various kinds can be combined so that your bed will flower continuously from early spring to mid-autumn. If the family vacations away for the summer, the border may display only spring and early summer flowers, or more color for early fall. A garden may require plants enduring a little shade or plants that thrive on a sandy soil. The perennial purist frowns on filling in with annuals during the difficult summer months, such resort being a sheer lack of thoughtful planning.

Be Choosy, They're Going to Be Around a Long Time

Continuous color from early spring to mid-fall can be yours with dependable flowering perennials. Standard kinds are started easily from seeds, but modern hybrids are best only from divisions. For continuous flowering all season, a combination of several varieties must be worked out; each species or variety has a definite period of flowering. Always remove seed heads of named varieties before they shatter; these are hybrids and will revert to their original state if allowed to seed themselves. The greatest number of perennials flower in May and June, an advantage to those who wish to be away all summer; another fine group flowers in September.

As a guide in selecting perennials suitable for various purposes and situations about the home, I recommend the following:

For Sunny Borders

Under 12″ (Edgings)

Alyssum, Basket of Gold
Arabis alpina fl. pl.
Artemisia, Silver Mound
Aster, Hardy Dwarf
Campanula, Wedgewood
Chrysanthemum, Cushion

Dicentra, Bountiful
Gaillardia, Dwarf
Iberis sempervirens
Iris pumila
Phlox subulata
Platycodon mariesi

12″ to 30″

Chrysanthemum
Gaillardia
Geum, Lady Strathenden
Gypsophila
Heuchera
Monarda

Peony
Pyrethrum
Rudbeckia, Gold Sturm
Shasta Daisy
Tritoma
Veronica, Crater Lake

30″ and Up (Backgrounds)

Achillea, Coronation Gold
Aster, Hardy Tall
Baptisia, False Indigo
Campanula, Brantwood
Delphinium, Hybrids
Hemerocallis, Day Lilies

Hibiscus
Liatris, September Glory
Lupine, Russell Hybrids
Phlox, Tall Border
Physostegia
Yucca

For Light Shade

Ajuga
Aquilegia (Columbine)
Astilbe
Bleeding Heart, Old-
    fashioned
Epimedium
Fern

Heleborus (Lenten Rose)
Heuchera
Hosta
Primrose
Pulmonaria, Mrs. Moon
Trollius

For Poor (light) Soil

Achillea
Artemisia
Catananche
Coreopsis
Gaillardia
Gypsophila

Lavender
Liatris
Penstemon
Sempervivum and Sedum
Spiderwort

For Cut Flowers

Achillea
Chrysanthemum
Delphinium
Gaillardia
Gypsophila
Lily-of-the-Valley

Peony
Pyrethrum
Shasta Daisy
Statice
Tritoma
Trollius

For Fragrance

Carnations
Dianthus, Old Spice
Lily-of-the-Valley

Peony
Phlox
Violets

For Rock Gardens

Alyssum, Basket-of-Gold
Arabis
Campanula, Wedgewood
Cerastium (Snow-in-Summer)
Dianthus, Tiny Rubies

Dwarf Iris
Epimedium
Moss Phlox
Sempervivums and Sedums

For Waterside (damp but not wet)

Aconitum
Astilbe
Cypripedium spectabile
Gentian
Helenium
Hibiscus

Japanese Iris
Lobelia, Cardinal Flower
  and Giant
Lythrum
Thalictrum
Trollius

For Wild Borders

Anemone pulsatilla
Aquilegia canadensis
Cimicifuga
Cypripedium pubescens
Fern
Forget-Me-Not

Sanguinaria (Bloodroot)
Tiarella
Trillium
Violet
Yucca

For Foliage Colors

Ajuga metallica
Apple Mint
Artemisia
Chrysanthemum
  ptarmicaefolium

Hosta
Pulmonaria, Mrs. Moon
Ruta Blue Beauty
Sage (purple and green)
Variegated Grasses

Continuous Blooming Throughout Growing Season

Asker frikarti
Campanula, Wedgewood
Dianthus, Allwood Hybrids

Dicentra, Bountiful
Gaillardia
Wonder of Staffa

Start With a Plan

Use a carefully designed bed or border plan that meets your particular site requirements as to soil, shade, moisture, and air drainage, and gives exact positions and spacings for plants. Buy plants to fill out as the budget allows; low plants will be shown in front, taller kinds in rear, and all making pleasant color harmonies.

Stage perennials according to height

Soils and Drainage

Existing soils can be improved by copious additions of compost, peat, and stable manure, well mixed to a depth of 2 feet. Beds 4 to 6 feet in width are easiest to maintain. With very shallow, sandy, or hard clay soils it is best to remove all earth to 2 feet deep and replace it with a loamy mixture containing the suitable organic ingredients. Provide perfect bottom drainage by tiling if needed; quick surface moisture drainage is essential, too, as is good air circulation to ward off disease.

Lime or Acid Lovers

Most perennials do well in neutral soils. A very distinguished group enjoys lime or alkaline soils: Christmas rose, anemone, peony, columbine, delphinium, clematis, and monkshood. On the other hand, only an acid soil will do for gentians and many of our choice wild flowers.

Backgrounds Are Important

Perennials show off best against a natural shrub or evergreen background. Make certain the roots of shrubs don't enter the bed; a 2-foot deep continuous metal shield between the shrubs and the flower bed will help keep them out. A handsome ornamental wood screen or fence makes a neat background with no root problems. The side of a garage or other such structure distracts from the floral picture, and seldom makes a suitable background.

Labor Savers

As a further labor-saving device, use metal edging, preferably 6 inches wide, sunk flush on the lawn side of the bed; lawn grasses will otherwise require hand edging or they will creep rapidly and soon entangle the plants. Provide supports for delphiniums before wind and hard rains break them down, and for peonies lest heavy blooms be bent into the mud. Get the mulching habit to save on weeding and watering.

Keep Beds Clean

Sanitation in the border planting can reduce insect and disease troubles; make sure that all top growth of delphiniums, peonies, and irises is removed in autumn and burned. Through the season, remove old flowers as they fade; many perennials will thus continue to flower a longer time and seeds will not be formed. Use nondiseased foliage for compost. If the beds become crowded, divide clumps of plants and dig up the extras to be transplanted or disposed of.

General Care Schedule for Perennials

1. As early as you can get into your perennial garden in the spring, cut back and remove all of last year's dead foliage.
2. In early spring, before new growth begins, sprinkle on the soil one pound of Epsom salt crystals per 100 square feet of garden.
3. Start to feed early in the spring with any of the liquid fish emulsions. Repeat every three weeks throughout the growing season.
4. Spray young new foliage with soap, water, and tobacco juice solution (see page 120 for recipe).
5. A week later, use an all-purpose fruit tree and garden spray. Repeat every 14 days throughout the growing season.
6. The amount of light the plants receive will dictate water needs. Keep the soil slightly damp but not soggy. In full sun you will need to water often; in shade seldom.

If these steps are followed religiously, your perennials will thrive. In fact, they may thrive a bit too much. Don't be afraid to thin, trim, clip, and pinch, or your perennials may take over the whole garden.

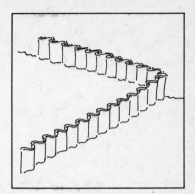
Six-inch-wide metal edging will keep grass out of beds

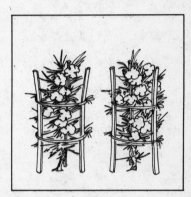
Stake tall perennials

In spring, cut back dead foliage

Bulbs

Why do most of you insist on overlooking one of the great rewards of the flower season—Dutch bulbs? Take a second look at these fabulous beauties. In the fall of the year, after you have removed all of this year's annuals and cleaned up the flower beds, you can take a few more minutes and plant the best imported bulbs from Holland, to come up next spring (from early March through the middle of June). With a little care each season, they will last for years. You don't even need to feed them the first year because these healthy bulbs carry their next season's food with them.

Bulbs Can't Swim

Bulbs are like flower and vegetable seeds; they want rich, organic, light, well-drained soil.

Check Your Calendar

Bulbs must be planted in the fall if you want to be assured of flowers next spring. Bulb planting begins in September in Zones 2 and 3, in October or November in Zones 4, 5, 6, and in December or January in Zones 7, 8, 9, 10. Remember, your bulbs must be in the ground for at least four weeks before the first heavy frost.

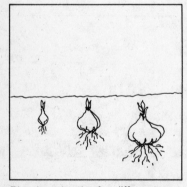

Plant bulbs with bulb planter or dig hole with trowel

How Deep Is Deep?

Different bulbs like different depths. Tulips, hyacinths, and daffodils are planted 6 inches deep. Crocus, scilla, muscari, and other small bulbs are comfortable at 3 inches deep.

Give Them Room to Grow

Leave 5 inches between the big bulbs and 2 inches between the little ones. Bulbs (large or small) can be planted in rows or patterns very easily, because they are big enough to handle comfortably. Visit your local garden department in early fall and pick up the beautiful bulb booklets supplied by the Dutch bulb growers for ideas—they're free in some places.

Plan for Long-lasting Beauty

Place bulbs in many locations throughout the garden so that bulbs and other flowers complement each other and don't step on one another's feet. Check the flowering times of some of the more popular flowers.

Planting depths for different sizes of bulbs

Timetable for Bulb Blooms

VARIETY OF BULB	March		April		May		June	
Galanthus (Snowdrop)	▓							
Eranthis (Winter Aconite)	▓							
Crocus		▓						
Chionodoxa (Glory of the Snow)		▓						
Tulip Species (see Note)			▓					
Red Emperor Tulip			▓					
Muscari (Grape Hyacinth)				▓				
Trumpet Daffodil				▓				
Tulips: Single and Double Early				▓				
Hyacinth				▓				
Medium-Cupped Daffodil				▓				
Breeder Tulip					▓			
Scilla Campanulata					▓			
Lily-Flowered Tulip					▓	▓		
Double Late Tulip					▓	▓		
Darwin Tulip					▓	▓		
Parrot Tulip					▓	▓		
Cottage Tulip					▓	▓		
Dutch Iris						▓	▓	

Note: Tulip species include such varieties as kaufmanniana, fosteriana, peacock, multiflowered, and rock garden varieties.

No Seedy Characters

As soon as the flower has faded, remove the head so that seeds don't form. When foliage has dried up, cut off. Work a small amount of bonemeal into the soil after flowers are through blooming to ensure a repeat performance next year.

Natural Perfume

Hyacinth aroma can fill the house in late winter and take the ache out of your green thumb. How? Plant hyacinth bulbs in pots, place the pots outside in fall, harvest them from under the snow in winter, and bring them into the house to bloom and brighten any room. Ask your local Holland bulb garden center for the free booklet that tells you how you can enjoy spring color and fragrance next winter.

Wild Flowers   In this day of mad hybridizing, the craze among gardeners to possess the latest in roses, irises, peonies, lilies, glads, and other haughty lords and ladies of the transient flower world often becomes oppressive. As we compete frantically for the newest man-made glamour, we're missing out on the simple, unspoilt beauty of our nation's wild flowers.

Take that long put-off look at the wild flowers of our great land; our priceless heritage of natural beauty awaits us in secluded woodland glades. We are rediscovering the charm of these flowers, some common, some excitingly elusive; few hybrids ever gave greater challenge or satisfaction.

Although we have grown field wild flowers and their European "improvements" in our open borders for many years—butterflyweed, spiderflower, bee balm, various daisies, and others—there remains a host of woodland plants to befriend. Their culture is unlike that for meadow plants and few of us are fortunate enough to have a shady grove well suited to them. But if you can provide them with a suitable environment, nurturing these lovely flowers is a whole new adventure.

Where to Find Plants Legally

Our most choice wild flowers are now protected by law. Only with permission of the property owner can one collect plants from the wild. Fortunately for their admirers, plant dealers are now increasing their offerings of started plants, available in spring. Numerous wild-flower specialists issue catalogs with wide selections for mail order; these are dormant plants, best ordered for planting in the fall.

Do not try to take a stray wild flower from our national forests; if you do, you could be in real hot water. These plants are protected, because many of them are in danger of extinction; taking them from public lands is not only illegal, it is immoral.

Where to Plant Safely

The north and sometimes east sides of a dwelling afford cool shade, especially if surrounded by trees. Here the ferns—Ostrich plume, lady fern, maidenhair, and evergreen Christmas fern—do nicely when soil is constantly moist and deeply prepared with leaf mold. Where ferns prosper, you may introduce bloodroot, Trillium, jack-in-the-pulpit, and Virginia bluebells. For the most perfect spot among ferns, the enchanting yellow lady-slipper may succeed, though it is rare and expensive and not the easiest to grow.

The beginner should try green dragon, merrybells, Turk's-cap lily, trout lily, blue-eyed grass, wild ginger, spring beauty, Hepatica, pasqueflower, twinleaf, Dutchman's-breeches, false indigo, shooting star, blue phlox, puccoon, and turtlehead. Alongside an old, "set" stream bank with firm soil many others are possible. They all require bright shade and moist soil.

The Garden for Wild Flowers

A shade tree, with its naturally acid soil, is the ideal starting point for a wild-flower bed. Don't try to grow under a maple, however, as it is too alkalizing and develops vigorous surface roots. As the level of acid humus in the soil builds up to 6 or 8 inches in depth, it's a good idea to plant flowering dogwoods as space allows; they look lovely with wild flowers and their shading foliage helps the soil retain moisture. Azaleas and viburnums make fine backgrounds for the flower borders.

How to Arrange Them So Folks Don't Laugh

Wild flowers always look their best when staged according to height. Taller ones may be used singly or in small groups at the rear; short ones are best in colonies, or "drifts," near the path.

Constant Mulch Is a Wild Flower's Best Friend

Mother Nature lays down a new mulch each autumn with the falling leaves. If you sweep these off in spring (oak leaves may smother), they must be replaced at once with an inch or so of shredded, composted leaf mold. Woodland flowers must have plenty of moisture in spring; most disappear by summer, so they can't be harmed by drought.

Wild flowers attractively arranged

Caution with These or Your Neighbors Will Hate You

Violets, Solomon's seal, columbine, and wild geranium seed freely and may spread beyond control. Avoid bracken fern and mayapple, as these are rampant spreaders by underground stems. Until the gardener is very experienced, he or she should not attempt the pink Lady-slipper or the cherished trailing arbutus because they can become a serious weed problem.

Gardening Nature's Way

Other than the few hints above regarding the proper environment for wild flowers, I am not going to tell you a single thing about their care. These plants are truly wild, and fussing and fawning over them defeats the purpose of growing them. Unlike our domesticated flowers, they are highly resistant to disease and insects, and they know how to live off the land in comfort and style without your help. Keep the chemicals in your shed, and just give them your admiration. Given half a chance, they will take care of themselves.

CHAPTER 7 Vegetable Gardening

Home-grown Tomatoes Don't Have to Cost $10 a Pound!

Home gardeners are constantly being made fun of for their efforts to save money by growing their own food. If you calculated the time they spent in the garden, claim their critics, you'd find their produce was worth its weight in gold. The quality of their goods is also criticized by the commercial grower and food broker. In a recent article in *Newsweek*, "Poking Fun at the Home Gardener," the director of a produce advisory board was quoted as saying that if the produce home gardeners grew were for sale at their local markets, they would never buy it. Well, when I see hundreds of roadside vegetable stands crowded with cars each weekend, and when a produce buyer for a 40-store supermarket chain tells me his sales are off considerably because of the home-grown produce for sale at the stands, I wonder what these food brokers have in place of normal taste buds. These guys also continuously try to play the organic gardener against those who use chemical fertilizers and controls, as if both groups weren't involved equally in the trials and rewards of growing their own food.

I feel sorry for the critics because they will never experience the personal satisfaction of seeing their shelves filled with canned goods, frozen foods, and dried produce resulting from their own blood, sweat, and tears.

It is true that beginning vegetable gardeners do make their share of mistakes (some very expensive), but most soon learn from these mistakes and become a real asset to their communities.

In this chapter, I would like to give you the benefit of my experience to help you keep down the cost to produce, the effort to grow, and the time to harvest your vegetables.

As for the debate over organic versus chemical methods, I refuse to take part. I use the natural methods as much and as long as I can. When they fail, I use the best plant medication available as directed. I believe that in this area, each gardener must follow his or her own conscience.

Enough—let's grow vegetables!

Minigardens for City Dwellers

City people, the cliff dwellers of today, need not abandon the good earth entirely, and children can thrill to the adventure of growing fresh things to eat, even with only a balcony or doorstep. Plenty of sunshine is the basic requirement. Balconies may need some sort of screen to break the wind; this can be ornamental as well as functional.

Gardeners whose yards are too shady or soils too poor for vegetables may also devise minigardens for both vegetables and flowers. For some, it may begin with, and go no farther than, the kitchen windowsill.

Planters

A multitude of inexpensive planters can be contrived from bushel and half-bushel baskets, wood shipping crates for vegetables and fruits, clay flowerpots, cut-down plastic waste baskets, bleach bottles, and sturdy plastic bags with the tops rolled down. Wood containers last longer if lined with large

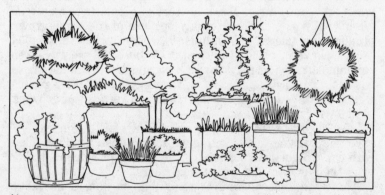

Almost any container can be a planter

plastic bags, with the tops rolled down over the edges of the wood sides.

Drainage

Since there must be a daily watering, punch or cut drain holes around the sides of the container, near the bottom, but not on the underside. If you are gardening on a balcony, place an inch of gravel, pottery, or stone chips in the bottom of the planter, as well as a saucer of some sort underneath it. This inch of gravel will help maintain the proper moisture level and allow excess water from rainstorms to drain into the saucer without carrying the soil out with it.

Growing Medium

There is no need to lug heavy loads of soil upstairs. Instead, use the lightweight prepared growing mixtures that are available at garden stores. These contain vermiculite or perlite, peat, and odorless organic fertilizer. Such mixes are free of weed seeds and plant diseases, and retain moisture and liquid feedings. Compact the growing medium to 1 inch below pot rims, 1½ to 2 inches below the edges of boxes and baskets.

Starting Seeds or Buying Plants

Quick-growing vegetables are started indoors from seeds in the containers where they are to remain without transplanting. Distribute seeds thinly over the growing medium and cover lightly with more of the medium, sprinkle until damp, then cover each planter with a clear plastic bag until growth is up. You can place them outside once the danger of frost has passed.

For late-producing vegetables, you may start seeds indoors early in peat pellets (compressed peat moss discs that expand and soften in water), or buy started plants from mid-May on. In Zone 5, outdoor growing can begin in late April for hardy types, mid-May for tender ones, but with frost-proof covers handy. To figure out the time to set plants out in your region, use this formula: Wait two weeks longer for each zone north of Zone 5 (e.g., if you live in Zone 2, you'll wait until mid-June to set your hardy plants out); set them out two weeks earlier for each zone south of Zone 5 (e.g., in Zone 7 you can place hardy plants outside in late March).

Plants for 6-inch Pots

The gourmet can enjoy fresh, home-grown herbs with very

little effort. Parsley, watercress, and chives grow in small pots year round; new plants can be started before the old ones wear out, anytime. Annual herbs may also be grown in small containers outside in the summer; use them fresh in season and then dry a winter's supply. Potted perennial herbs will not survive the winter outside, so bring them inside in fall.

Small containers 4 inches in diameter and 6 inches deep are also ideal for growing small lots of radishes and lettuce. Start them outdoors (in late April in Zone 5; adjust for your region).

Plants for 10-quart Pails

All the following plants do well in partial shade, indoors or out. They can also be grown in boxes. Planting dates are for Zone 5. Adjust for your region.

	When to Plant	Days from Seed to Harvest	Space Apart	When to Harvest
Beets, Detroit dark red (short top)	May 10, seeds	50 to 60	2 to 3″	Roots are 1 to 2″ in diameter. Use leaves for greens
Cabbage, midgets, earlies	May 1, plants	65 to 90	1 per pail	Head is round and hard
Carrots, short, sweet, Goldinheart	May 10, seeds	65 to 80	2 to 3″	Roots are ½ to 1″ in diameter
Chard, Rhubarb, Swiss	May 10, seeds	30 to 40	4 to 5″	Leaves are 3″ or more long; grows all summer
Kale, Dw, Siberian	May 1, plants	50 to 65	1 per pail	Remove leaves when large enough for greens
Onions	May 1, sets April 20, seeds	50	1½ to 2″	8 to 12″ as green onions
Tomatoes, Tiny Tim	May 20, plants April 10, seeds	55 to 75	1 per pail	Fruit in full color
Turnips, Shogoin	May 1, August 20	30 for greens 60 for roots	3 to 4″	Greens are big and deep green; use greens as well as roots

In Baskets or Boxes

These plants require full sunlight 12 hours a day. After larger plants are well established, the growing medium may be covered with plastic to reduce rapid moisture loss in hot weather. Use a liquid, balanced plant food every three weeks.

	When to Plant	Days from Seed to Harvest	Space Apart	When to Harvest
Cucumbers, mini	June 1, plants May 1, seeds	55 days (indoors)	1 per basket, provide trellis	Reach 4" long
Eggplants, Early Beauty	June 1, plants	65 to 80	3 per bushel basket	Purple/black fruit
Peppers, King of the North	June 1, plants	75 to 90	4 per bushel	Red or green
Squash, bush types only (e.g., Golden Nugget)	June 1, seeds	80	1 per bushel	Best when not too large—about 6 to 8" long
Tomatoes	May 20 to June 10, plants	45 Early Salad	1 per bushel	Deep red fruit
		60 Early Wonder		Use 3' stake
		85 Early Rutgers		Use 6' stake and prune to one stem

Call It Dirt or Soil; but Make It Soft

When I was a youngster, I worked for an old landscape superintendent who used to correct me constantly when I referred to garden soil as *dirt*. "Gosh darn kid," he would yell, "Dirt you sweep under the carpet and soil you grow in." You call it what you want but if you want vegetables to grow in it, it should be soft, fertile and well drained, with as few stones as possible.

Since it will be almost impossible for you to pick a location with perfect soil, it will be your responsibility to build perfect soil.

Walk slowly back and forth across your garden patch with a thin-soled pair of shoes, looking and feeling for rocks, large stones, metal, wood, glass, nails, tar paper. Anything that would make you uncomfortable will do the same to your garden friends, so get rid of it.

Now get the soil ready for the seeds or baby plants. You must break up the big chunks of soil and get the rest of the dirt as fine as though you were going to plant grass seeds. Use a hoe, rake, pick, rototiller, or neighborhood weasel. Spade at least 9 to 10 inches deep if you want long, strong carrots and other root crops. If the soil is heavy clay, add 50 pounds of sawdust, sand, or peat moss per 100 square feet. If the soil is sandy, add 5 to 6 bushels of clay per 100 square feet. To any type of soil, add 50 pounds of agricultural gyp-

Bigger Gardens for Bigger Spaces

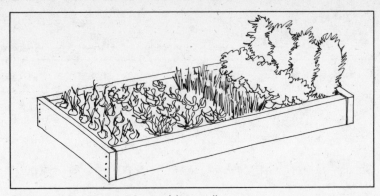

Raised vegetable bed for problem soils

Deep-spade bed in fall and spring

Add lime, gypsum, fertilizer, and organic matter

sum per 100 square feet. Gypsum breaks up heavy clay, neutralizes sodium salts, kills soil insects, and makes fertilizer act faster and longer.

If you are on a solid base of clay, save your digging effort and build a big kid's playbox out of 2-inch by 12-inch boards that are wolminized (treated to prevent rotting). Fill it with a good sandy loam, homemade or purchased compost, peat moss, dried leaves, and any other organic material you can get your hands on. Grow your vegetables in this playbox. If the soil is heavy but not clay, lighten it up with all of the above.

Turn It Over, Don't Just Tickle It

Grandma Putt is the lady who taught me the difference between a pig and a plow. I was five years old when I went to live with her, a grand lady who lived in her garden and by the Bible. She taught me that in order to get the most from the soil you must pamper it, put back into it each season what the plants took out. The one thing she insisted my uncles do every fall was deep-spade the earth, turning it over and then sweetening it with gypsum and lime to brew through the winter. Come spring, it was turned again and fertilized. Rototilling or raking is fine after you have turned the soil but is not a substitute. The results will be worth the effort.

The Big Three Soil Builders

After you have turned the soil in the late fall, add 25 pounds of lime, 25 pounds of gypsum, and 25 pounds of fertilizer per 100 square feet of soil and let it set for the winter. In spring these three will end up on the bottom, where they

Break up clumps of soil in spring after deep-spading

Scatter fertilizer

Till

belong. In spring, after deep-spading, hand scatter 10 pounds of fertilizer per 100 square feet and rake it into the soil lightly.

The Three Numbers on a Fertilizer Bag Are the Odds to Win or Lose

Every time you turn around there's a new advertisement for a new super-duper garden food. Don't waste your money; 5-10-5 will do just fine. For you newcomers to gardening, 5-10-5 means five parts of nitrogen to ten of phosphorus to five of potash; just look for 5-10-5 on the label and buy the cheapest brands. It seems to me that the only thing about fertilizer that has really changed over the years is the cost of the packaging and advertising. Manure is still the best if you have the time to wait; it takes four to six months to break down in the soil. If you are in a hurry, the inexpensive commercial fertilizers will get the job done quicker.

Rake

Keep the Compost Pile Cooking

There's nothing that enriches soil like generous applications of compost. Later in this chapter there's a section describing how to make compost in your yard. Check out the compost recipe and use it—for shrubs, trees, and flower beds as well as your vegetables. It will save you money, time, and, very likely, a crop or two.

Start off Weed-free, the Easy Way

If I told you that there is a chemical that will safely and easily kill weeds, weed seeds, soil fungi, nematodes, and many soil insects, leaving your garden ready to plant within three or four weeks, would you believe me? There is such a chemical. It's called Vapam; you can purchase it under many brand names. Vapam is a professional soil fumigant manufactured by the Stouffer Chemical Company of Westport, Connecticut. You mix it with water and apply it to your spaded or tilled garden plot with a sprinkling can or hose-end sprayer. The chemical turns into a gas that kills the various pests in the soil, then disappears. Once the gas has escaped, no harmful residue remains in the soil.

When you rid your garden soil of pests with Vapam, plants grow evenly and quickly. The difference in vigor between plants grown on Vapam-treated soil and those grown on untreated soil is striking. Just follow the directions on the label.

Never Take a Trip without a Map

I have given this little piece of advice so many times that I have lost count. You have *got* to have a plan in every phase of home gardening, from lawn layout to zucchini placement.

Take a large brown paper grocery bag and split it open so

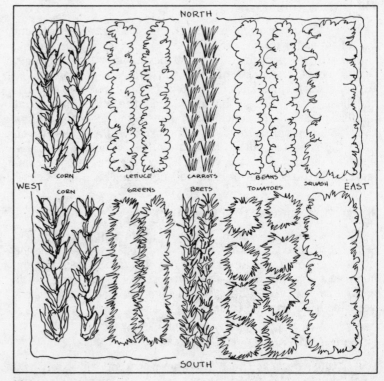

Make a garden plan

you have plenty of room to draw. Mark the four directions on your paper-sack plan: north, south, east, and west.

Plan your garden from west to east, as the dry, hot summer winds come from the southwest and can dry your garden out in a hurry. The rows themselves will run north-south. I have found from experience that corn should be planted on the west and south side of your garden as a wind barrier to protect the more fragile plants. Next, lettuce and the greens. Then any of these in any order: potatoes, carrots, radishes, parsnips, turnips, cabbage, peppers, cauliflower, onions, broccoli, Brussels sprouts, beets, peas, beans, tomatoes. Squash, cantaloupe and cucumbers are always planted on the east of your garden, as they grow to the morning sun and will grow over the top of your other plants if they're not on the east side. Mark the position of each crop on your plan.

Keep this plan after you've planted so you'll know where everything is; otherwise you may pull up the lettuce and cultivate the dandelions by mistake.

Plants Who Enjoy One Another's Company: Natural Insect Control in the Vegetable Garden

Those who take great pride in cultivated, weed-free gardens may unwittingly be inviting insect hordes to dine on succulent plants. Note the stray tomato or squash that has sprouted in tall grass and weeds where unwanteds were tossed last year: Competition is difficult here, growth is slow from a late start—but in most cases these strays have no insect damage. Certain weeds attract chewing insects, leaf hoppers, and aphids away from vegetables, yet can be restrained from choking plantings by selection and limited cultivation. So when you lay out your vegetable garden, take advantage of the natural protection afforded by having your plants keep the right company.

The virtues of marigolds are now widely recognized; their roots exude a substance that has been shown by scientists to repel and kill nematodes. Some species of nematodes cause root problems that deform and stunt many plants, both herbaceous and woody. Marigolds also repel slugs. Plant marigolds lavishly between all susceptible vegetables.

Herbs like rosemary, sage, basil, garlic, and chives give off heavy aromas that upset insects' sensory organs and drive them away.

Leguminous plants such as peas and beans produce extra nitrogen, spurring more productive development in other plants within root reach. Healthy, strong plants best resist insect and disease attack, so mingling legumes with other plants will help the pest problem. Horseradish is reported to keep potatoes free of beetles, and onions protect beans from ants. Borage, bee balm, and comfrey near any plants assure good pollination by bees.

Caution: Reports state that onions stunt pepper plants and may stunt tomatoes.

PLANT	COMPANION PLANTINGS
Asparagus	Tomatoes, parsley, basil
Beans	Potatoes, carrots, corn, cauliflower, cabbage, celery, cucumbers, most other vegetables and herbs
Borage	Tomatoes (borage attracts bees, deters tomato worm, improves growth and flavor), squash, strawberries
Cabbage family, including: Cauliflower Broccoli Brussels Sprouts Kohlrabi	Potatoes, celery, dill, chamomile, sage, thyme, mint, rosemary, lavender, beets, onions. Aromatic plants deter cabbage worms.
Carrots	Peas, lettuce, chives, onions, leeks, rosemary, sage, tomatoes
Catnip	Plant in borders; protects against flea beetles
Celery	Leeks, tomatoes, bush beans, cabbage, cauliflower
Chamomile	Cabbage, onions
Chives	Carrots; at base of fruit trees to discourage insects from climbing
Corn	Potatoes, peas, beans, cucumbers, pumpkins, squash
Cucumbers	Beans, corn, peas, radishes, sunflowers
Dill	Cabbage (they improve each other's growth and health), carrots
Eggplants	Beans
Fennel	Most vegetables are supposed to dislike it—confine it to your herb or flower garden
Garlic	Roses and raspberries (garlic deters Japanese beetles); with herbs to enhance their production of essential oils; plant liberally throughout garden to deter pests
Horseradish	Potatoes (horseradish deters potato beetle); under plum trees to discourage curculios
Leeks	Onions, celery, carrots

Lettuce	Carrots and radishes (lettuce, carrots, and radishes make a strong companion team), strawberries, cucumbers
Marigolds	See above. Discourages many insects, slugs. Interplant freely
Mint	Cabbage family (deters cabbage moth), tomatoes
Nasturtiums	Tomatoes, radishes, cabbage, cucumbers; under fruit trees to deter aphids and pests
Onions	Beets, strawberries, tomato, lettuce (onion protects against slugs), beans (against ants), summer savory
Parsley	Tomatoes, asparagus
Peas	Grow well with almost any vegetable, add nitrogen to soil
Petunias	Protects beans; beneficial throughout garden because they distract insects from your vegetables
Pigweed	Brings nutrients to topsoil; beneficial with potatoes, onions, and corn if kept well trimmed
Potatoes	Horseradish (as trap crop for beetle), beans, corn, cabbage, marigolds, limas, eggplants
Pumpkins	Corn
Radishes	Peas, nasturtiums, lettuce, cucumbers; general aid in repelling insects
Rosemary	Carrots, beans, cabbage, sage (deters cabbage moth, bean beetles, carrot flies)
Sage	Rosemary, carrots, cabbage, peas, beans (deters some insects)
Spinach	Strawberries
Squash	Nasturtiums, corn
Strawberries	Bush beans, spinach, borage, lettuce
Summer Savory	Beans (deters bean beetles), onions
Tansies	Roses, raspberries, cucumbers, squash; under fruit trees (deter pests of roses and raspberries, flying insects, Japanese beetles, stripped cucumber beetles, squash bugs, ants)
Tomatoes	Parsley, asparagus, marigolds, nasturtiums, carrots, limas
Yarrow	Plant along borders; enhances essential oil production in herbs

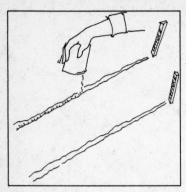

Planting seeds

Setting out plants

Raise replacement plants in a planter or paper cups

Seeds Versus Plants

The first consideration here is money; the second is time. If you have the spare time and growing season, you'll save money if you plant seeds. If your area has a short growing season (Alaska, the Dakotas, the Northeast), you should start seeds indoors or buy plants. The end results are the same either way.

If you are going to start from seeds, you must be prepared to wait a bit longer for your harvest. To speed up sprouting, soak your seeds in a cup of tea in the refrigerator for at least three days. This will fool the seeds into thinking it's later than they think and they will grow faster.

If you are planting seeds in the city, you have a problem that most country and suburban folks don't, and that is the unending appetite of pigeons and many other birds for your corn and large seeds. To stop them from gobbling up your unborn crops, collect paper, plastic, or styrofoam cups and cut the bottoms out of them. Plant the seeds and place the cups over the top, forcing them down into the ground an inch or so. The birds won't be able to reach far enough into the cups to get the seeds.

When to Plant Is a Guessing Game

I have included the standard planting table at the end of the chapter to give you something to blame a screw-up on, but in reality you never know for sure when it's safe to plant. Here are a few sugestions to even out the odds:

Real Tough (Plant 5 to 6 weeks before last frost date)

Broccoli	Peas
Cabbage	Potatoes
Lettuce	Spinach
Onions	Turnips

Kind of Tough (Plant a couple of weeks before last frost date)

Beets	Mustard
Carrots	Parsnips
Chard	Radishes

Don't-Take-a-Chance Vegetables (Plant two weeks after last frost)

Beans	Peppers
Cucumbers	Squash
Eggplants	Sweet Corn
Melons	Sweet Potatoes
Okra	Tomatoes

To find out the last frost date in your area, consult the chart at the end of the chapter.

Plan for a Continual Harvest

Your vegetable garden should never have an empty spot. When you harvest one thing, plant another. See the planting table for planting and harvesting times.

So that you don't waste any time waiting for new seeds to sprout when you go to replace plants you have harvested, start the new seeds two or three weeks ahead of time in paper cups filled with a light soil mix:

1 part soil
1 part sand
1 part peat moss or sawdust

Keep the cups outside on the east side of the house and they will be raring to grow when you plant them in the soil.

Protect stems of tomato and pepper plants

Keep Them Clothed and Comfortable

As soon as your garden begins to sprout, lay two layers of newspaper between the rows, one on top of the other, right up next to the plants, and cover each layer of paper with a sprinkling of grass clippings. This will keep the weeds from growing and save on water and work.

Tomatoes and pepper plants should have small pieces of index card or aluminum foil wrapped firmly around the stems up to the first branch when first planted to keep the cut worms from chopping them down.

Since you will not have all the room in the world, it is a good idea to use stakes for supporting upright plants such as peppers and tomatoes. Cucumbers, peas, and beans can be grown on a chicken-wire fence tied to stakes. Tie plants with pieces of nylon cloth or stockings.

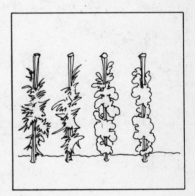

Stake tall plants

Start Them off Eating Right

As soon as you have planted your garden, apply a liquid starting food called Upstart. It contains a hormone that will mean the difference between a good crop and a super one.

After the starter feeding, leave the garden alone until the plants are well-established. At this point you will start to feed the appropriate type of fertilizer.

Boys and Girls Are Different

In order for you to better understand which plants get

which food, I have divided the plants into boys and girls. We are all aware that men and women need different nutrients in different quantities to look their best. Well, plants are no different.

Fertilizer contains 3 basic things that plants need:

1. Nitrogen—This makes lots of green leaves and long stems.
2. Phosphorus—This makes the stems strong and thick and stimulates the growth of flowers and fruit.
3. Potash—This grows thick, strong roots.

Girl plants need a little nitrogen and plenty of phosphorus and potash to produce flowers, which turn to fruit, or roots, which swell and turn into tubers like carrots and radishes. Boy plants need lots of nitrogen to grow green and leafy but not so much of the other two. Girl plants are those that bear flowers and fruit (such as tomatoes and squash) and the tubers (such as carrots, radishes, beets, parsnips). Boy plants include the cabbage family, all the greens, corn, peas, and beans. Garden food is used for girl plants because it is high in phosphorus and potash, and lawn food for boy plants because it is high in nitrogen.

Give Them Regular Meals

After your plants are up, you should side-dress. This means to sprinkle a small amount of the appropriate plant food on both sides of the rows 3 to 4 inches away from the plants. If you have not covered the soil with newspaper and grass clippings, then hoe the food in. If you have used newspaper and clippings, sprinkle the food on top and then take a sharp stick or rod and punch lightly into the soil. Leafy vegetables are side-dressed after they are well started, corn when it is 12 inches tall, and tomatoes, peppers, and vine plants after the first fruits are visible. Do not side-dress when foliage is damp. Keep the plant food off the leaves.

Wet Their Whistles

Don't let your garden get thirsty. If I could cut one rule into stone, it would be DON'T FORGET TO WATER. It sounds simple, but it's the simple things we forget. On a hot July or August day, a 10×10-foot garden will give 100 gallons of water back to the sky. Not only does some water evaporate from the soil, but plants, like people, sweat (respire), and that water has to be returned to the earth so that the plants can drink. It is best to water over the top of your garden (wetting the foliage as well as the soil) between 7:00 A.M. and

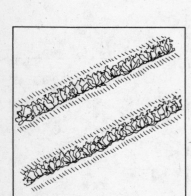
Side-dress

Don't forget to water!

10:00 A.M., and to soak water (wetting the soil only) when the sun is high and hot, between 11:00 A.M. and 3:00 P.M. Don't do both at one watering, and don't water after 3:00 P.M. or fungi may become a problem. Nelson sprinklers have a whirlee that is designed for vegetable and flower gardens. Keep the soil damp, but not soggy wet. If small pools of water lie on the surface, poke holes at least 10 inches deep in that area 1 foot apart for the water to drain into.

A Clean Garden Is a Healthy Garden

I have never seen a gardener yet who has not been bothered by one thing or the other, mainly bugs or sick plants. You'll have less of both if you keep your garden clean. Remove any trash that blows in, and don't smoke when you are gardening. Gardens need a bath occasionally, so wash your garden at least once every other week with soap and water; use ½ teaspoon of liquid soap per gallon of water. The easiest way to apply the soap and water is with a compression sprayer with an adjustable nozzle, because you can direct the spray right where it is needed.

Bathe your garden and spray against pests

When you need an insect and disease control, use one of the fruit and vegetable sprays, like Super K-Gro Fruit and Garden Spray, that are safe to use and will not hurt man, beast, or bird. Ask your local garden supplier about them and follow all the directions. Remember, a little goes a long way, so share the cost with your neighbors. Needless to say, you must always keep them out of reach of children. Your garden supplier may also recommend dusts. They should be applied early in the morning when the dew is still on the plants. As an extra precaution, a few empty beer cans scattered in your patch will catch slugs. Replace them weekly.

Don't Press Your Luck

"In sickness and in health" is a promise you only make in marriage; in gardening it does not count. I have seen a super-looking garden die in a matter of days because one plant got sick and, instead of removing it, the gardener thought he could save it, only to have it infect all the other plants. You are not an expert, so don't take a chance if a plant does not respond to food or water and you can't see bugs. Pull it out and burn it. Don't risk your whole garden for the sake of one plant.

Keep Them Company—but Not During Their Siesta

Your garden is like you. It likes some time to itself. There is a good time and a bad time to work in your garden. Try to work in the morning before noon or from 4:00 P.M. until dark, as the plants like to rest when the sun is hot. Plants sleep at night and that is when they grow.

When you are at work with the plants it will help to compliment the ones that are doing well and lightly shake the lazy ones. I find that humming helps us both, since I can't sing.

Be a Good Neighbor

Many of you will be gardening next to one another, and a natural competitive spirit will develop. This is good, but don't let it blind you to problems your garden neighbor might be having. Offer a helping hand or a word of advice from time to time. Remember, one of these days the shoe might be on the other foot.

You and your neighbors can cut down on a lot of expenses by sharing supplies and equipment. If you're on good terms with your neighbor, suggest splitting packets of seeds, garden sprays, and other products next season. Maybe he'll let you use his power lawn mower if you lend him your rototiller. You can both save money and get to know each other better in the process.

At Season's End . . .

When winter comes, don't just walk away from your garden. Say farewell to the last of your vegetable friends and clean up your garden patch. Pull up any remaining plants and put them in your compost pile. If you're going to use the same plot next year, you can get a headstart by applying lime, gypsum, and fertilizer now, before the snow comes. Then turn the soil and let it brew over the winter, and start over again next spring.

Tomatoes, the Top Contender

You home gardeners have made tomatoes your favorite vegetable; and from the looks of my daily mail, they appear to be the vegetable giving you the most trouble. Tomatoes can be grown indoors or out and in any kind of container you can find to hold soil and water, but they do need some special care.

Here Are My Tomato Choices

There are many varieties of tomatoes available to the home gardener today. These are my favorites.

Beefsteak	Extra big, not too acid.
Burpee VF	Firm, medium size, great taste.
Early Girl	Lots of 4-ounce size.
Fireball	Lots of 8-ounce size.
Italian Paste	Nice and thick for tomato paste.
Jubilee	Subtle color, not too acid.
Marglobe	The best all-around—hardy, easy to grow, lots of fruit, delicious.
Rutgers	Keeps on giving.
Supersonic	Early yield; bush type.

Tomato cages save work and worry

All of the above can be grown for pennies apiece, and they all put the big-mouth food broker I mentioned at the beginning of the chapter to shame.

Planting Time Is Iffy

Watch the weather reports, check the planting chart at the end of the chapter, and then wait two weeks to plant. If you miscalculate and there's a frost, cover the plant with a grocery bag for the night.

It's Place in the Sun

Tomatoes need sun all day, good circulation of air, and well-drained, light, rich, organic soil. It's not a good idea to plant tomatoes in the same spot each year, because they quickly deplete the trace minerals in the soil. Pull up the old plants and burn them; do not throw them into the compost pile or you will end up with millions of unwanted wild plants next season all over your garden. Use fresh soil each year for container-grown tomatoes.

Give Them Room

Tomatoes need 2 to 3 feet between one another, and it's a good idea to leave 4 feet between rows.

Using tomato cages will save you work and worry. They keep the plants from sprawling all over your patch. The plastic cages are somewhat better than metal ones, because the wire often gets too hot on sunny days and burns the vine. Plastic also can be cleaned more easily in fall.

Mulch tomatoes to a depth of 4 to 6 inches

Too Rich a Diet Is Bad for Any Tomato

Low-nitrogen garden food (5-10-5) will do nicely to produce more and larger fruit ("vegetable" in the United States, by an act of Congress). High nitrogen will give you too much soft, floppy foliage. You may also get too many suckers, which tax the plant's resources without bearing fruit. I have found that it's more work than it's worth to worry about pinching suckers—let 'em grow—but do correct your feeding if necessary.

Make Them Comfortable

Mulch beneath tomatoes to a depth of 4 to 6 inches with marsh hay or grass clippings. Mulch helps to prevent blossom-end rot and skin split.

The Worms Stop Here

Use Dipel™, a safe, organic control. For most other bugs, use K Mart's garden and fruit tree spray.

Compost—Your Garden's Best Friend

Compost Doesn't Have to Be Smelly—or Hard Work!

Composting is the simple, natural process of turning decaying plant and animal wastes into a loose, peatlike humus. Composting is a time-saver because it solves your surplus trash problems. It saves money that you would otherwise spend on fertilizer, because finished compost is one of the most complete plant foods known. Best of all, by reusing waste materials you will be doing your share to protect the environment.

Here's how composting works: Bacteria that live in the soil feed upon and digest plant and animal wastes. This process causes the decay of these wastes. The activity of the bacteria releases heat, which in turn speeds up the process of decay. As the wastes decay, they break down into the essential nu-

Styles of compost piles range from the open heap to neat, modern bins.

trients that your plants need to grow. Depending on how you treat your compost pile, it takes from 6 weeks to 6 months to make finished compost. A well-cared-for compost pile has a clean, fresh earth fragrance and need not cause any turned-up noses.

How to Build a Compost Pile

It's easy to learn how to compost. Pick a spot in the garden that is somewhat secluded. Plan on using a space about 4 × 6 feet. Put a 6- to 12-inch layer of waste material on the ground. Over this layer scatter 1 or 2 pounds of lawn or garden fertilizer. Better yet, use several handfuls of blood-meal or cottonseed meal mixed with bonemeal instead of the fertilizer. This hurries the process of decay and forms a richer compost. If the material that is used is dry, dampen it with water to the wetness of a squeezed sponge.

On the top of this area, sprinkle a 1- to 2-inch layer of ordinary topsoil. Good loam from a cultivated vegetable garden is ideal. Loam contains the starter bacteria.

Keep adding layers until the pile is 4 feet high. The pile can be enclosed on two or three sides by a cement block wall or all the way around by an open mesh fence.

Regulate moisture evenly; never depend on rainfall. The ideal way to accomplish this is to cover the heap with black plastic held down by stones. The plastic covering prevents the pile from drying out or getting rained on. When you turn the compost or add new waste, simply lift up the cover.

If you follow these steps and never touch your compost pile except to add new layers, you will have finished compost in about six months. Warm weather will speed up the process, but don't allow the pile to heat up beyond 150° F or it may start to burn.

Materials to Use in Making Compost

You can use grass clippings, leaves, weeds, sod, fall garden waste, shredded newsprint, kitchen waste of vegetable origin, tree trimmings, animal manure (not horse or dog or cat)—any organic waste that does not harbor insects, weed seeds, or disease. You can collect sawdust, hay, straw, and factory by-products of plant or animal origin, such as shells and hulls. But don't use fat, whether plant or animal. That means no bones or meat or greasy dishwater either.

How to Speed Up the Composting Process

There are a number of ways in which you can speed up the time it takes for nature to make finished compost. To work properly, compost piles need air, moisture, and heat in moderate quantities. Here's how you can provide these conditions:

Grind or shred all materials to be composted. There are shredding machines on the market that will grind up garden refuse—sometimes even branches up to 3 inches in diameter.

Turn the pile once a week until it is done. Fork it over from one end to the other.

Keep the pile moist. Cover it with a sheet of black plastic. Leaching by rainfall can reduce the concentration of effective nutrients in the compost. Don't let the pile lie exposed and unused.

Raise the pile off the ground on a screen for better aeration.

Use starter cultures of bacteria available commercially, or ½ bottle of beer per 5 bushels of material.

The Stylish Compost Pile

The open heap is still the least expensive method of composting, but it is not permitted in many communities, and there are also those homeowners who shrink at the thought of keeping an exposed pile of debris in their backyard. There are now a variety of composting methods designed to look more attractive, take less work, or use less space than the traditional open heap.

A small compost pile can be made by digging a shallow trench in your yard and filling it gradually. Spread a layer of raw compost material, sprinkle on some fertilizer, and cover with an inch of topsoil, as for the open heap. Turn the compost frequently, since it will not get as much air as an aboveground pile. Surround the little Eden with sturdy dog- and rabbit-proof fencing.

A covered pit built of concrete is durable, animal-proof, and fly-free. It looks good when built onto a retaining wall. A sheet of metal in front slides up and down to function as the door, and a hinged cover may be provided on top. If the pit is tightly closed, a cylinder of wire mesh should be inserted from bottom to top near the rear to allow air to circulate inside the pit. Dress up, if you like, with creeping vines and low-hanging shrubs.

Another method of making compost is to install a garbage digester below ground, with the top level with the lawn surface. This device is very inconspicuous and lasts many years before replacement is needed. A good, cheaper alternative is burying a heavy plastic garbage can up to the top.

Small quantities of compost can be made in heavy, sealed plastic bags, kept in the garage or basement. Maintain the proper moisture level, and flop the bags over each day. This method is helpful for making up potting soils throughout the year. Rub the finished material through a ¼-inch mesh sifting screen (hardware cloth, framed in wood) and sterilize before using for potting as described in Chapter 6.

A little plastic silo with removable staves and top looks neat at the edge of the garden, but is no more efficient than a homemade retainer, like the concrete pit. It has openings at the sides to admit air; the top keeps out rain and lifts off easily for adding refuse.

A compost maker with a rotating drum that holds several bushels can be stationed in the garage. A few turns are suggested each day, with the finished product ready in as little as fourteen days.

How to Use Finished Compost

The use of compost is the key to natural gardening. Compost loosens and aerates hard clay soils and builds up sandy ones. It also helps sandy soils hold water. Compost slowly releases its many nutrients for plant use. It also activates beneficial soil organisms. Here's how to use finished compost:

- Build up the soil by working a 2-inch layer into flower beds and vegetable gardens.
- Mulch around established plants with it.
- Top-dress your lawn with it.
- Mix it with an equal quantity of topsoil and use it as potting soil or tree planting mix.
- Side-dress growing plants with it.

Kiddy Cocktails for Little Plants

If the compost route is a little too much for you, here's a compromise. Save your table scraps each day (peels, vegetables, eggshells, etc.); no fat or salt, please. Place the table scraps in the food processor and cover to the top with water or dishwater. Add a tablespoon of Epsom salts and liquify. Now, pour this on the soil in the garden and lightly hoe in. This will do wonders!

How to Get Rid of Troublemakers

Roll call: moles, gophers, ground squirrels, mice, rats, chipmunks, squirrels, skunks, raccoons, foxes, woodchucks, groundhogs, deer, rabbits, dogs, cats, snakes, pigeons, and other birds (to name a few).

There is nothing that makes a home gardener's heart sink more than coming into your yard after you have spent time, effort, and money to have a healthy and attractive lawn, flower bed, or vegetable garden and finding the results of a mole or gopher family reunion. You find tunnels and mounds everywhere, and you feel so helpless. Well, my gardening friend, that need not be the case. You can fight back and guard your little corner of the world.

Gophers and moles are far and away the number-one concern from border to border and coast to coast; chipmunks, shrews, squirrels, mice, rats, woodchucks, raccoons, and skunks can also be a headache. Then there are the cute little bunny rabbits hopping all over the yard, eating the bark off fruit trees and shrubs in the winter and racing you for the garden each spring. Last, but not least, there are the beautiful but hungry deer and your neighbor's beloved Kitty and Fido. What's a body to do? Don't just hang up your hoe—stand up and fight! I am going to tell you how to trap, discourage, and aggravate most of the unwelcome guests that may venture into your yard or garden (what I call your "yarden").

I wish to go on record as being opposed to destroying any living creature that does not pose a danger to human or other animal life. I highly recommend that whenever possible these pests be humanely trapped and relocated to a more suitable habitat for both of you. In nine out of ten cases I have found that I can antagonize a varmint enough without harming it or me to make it move on. The real secret to success in fighting these pests is knowledge. Learn all you can about the intruder's diet, habits, and living preference, and in every case you will find a way to beat it.

Professional traps can be rented in many suburban or rural area garden shops, feed stores, equipment rental shops, and hardware stores. Traps can be purchased through most of the large retail catalog houses or from Havahart Traps, Box 551, Ossining, New York 10652. They have a humane trap for every situation.

I don't believe in unnecessary poisoning of animals but in some cases you may get so frustrated with your garden pests that you start to wonder how it's done. I have some suggestions for using poisons effectively to get the culprit (and not your dog, your kids, or your mother-in-law), but it's up to you to decide when to use them.

Moles

To begin with, moles have no interest whatsoever in vegetation as a food source, and only gather grass clippings and leaves to line their nests. The mole's diet consists primarily of insects, and as a last resort they will eat snakes, frogs, and even weaker moles. A mole can go without food only for about twelve hours, as its appetite is endless, and it will eat as much as three times its own body weight daily. The mole is nearly blind and seldom, if ever, comes above the ground. With its powerful front paws with strong clawlike nails that resemble human hands, it can excavate 200 to 300 feet of new tunnel in a day's work. Moles are extremely sensitive to sound, avoiding unfamiliar noises whenever possible. A little-known fact about moles is that they are darn good swimmers when necessary—they can easily paddle 100 to 200 yards. One last thing you should know is that the mole's tail is very sensitive and guides it when it crawls backwards in its tunnels. The mole makes hundreds of yards of tunnels in search of food, and continually maintains them. The mole maintains them so well that mice, snakes, and voles (small mouselike creatures) use them to get to your garden plants and roots, leaving the mole to take the blame.

CONTROLS: Since moles eat insects, get rid of the insects and you get rid of the moles. It's that simple. To do this, apply Diazinon liquid or granules to the soil in the early fall and/or early spring. There is also a super new chemical called Oftanol, which is manufactured by Mobay Chemical Corporation of Kansas City, Missouri and is available in many garden centers.

To discourage the moles, place decorative plastic daisy pinwheels in various spots on their runs. As the pinwheels spin, they set off vibrations in the ground, which drive the moles nuts. Or you might want to bury a few wine bottles at a 20° to 30° angle with only the necks sticking out in different directions. The open bottles catch the wind and make a strange and aggravating noise. Firecrackers placed in the nest or mound area (which you will probably find in a shrubbed area, on a hillside, or between the roots of a tree) really annoy them and the air compression caused by the explosion in the tunnel can give them a concussion, which is generally fatal. Burning road flares placed fire side down into the run or a garden hose attached to the exhaust pipe of a car for 15 minutes and placed into the run will end their lives in a hurry, but your car might meet the same fate. Gopher gassers, made by Dexol Corporation, are available in most garden departments. They let off a poisonous gas when you light the gas cartridge; place them in the runs of moles, gophers, and ground squirrels. Golf courses, parks, and cemeteries use these very effectively. I prefer Grandma Putt's method of discouraging them while I wait for the insects to die. She had my Aunt Jane and I place a tablespoon of Paradichlorobenzene (don't fret, folks, that's moth crystals) every 6 or 8 feet apart in the tunnels. In between the small piles of crystals we placed a three-finger measure of hair clippings. The hair gets stuck to their velvety fur and makes them scratch to get it off. Their claws are so sharp that they sometimes claw themselves to death. As a last resort you can use the Victor Harpoon Spear Trap to kill them. You can also use a chemical called Mercaptans as a repellent. Ask your druggist about it.

Gophers

These critters are another story. Gophers eat a whole selection of garden produce as well as make a mess out of the garden patch. You can trap them with a number 0 Havahart Trap baited with peanut butter mixed with molasses and spread on whole-wheat toast. Some folks then drown them. I prefer to take them to a large wooded area four or five miles from my home. Since they don't eat insects, forget the chemicals, but all of the other suggestions for moles will work.

Ground Squirrels

These beasties are akin to the gopher and can be captured or destroyed in the same way. Use unroasted peanuts as trap bait.

Mice

I don't need to tell you about these critters, except that fall is generally when they become a problem indoors, and that is also when they are easiest to destroy. Here I recommend forceful methods of eradication. They may look cute and innocent, but the damage they do to food crops and property, the diseases they spread, and the bites they inflict on children and small animals should clear your conscience.

The best way to bait mice is to use a D-Con Mouse Bait inside of a milk carton with the bottom cut out and laid on its side next to an outside wall behind boxes or cans. Do not wash out the milk carton; the sour milk will attract the mice. To trap them, coat a 2-inch wide board, 3 feet long, or 4 × 30-inch pieces of roofing felt paper, with Rat and Mouse Tanglefoot, manufactured by the Tanglefoot Company of Grand Rapids, Michigan. This is a trapping adhesive and is used to prepare sticky traps to catch and hold rats and mice. This product is extremely tacky, nonpoisonous, odorless, nonflammable, nondrying, and nonflowing. Place the coated boards or felt paper in rodent runways leading to the milk cartons, especially just inside garage doors on either side in mid-September.

Rats

It gives me the creeps to even write about these pests. Ramik Green Rodenticide by Velsicol Chemical Company, Chicago, Illinois, really does the job on these guys and is available in almost any farm or feed store. It is an extremely dangerous poison and should not be used near children or pets. It is, however, safer and faster-acting than older rat poisons like warfarin. Use where you suspect the rats of nesting. To trap the rats, use the Rat and Mouse Tanglefoot mentioned before—but be careful; everything that you have heard about a trapped rat is true. If you are weak at heart about banging these nasties on the head with a shovel, call your local PCO (pest control operator). Terrier dogs and some cats are super critter killers. Don't get a cat just to kill rats, though; most cats won't go near a full-grown rat.

Chipmunks

These cute little fellows are a pleasure to watch as they dart here and there with their cheek pouches so full they look like a couple of balloons. Chipmunks eat seeds, berries, nuts, and plant buds. They live in nests underground near walls, rock piles, and tree roots or stumps. They are, however, incredibly destructive in the garden and make a mess out of the bulbs planted in fall for spring blossoms. They are easily trapped with a number 1 Havahart Trap; they should be baited with cracked nuts left in their shells or peanut butter and molasses on crackers or whole-wheat toast. Make a trail of the bait to and through the trap and lock the door open so it won't spring shut. After a few days they'll get to trust the trap. That's when you unlock the door and get 'em. To discourage them from eating your bulbs, mix Paradichlorobenzene (moth crystals) into the soil when planting. Disposing of chipmunks is rather difficult for most folks; even the toughest of trappers are moved by their personality and cart them a good distance away from their garden instead of killing them.

Squirrels

This mammal is pretty stupid and easily caught. Use a number 2 Havahart Trap. Tie the end open for a few days and keep it well baited with sunflower seeds, nuts, or acorns. After a few days the squirrels will get used to the trap and go in and out without concern. Then untie the doors and you can catch one after the other. If you know of a hunter or two you will have no problem getting rid of your catch, as the meat is delicious. Don't try to make pets out of them; they can't be tamed.

Skunks

Wow! What a challenge this critter is. No, not because it is tough to catch. That's a snap. It's what you do with it after you have it in a trap. If you shoot it in the trap, it will release its odor as it relaxes in death. Fortunately, there is a special type of trap, the Havahart Trap number 4, that won't let the skunk raise its tail to spray, so the scent is kept down to tolerable (P.U.). Bait the trap with canned fish-flavored cat food. You may have to release the neighbor's cat while you are waiting for your local stinker to make an appearance. Ricky Raccoon may also pay your trap a visit. You can approach the trapped animal from either end of the trap and move it away from the house. Placing a plastic bag over it and then gassing it with the exhaust from your automobile will destroy the animal without too much of a stench. By the way, the trap will be even better for trapping other animals after a skunk has been in it.

Raccoons

If you have ever had a mama raccoon give birth in your attic and watched her bring her babies out at night to play and eat, it is hard to think of them as being troublemakers. Drive down the road on the morning of the day that the garbage man makes pickups and you'll change your thinking—it sometimes looks like a garbage war has been fought. Or, maybe you've been kept awake half the night from the noise as Ricky Raccoon, family, and friends shop in your garbage can; you will soon find it easy to think about trapping him and sending him on a one-way ride. Use a number 3 Havahart Trap and set only one end. Lock the other in place and bait the trap with smoked fish. Raccoons can't resist it, nor can possums. Again, hunters will relieve you of your catch. If you live in a community that has a branch of the Humane Society, you can give them a call; they may be able to find a home for the raccoon.

Foxes

Here you are going up against a real thinker. It will take awhile to trap a fox. The number 7 Havahart Trap should be baited with a live chicken or rabbit. Make sure that the fox has to pass through the trap to get to the bait. The fox must be destroyed. If you prefer, turn it over to an animal shelter. Foxes (like dogs) will return to their home from miles away, so you can't just relocate your catch.

Woodchucks

Boy, oh boy, can these varmints tear up, or rather eat up, a garden in a hurry! The best time to trap a woodchuck is in early spring, right after it wakes up from hibernation. Seed a couple of plastic flats with oats, four or five days apart, so you'll have plenty of bait. Locate the hole (usually you can't miss it) and place a number 3 Havahart Trap over the flat of oat sprouts. Bang! You got 'em. Sweet corn, fresh peas, string beans, or lettuce are also good baits. The woodchuck will have to be transported to a wooded area as far away as possible, shot, or drowned.

Groundhogs

Trap the weather predictor the same way you do woodchucks, but only if it sees its shadow.

Deer

These beautiful animals can be a pain when a hard winter sets in and food is hard to find. A deer will think nothing of wandering into your yard and eating all your evergreens in one night. Spray your trees, shrubs, and garden with bone tar oil, a deer repellent manufactured by Plantabbs Corporation, Timonium, Maryland. This repellent can be purchased in most garden departments and feed stores. It doesn't smell great, but it does the job.

Rabbits

They may be cute-looking but there is nothing cute about the damage they do to gardens, trees, and shrubs in summer and winter. For gardens, the best control is still a fence of 1-inch mesh chicken wire, 3 feet high with 1 or 2 inches buried under the ground. It is also advisable to wrap the trunks of young trees with chicken wire or plastic guards. In the early garden season, a solution of 3 tablespoons of Epsom salts sprayed once a week or so over young foliage will keep your garden rabbit-free. You can also trap them and eat them; they're delicious (similar to chicken). Use the Havahart Trap number 2 baited with Brussels sprouts, apples in winter, and bread. Rabbit pellets are also good bait; they are available in any pet store. There are several dozen rabbit repellents available, but most don't work. Thiram-based rabbit repellents, like the one Plantabbs sells, do work and are available in most garden departments. Marigolds are an excellent rabbit repellent and make an attractive border.

Dogs

It's just the nuisance of their droppings and the inconsideration of their owners that bother most folks. If you have been unable to get satisfactory action from the animal's owner, call your local animal control officer. If that doesn't work, try one of the repellents on the market, like Plantabbs Scent-Off Pellets and Twist-ons. Naptholene, Paradichlorobenzene (moth crystals), tobacco dust, a swift kick, and a swat with a long broom or fat rolled paper all work as well. You might also try this formula from *Garden Ways:*

> 1 garlic bulb or large onion
> 1 tablespoon of cayenne pepper
> 1 quart of hot water
> 1 teaspoon of liquid soap

Finely chop the onion and/or garlic, place it in a piece of nylon stocking, and tie the bundle. Steep for an hour or two in the hot water. Add the cayenne pepper and liquid soap. Strain through cheesecloth and use a hose-end sprayer to spray the liquid on shrubs and lawn edge. Other repellents are oil of lemon and oil of mustard. Obviously poisoning and shooting are *not* options; no matter how much you hate your neighbor's dog, killing it is strictly against the law.

For those of you who own dogs, an application of Sof 'N Soil Garden Gypsum in the fall on the lawn and garden area and again in the spring will prevent burn from animal waste or rock salt.

If you are thinking of getting a dog, you might be interested to know that terriers, even the small ones, are determined killers of rats and other rodents.

Cats

In farm areas or new suburban developments, cats are a farmer's or gardener's best friend. They are excellent for controlling mice, rabbits, and sometimes rats. The only problem they cause is digging in the seed, bulb, or flower beds as a toilet practice.

If you are thinking about having a cat or two around, keep in mind that these animals are pets, not killing machines. The old wives' tale about how they should be kept hungry and raised outdoors if they are to be effective rodent killers is simply not true. The best mousers are healthy cats who are fed plenty of balanced commercial cat food and see a veterinarian regularly. Cats hunt for fun, not hunger, so the stronger and more energetic your cat, the more animals it will kill (if it's not hungry, it won't eat them, but they'll be dead just the same). Cats have strong territorial instincts, so they will hunt most vigilantly in their home turf. That means that if you want your cat to mouse in the house, raise it in the house; if you want it to mouse in the barn, raise it in the barn—don't keep it in a shed or garage. Cats are not faithful like dogs, so if you don't give your cat a comfortable place to live, a little affection, and a wholesome diet, it'll just take off for greener pastures.

If you're a gardener and you have cats, whether they mouse for you or not, you should remember that they dig in the yard and then lick themselves clean. Consequently you should never apply poisons to the soil because the cat will ingest them. More than one cat has died from the arsenic meant to do in the grubs.

Excellent repellents for cats are a nicotine sulphate spray, oil of mustard, and Paradichlorobenzene crystals.

Snakes

I will bet that you can't find one in ten people (except maybe boys under the age of ten or twelve) who want anything to do with snakes, even though they won't bother you unless you disturb them. Snakes play an important part in nature's balance, by eating mice and other destructive rodents, so even if they give you the creeps, you're best off giving them a free rein in your garden. If they become an unbearable problem, or they are nested where you do not want them, you can repel them with a chemical called Mercaptans (available from your pharmacy). Mercaptans is a synthetic skunk odor. Skunks eats snakes, rats, and mice, so apply Mercaptans in areas where you don't want these varmints.

Pigeons

These B-19s of the bird world are just plain messy. You can discourage pigeons, as well as most other birds, by simply placing a plaster, wood, or plastic replica of an owl where you don't want them. They are scared to death of owls. You might consider treating windowsills, ridges, building ledges, gutter edges, and tops of signs with Bird Tanglefoot, manufactured by the Tanglefoot Company of Grand Rapids, Michigan, and available in most garden centers. Bird Tanglefoot is a nondrying, long-lasting, weatherproof, sticky material that doesn't trap the birds, but it makes them darned uncomfortable; they'll soon leave.

Other Birds

Robins, catbirds, and brown thrashers in particular love tender young vegetables as much as you do. The problem becomes apparent when sweet corn begins to break the surface—the tiny shoots are found lying beside a little cone-shaped hole. On finding one, Mr. Thrasher goes down the row probing with his sharp beak for the plump, soft kernels we so carefully planted, casting aside the new corn sprouts.

One method to protect corn is to enclose the rows under special plastic netting when first planted. Or you can start corn in boxes (extra-deep wooden flats) or deep peat pots, covered with pieces of screen wire. Seeds can be spaced 2 inches apart in the box. When 5 inches tall, the corn is transplanted to the garden in a little block of soil, too late to interest the birds. A starter plant food like Upstart will help the young plants make good recovery from any transplant shock in a week to ten days. The starter food will also produce a more even strand of corn.

Other succulent sprouts, such as beans, also fall to the birds. Since beans do not transplant well, unless started in peat pots, rows should be blocked together, with netting stretched over 6-inch-tall stakes. Follow the instructions in Chapter 3 (pages 77 to 80).

I have tried to give you a little insight and a few simple suggestions about some of the creatures you will come in contact with in your everyday gardening, and for the most part a humane way to discourage or trap them. Your local garden department, farm feed store, co-op elevator, or hardware store may have some more suggestions. Whenever you try out a new method of pest eradication, consider whether it will harm you, your children, your pets, desirable wild animals, and the ecology of your area in any way before you use it.

VEGETABLE PLANTING TABLE

(May be started indoors 1–2 months before outdoor seeding date)

Name of vegetable	Time to plant or seed outdoors	Seeds or plants for 100-foot row	Distance apart in rows in inches	Depth planting in inches	Rows apart hand cultivation in inches	Rows apart field cultivation in inches
Asparagus Plants	April	75 plants	18	8	24–36	36–48
Beans, Bush	May 10–July 20	1 pound	3–4	2	24–30	30–36
Beans, Pole	May 15–July 20	½ pound	18–24	2	30–36	30–36
Beans, Bush Lima	May 15–June 10	1 pound	6–10	1	30	30–36
Beans, Pole Lima	May 15–June 20	½ pound	24–36	2	30–36	36–48
Beets, Table	April 1–July 20	2 ounces	2–3	½	12–15	30–36
Broccoli	April 1–June 30	75 plants	18–30	½	30–48	30–48
Brussels Sprouts	April	100 plants	12–18	½	30	30–36
Cabbage Seed, Early	April	¼ ounce	14–18	½	30	30–36
Cabbage Seed, Late	May 1–June 10	¼ ounce	18–24	½	30	30–36
Cabbage Plants	April 1–July 10	75–80 plants	14–18	——	30–36	30–36
Carrots	April 1–July 15	1 ounce	2–3	½	12–15	30–36
Cauliflower	April 1–July 10	75 plants	18–24	½	30–36	30–36
Celeriac (seeds and plants)	May 1–June 10	150–200	6–8	1	18	30–36
Celery Plants	May 1–June 10	150–200 plants	6–8	——	12–30	36–42
Celery Seed	April	¼ ounce	——	1	12–30	36–42
Corn, Sweet	May 10–July 10	¼ pound	14–36	1–2	30–36	36–42
Cucumbers	May 15–July 10	½ ounce	48–72	½–1	48	48–72
Eggplants	May 30	50 plants	18–24	¼	30	36–42
Endives	April 1–July 5	1 ounce	8–10	½	18–24	24–30
Kale	April 1–August	1 ounce	2–4	½	18–24	30–36
Kohlrabi	April–July 15	½ ounce	6–8	½	15–18	30–36
Leeks	April	1 ounce	6–10	½	18–24	30–36
Lettuce Seed, Loose	April–August	½ ounce	2–4	¼	12–15	24–30
Lettuce Seed, Head	April–July 10	½ ounce	12–15	¼	12–15	24–30
Melon, Musk	May 15–May 30	½ ounce	48–72	1–1½	48–72	48–72
Melon, Water	May 20–May 30	1 ounce	72–90	1–2	72–90	72–90
Mustard	April–August 10	1 ounce	4–6	½	12–15	30
Okra	May	1 ounce	18–24	½	24	30–36
Onion Seed	April–May	6 ounces	2–3	½–1	12–15	30
Onion Sets	March–June 15	1–2 pounds	2–3	1	12–15	30

Name of vegetable	Time to plant or seed outdoors	Seeds or plants for 100-foot row	Distance apart in rows in inches	Depth planting in inches	Rows apart hand cultivation in inches	Rows apart field cultivation in inches
Parsley	April–May	½ ounce	3–6	¼	12–15	30
Parsnips	March–April	½ ounce	5–12	½	12–15	30–36
Peas, Early	March–April	2 pounds	2–3	2–3	15–24	30–36
Peas, Late	April–May	2 pounds	2–3	2–3	15–36	30–36
Peppers	May 15–30	50 plants	18–24	——	24–36	30–36
Potatoes	April–June	10 pounds	12–14	4	24–30	30–36
Pumpkins	May 20–May 30	1 ounce-15 hills	72–86	1	96	——
Radishes	April–August	1 ounce	2–3	½	12–15	——
Rutabaga	July	1 ounce	3–6	1	12–15	30–36
Salsify	April	½ ounce	3–5	1	12–15	30–36
Spinach	April–July	2 ounces	2–3	1	12–15	——
Squash, Bush	May 20	1 ounce-40 hills	48	1 to 2	48–72	48–72
Squash, Vining	May 20	1 ounce-40 hills	96	1 to 2	72–96	96
Swiss Chard	April–June	1 ounce	8–10	1 to 2	12–18	30–36
Tomato Plants	May 10–June 30	30–40	24–48	——	24–48	36–48
Tomato Seeds	May	1 packet	——	½	——	
Turnips	April–July 20	1 ounce	3–4	½	12–15	30

HARD-FROST DATES

(From USDA Weather Records)

State	First Frost in Fall	Last Frost in Spring
Arkansas, N.	Oct. 23	Apr. 7
Arkansas, S.	Nov. 3	Mar. 25
California		
Imperial Valley	Dec. 15	Jan. 25
Interior Valley	Nov. 15	Mar. 1
Southern Coast	Dec. 15	Jan. 15
Central Coast	Dec. 1	Feb. 25
Mountain Sections	Sept. 1	Apr. 25
Colorado, W.	Sept. 18	May 25
Colorado, N.E.	Sept. 27	May 11

State	First Frost in Fall	Last Frost in Spring
Colorado, S.E.	Oct. 15	May 1
Connecticut	Oct. 20	Apr. 25
Delaware	Oct. 25	Apr. 15
District of Columbia	Oct. 23	Apr. 11
Florida, N.	Dec. 5	Feb. 25
Florida, Cen.	Dec. 28	Feb. 11
Florida, South of Lake Okeechobee	—almost frost-free—	
Georgia, N.	Nov. 1	Apr. 1
Georgia, S.	Nov. 15	Mar. 15
Idaho	Sept. 22	May 21
Illinois, N.	Oct. 8	May 1
Illinois, S.	Oct. 20	Apr. 15
Indiana, N.	Oct. 8	May 1
Indiana, S.	Oct. 20	Apr. 15
Iowa, N.	Oct. 2	May 1
Iowa, S.	Oct. 9	Apr. 15
Kansas	Oct. 15	Apr. 20
Kentucky	Oct. 20	Apr. 15
Louisiana, N.	Nov. 10	Mar. 13
Louisiana, S.	Nov. 20	Feb. 20
Maine	Sept. 25	May 25
Maryland	Oct. 20	Apr. 19
Massachusetts	Oct. 25	Apr. 25
Michigan, Upper Penn.	Sept. 15	May 25
Michigan, N.	Sept. 25	May 17
Michigan, S.	Oct. 8	May 10
Minnesota, N.	Sept. 15	May 25
Minnesota, S.	Oct. 1	May 11
Mississippi, N.	Oct. 30	Mar. 25
Mississippi, S.	Nov. 15	Mar. 15
Missouri	Oct. 20	Apr. 20
Montana	Sept. 22	May 21
Nebraska, W.	Oct. 4	May 11
Nebraska, E.	Oct. 15	Apr. 15
Nevada, W.	Sept. 22	May 19
Nevada, E.	Sept. 14	June 1
New Hampshire	Sept. 25	May 23
New Jersey	Oct. 25	Apr. 20
New Mexico, N.	Oct. 17	Apr. 23
New Mexico, S.	Nov. 1	Apr. 1
New York, W.	Oct. 8	May 10
New York, E.	Oct. 15	May 1
New York, N.	Oct. 1	May 15

State	First Frost in Fall	Last Frost in Spring
N. Carolina, W.	Oct. 25	Apr. 15
N. Carolina, E.	Nov. 1	Apr. 8
N. Dakota, W.	Sept. 13	May 21
N. Dakota, E.	Sept. 20	May 16
Ohio, N.	Oct. 15	May 6
Ohio, S.	Oct. 20	Apr. 20
Oklahoma	Nov. 2	Apr. 2
Oregon, W.	Oct. 25	Apr. 17
Oregon, E.	Sept. 22	June 4
Pennsylvania, W.	Oct. 10	Apr. 20
Pennsylvania, Cen.	Oct. 15	May 1
Pennsylvania, E.	Oct. 15	Apr. 17
Rhode Island	Oct. 25	Apr. 25
S. Carolina, N.W.	Nov. 8	Apr. 1
S. Carolina, S.E.	Nov. 15	Mar. 15
S. Dakota	Sept. 25	May 15
Tennessee	Oct. 25	Apr. 10
Texas, N.W.	Nov. 1	Apr. 15
Texas, N.E.	Nov. 10	Mar. 21
Texas, S.	Dec. 15	Feb. 10
Utah	Oct. 19	Apr. 26
Vermont	Sept. 25	May 23
Virginia, N.	Oct. 25	Apr. 15
Virginia, S.	Oct. 30	Apr. 10
Washington, W.	Nov. 15	Apr. 10
Washington, E.	Oct. 1	May 15
W. Virginia, W.	Oct. 15	May 1
W. Virginia, E.	Oct. 1	May 15
Wisconsin, N.	Sept. 25	May 17
Wisconsin, S.	Oct. 10	May 1
Wyoming, W.	Aug. 20	June 20
Wyoming, E.	Sept. 20	May 21

CHAPTER 8 House Plant Care

House Plants Are No More Trouble than Pets or Kids!

Every time I sit down to write about house plants, as I am now doing, I take my lap desk, pen, and pad, and plop down in a chair in the family room. I always begin by looking around the room at Duke, Toby, Queen Elizabeth, Ben Franklin, Tarzan, and the Girls in the Bridge Club for inspiration as I try to get you folks to enjoy everyday living with house plants. House plant care doesn't have to be a source of aggravation and frustration. There are lots of ways to make it easy and fun.

I guess I had better begin by satisfying your curiosity as to who the crowd in the family room is. They are my house plants. Naming them makes it easier to remember and relate to them. I have in past books gone into the advantages of this practice in great detail. We are concentrating on expedience here, so I'll just mention it in passing. And I should also mention Willy (the parakeet), Bob (the hamster), and Rudolph B of Troy (the dachshund); they're also on hand for consultation. Don't worry! I left Walter, my desk, down in my office.

I hope that by now you are chuckling, because that is step one. Relax, enjoy, and have some fun with any job you undertake and it will become a pleasure, not a burden. The naming idea is just one of the fun things you can do.

The More the Merrier

You can never have too many house plants in your living

quarters or place of employment. Well, *never* is a big word. The time and space available play the biggest part in determining the size of your plant entourage. Follow this simple rule: No plant should be allowed to touch another. Plants, like people, each require their own room to grow and must receive full exposure to light on all sides, adequate protection from insects, and good air circulation. Each plant should also receive its fair share of TLC.

By the way, that old wives' tale about too many plants burning up the oxygen is hogwash. Science has proven that plants manufacture oxygen—so the more plants, the more oxygen.

Cheap Decor—Plants

What do I mean by cheap? Haven't I seen the prices they get for plants nowadays? I sure have, but I don't buy at fancy florists and garden shops. I buy inexpensive, healthy, large plants in K Mart stores, grocery stores, gas stations, flea markets, and drug stores. A half-dozen growers supply most of the plants for sale in this country, so the cheap plant at the dimestore probably came from the same source as the expensive plant at the florist. If the price is right, the leaves are the right color, and nothing moves, buy it!

Okay, so plants can be cheap—but are they decor? Let me tell you a story. I have a friend who is famous, rich, and extremely good-looking. He entertains a great deal. He has less than ten pieces of furniture. Four pieces are chairs for the dining table, one is a 10 × 12-foot oriental rug from Iran, and all the rest are from resale shops and cost him less than what some kids pay to furnish their rooms in the dorm. Is he a skinflint? Quite the contrary. One last piece to the puzzle: A magazine wanted to feature his beautiful apartment. He also has 146 house plants.

What Is a House Plant?

A house plant is any plant that will stay alive when grown in a container indoors. This goes to show you that there is almost no limit to your selection. Just make sure that you can provide the plant of your choice with the proper amount of sunlight and care.

Your choice may be somewhat more limited if you have small children or pets. As every mother knows, toddlers will put almost anything into their mouths, and the leaves or berries of many common house plants are poisonous. Some dogs and cats also nibble on house plants. Plants to avoid include croton, dumb cane, Jerusalem cherry, ornamental pepper, and poinsettia. Keep them out of reach, or don't keep them at all.

I've listed below some of the most popular house plants according to the conditions of light and moisture they like best. You have a lot of control over how much moisture your plants get, but providing enough light may be more of a problem, so keep in mind the amount of sunlight your home gets as well as the number of plant lamps you plan to buy as you make your selection.

Bright Light: South or West with a Sheer Curtain

African Violet
Amaryllis
Aphelandra
Azalea
Baby's Tears
Cacti and Succulents
Christmas Cactus
Chrysanthemum
Citrus (all)
Croton
Cyclamen
Gardenia
Gloxinia
Hedera (Ivy)
Hibiscus
Hoya (Wax Plant)
Jade Plant
Jerusalem Cherry
Kalanchoe
Lanpranthus
Pittosporum
Poinsettia
Yucca

Medium Light: East Window

Anthurium
Asparagus Fern
Begonia
Bromeliads
Caladium
Chlorophytum (Spider Plant)
Dieffenbachia (Dumb Cane)
Dracaena godseffiana and
    sanderiana
Fiddle-leaf Fig
Fuchsia
Grape Ivy
Hydrangea
Maranta (Prayer Plant)
Nephthytis
Orchids (all)
Palms
Peperomia
Piggyback Plant
Pothos (Marble Queen)
Rubber Plant
Schefflera
Wandering Jew

Shade: North Window

Aspidistra
Bamboo Palm
Dracaena marginata and
    massangeana
Kentia Palm
Nephrolepsis
Philodendron
Sansevieria
Spathiphyllum

House Plants That Like It Dry

Aloe
Cacti
Crassula

Echeveria
Euphorbia
Sedum

House Plants That Like It Wet, But Not Soggy

Bromeliads
Century Plant
Crypanthus
Dieffenbachia
Geranium
Hoya
Impatiens
Kalanchoe
Lily

Orchid
Peperomia
Poinsettia
Pothos
Sansevieria
Saxifraga
Schefflera
Scindapsus
Shrimp Plant

Mildly Damp Will Do For The Rest

African Violets
Amaryllis
Anemone
Aphelandra
Aralia
Ardisia
Asparagus Fern
Aspidistra
Aucuba
Azalea
Baby's Tears
Bamboo
Begonia Wax
Bird-of-Paradise
Bougainvillea
Caladium
Calceolaria
Chinese Evergreen
Chlorophytum
Chrysanthemums
Cineraria
Coffee
Coleus
Creeping Charlie
Creeping Fig
Crossandra
Cyclamen

Cycas Fern/Palm
Dipladenia
Dracaena
Euonymus
Fatshedera
Ferns
Ficus
Fittonia
Fuchsia
Gardenia
Gerbera
Glounia
Gynura
Hawaiian Ti
Hibiscus
Hydrangea
Jerusalem Cherry
Joseph's Coat
Lipstick Vine
Nepthytis
Norfolk Island Pine
Oleander
Oralis
Palms
Pandanus
Pellionia
Philodendron

Pilea
Pittosporum
Podocarpus
Ponytail
Prayer Plant
Primrose
Selaginella

Sensitivity Plant
Spathiphyllum
Stephanotis
Swedish Ivy
Tolmeria
Wandering Jew
Zebra Plant

Light Up Your Plant's Life

Plants grow in the dark, like babies and puppies, but they need light in order to make their food. Unlike animals, plants manufacture their own food through a process called photosynthesis. Using carbon dioxide from the air and water and minerals from the soil as the basic ingredients, plants draw on the energy in sunlight to synthesize these ingredients into food. (What we call "plant food," by the way, is not really food because it does not provide the plant with energy—calories—to carry on its life processes. "Plant food" just adds nutrients to the soil that the plant can use as building blocks in manufacturing its own food.) Photosynthesis is activated by a chemical in plants called chlorophyll, which gives plants their green color.

Provide extra light with plant lamps

That's a very simple explanation of a very complicated chemical process. All you, the Impatient Gardener, need know about photosynthesis is that your house plants need plenty of sunlight each day. Most plants need between 12 and 16 hours of light a day.

I have found that a good northeast exposure, with extra light during the fall and winter months from lamps, will generally keep most of my plants happy, including cacti and succulents. Plants that like bright sun will be happier in a southern exposure. True east and west windows may have the intensity but lack the length of light necessary. If you can't give your plants enough light naturally, there are a great number of plant lights on the market designed to meet their needs. I have had excellent results with the Sylvania Gro-Lux lights available in almost any plant department.

What's So Hard about Watering Plants?

Once or twice a week, you pour in a cup or two of good old H_2O. What's so hard about that? The water, maybe. When it comes to plants, there is good water and bad water. It may be too "hard," or high in minerals; this is often true of deep-well water. Or the water in your region may be too "soft," and it may slowly kill off your plants. Many homeowners and communities "soften" their water by filtering it through a

Test soil for moisture content before watering

container filled with rock salt. The rock salt breaks down the harmful minerals in "hard" water, but the rock salt residue in "soft" water is even worse for your plants. The very best water is rain, melted snow or ice, and water from the dehumidifier or air conditioner. City water is usually good too. Collect it in buckets, and store it in a cool place. Before you use it to water the plants, let it warm up to room temperature.

There is also a right time and wrong time to water plants. As a rule, all plants purchased commercially have an instruction tag attached—follow the directions to the letter. To check the soil for moisture content, poke your finger down into the soil about an inch or so. Water and fertilize early in the morning so that the plant will have enough moisture and nutrients on hand to make plenty of food during the sunlit hours. Let the water run all the way through the soil. Let the excess soak in for five or ten minutes; then pour off any remaining standing water.

Don't water a fixed amount on predetermined days without paying attention to the actual dryness of the soil. The needs of the plants vary from day to day, depending on such factors as heat and humidity, so read the signs—let the plant's thirst determine how much you pour.

These charts will help you determine the proper watering method for these popular house plants:

FOLIAGE HOUSE PLANTS

	Drench; Let Dry	Drench; Let Dry Slightly	Keep Soil Moist	Mist Foliage Often
Aluminum Plant		x		
Asparagus Fern		x		x
Baby's Tears			x	x
Boston Fern			x	x
Cast-iron Plant		x		
Chinese Evergreen			x	
Coleus			x	
Corn Plant	x			
Dumb Cane		x		
English Ivy		x		
Fittonia		x		x
Grape Ivy		x		
Maidenhair Fern			x	x
Norfolk Island Pine		x		

	Drench; Let Dry	Drench; Let Dry Slightly	Keep Soil Moist	Mist Foliage Often
Peperomia		x		
Philodendron		x		x
Piggyback Plant		x		
Prayer Plant			x	x
Snake Plant	x			
Spider Plant		x		
Umbrella Tree		x		
Wandering Jew		x		
Zebra Plant		x		

FLOWERING HOUSE PLANTS

	Drench; Let Dry	Drench; Let Dry Slightly	Keep Soil Moist	Mist Foliage Often
African Violets			x	
Aloe	x			
Anthurium			x	
Azalea		x		
Begonia		x		
Cacti	x			
Century Plant	x			
Christmas Cactus	x			
Crown of Thorns	x			
Cyclamen	x			
Firecracker Flower		x		x
Flowering Maple		x		
Fuchsia		x		
Gardenia		x		x
Geranium	x			
Gloxinia			x	
Hens and Chicks	x			
Hoya		x		
Hydrangea			x	x
Impatiens			x	
Jade Plant	x			
Kalanchoe		x		
Orchid Cactus	x			
Oxalis		x		
Shrimp Plant		x		

Plants Can't Live by Water Alone

Plants, like people, need a balanced diet. *Every* time you water your plants, add 10 percent of the amount of plant food recommended by the manufacturer to the water along with 3 or 4 drops of liquid dishsoap. The soap softens up the soil and allows the water to penetrate fully, instead of running down the side of the pot to the bottom. Use only 10% of the recommended amount each time because you are feeding more often than the manufacturer recommends. Plants can only ingest so much food at a time. You'd probably rather eat several snacks a day than a huge feast every three days; by the same token your plant would rather snack twice a week than feast once a month.

Vary Your Plant's Menu

There are more ways of feeding plants today than you can shake a stick at: plant pills, sticks, drops, and granules. All of these foods work to some degree. However, I always stick to the greenhouse way: add food to the water. Day to day, I use soluble house plant food for all my flowering or color foliage plants—even for my African violets. Plants like organic plant food from time to time, so I vary their daily diet with fish fertilizers, liquid seaweed or, homemade barnyard tea (manure water). These don't smell delightful but the plants love them.

Once a month my plants get a liberal helping of Grandma Putt's homemade plant food. To one gallon water (preferably collected rainwater or melted snow), add one cup of the following formula:

> 1 tablespoon of household ammonia
> 1 tablespoon of baking powder
> 1 tablespoon of saltpeter
> 1 tablespoon of druggist sulphur
> 2 tablespoons of Epsom salts
> 1 very rusty nail (or 1 Femiron tablet)
> 2 tablespoons of liquid soap

Use once a month to perk up your plants. For acid-loving plants, add 5 tablespoons of black coffee or 4 drops of white vinegar per gallon of Grandma Putt's recipe.

Dry Skin Will Drive You Both Nuts

If you wake up in the morning with dry skin, brittle hair, and a shock every time you touch the doorknob, your plants are in trouble. What's your discomfort got to do with your plants? They are suffering from the same problem—lack of humidity. Both heating and cooling your house extract moisture from the air, so any time a furnace, air conditioner, or dehumidifier is on in your home, not only the air and you but also your pets, plants, drapes, wall coverings, furniture, fabrics, wood, and carpeting will dry out. Some symptoms of excessive dryness are squeaky floors, rungs on chairs coming unglued, tips of leaves turning brown, and your cat avoiding being petted.

To correct this condition, get a humidifier or spray the foliage of your plants daily with a weak solution of tea (what you get when you use a tea bag for the third time), with three drops of any liquid soap added per quart of tea. Spray top and bottom.

Fresh Air or Forget It

Friends of ours have a "smoking" and "no smoking" section in their living room. Their plants and I always request the "no smoking" section. I kid you not. Here is how it works. They have installed a very inexpensive window fan (one of those 8-inch or 10-inch adjustable window fans) on one side of the living room to blow in fresh air. In a window in an adjoining room they have the same type of fan placed backward in the window so it is drawing the air out of the room. This setup creates strong cross-ventilation. All of their plants are placed in the side of the living room away from the fan so they are in the cross-current.

Even if you can't set up a cross-ventilation system like this one, you can use an oscillating fan to move the air around, or open windows when possible to give your plants (and yourself) some fresh air.

From Indoors Out or Vice Versa

Plants that live indoors for a good part of the year deserve a little time outside. After the last frost date plus a week, make sure they have been vaccinated before putting them outside. Poke pencil holes into the soil and feed with a systemic insect control and food combination. I use the K Mart Systemic Insect, Rose and Flower Plant Food.

Next, spray the foliage with Benomyl, a systemic fungicide, and pour whatever is left over in the container through the soil.

A week later, spray the foliage with Kelthane and pour Diazinon through the soil until it's quite wet. Then bring them outside. Just before you bring them back in, repeat the Kelthane and Diazinon treatment.

Mist foliage daily when the air is dry

A Pest Is a Pest

Bugs or diseases can discourage any of us. Just when you're starting to think you're really good, Mother Nature puts you in your place. So, be ready. Keep this arsenal in your potting shed:

1 bottle of Benomyl (Benomyl controls most fungi)
1 bottle of Kelthane (Kelthane controls most mites)
1 bottle of Safer Agro-Chem Insecticide Soap (good for most everything)
1 bottle of Diazinon (controls many soil insects)
1 container of systemic insect granules (makes your plants' foliage no-man's land for bugs)

As soon as you suspect a problem, isolate the plant and begin the appropriate treatment. If the plant doesn't respond before your patience wears out, get rid of it. You don't want your whole house plant family catching the same thing.

Dress Them in the Right Pot

Plants, like babies, go from infant size to toddlers, to children, to juniors, and up the growing ladder. When a plant outgrows the pot it's in, it has to be moved to a new one the next size bigger.

Plants must be slightly pot-bound but not root-strangled. Pot-bound means there is a slight web of roots around the soil ball when it is lifted from the pot. Root-strangled means that the root ball is bound so tight that water and food just run down the side of the pot and out the hole in the bottom instead of soaking into the soil so the plant can eat and drink. The simple rule is to move a plant up to the next size pot when the roots show in the bottom hole or growth stands still.

Transplanting a seedling into its own pot

Repotitis is Curable

There's no need to get the blues when you have to transplant or repot. No, they are not the same thing, but they are accomplished the same way.

Transplanting is the placement of a new, young plant that's been seeded in a flat or pan into its own container, where it will grow until it has outgrown this container and has to be repotted.

Repotting is moving a plant into a larger container so that it can continue to grow. Sometimes you may also repot a plant simply because you are tired of looking at its old container and want to try it in something new. Lastly, you may

Repotting a plant into a larger pot

repot a plant from a planter contaminated by disease, insects, or general cruddiness into a fresh, clean one. Normally, however, you repot because the plant has outgrown its old container.

Always repot with a specific purpose in mind, never just because your green thumb is itching and you have some time to kill. Usually what you end up killing is the plant.

The rules for transplanting and repotting are the same.

Containers Make It or Break It

A plant's life depends on the container it is grown in.

Clay pots are the best containers for a variety of reasons. They are porous, so excess water and built-up chemical salts from plant food can escape. They are easy to clean, fairly inexpensive, and great-looking. If you prefer to use another type of decorative container, pot the plant in clay and then place the clay pot inside the container of your choice.

Clay pots should be soaked in water for several hours before use. Never use dry clay pots. They will draw the moisture out of the growing medium and force the plant into shock.

Don't Overdo It

Do not place a plant in a container that is too large. If you put it in too big a pot, it will spend all its time growing more roots to fill up the pot and too little time growing foliage. A good size to transplant seedlings into is a 2¼-inch pot. When they're ready, move them into a 3-inch pot, then a 4-inch pot, and so on. Older plants should also move up only one to one-and-a-half pot sizes each time.

Plants Don't Grow in Dirt

Get out of the habit of thinking plants grow in dirt. They grow in soil, which is sweet and clean. Don't go out to your vegetable or flower bed and dig up soil to use as is for house plants or outdoor planters. Soil from an outdoor bed is too heavy for planters and will settle in the pot until it chokes the plant to death. Instead, use a soil mix designed especially for planters. For most house plants, the following all-purpose blend will do quite well:

> 25% sharp sand (not sandbox type—sharp sand has bigger granules and won't compact)
> 25% peat moss
> 25% garden soil (sterilized)
> 25% perlite

Soilless Mixes Are a Dream Come True

You can also use one of the relatively new soilless mixes for your house plants. They are formulated to provide a sterile, disease- and insect-free growing medium to ensure that your plant gets off to a good start in its new home. Buy them at any garden center under one of their many brand names; Pro Mix and Jiffy Mix are among the most popular. They contain peat moss, perlite, vermiculite, and a starter fertilizer. Make sure the mix is well-moistened before use.

Early to Rise Used to Be the Rule

You'll hear it said that transplanting and repotting should be done in the early morning. Not true. Do it in the late afternoon or early evening. Plants grow at night. Planting late in the day gives them just enough time to settle down before getting off to a growing start the same evening. If you don't believe me, try repotting two plants of the same size and variety into the same soil mix in the same size and type of pot. Repot one in the morning and one in the evening. See which begins to grow first.

Spare the Food and Save a Plant

If you are using a soilless mix, you don't need to use any plant food for a week or two after repotting because the mix contains a starter food. If you are using a soil mix, use one of the plant starter foods as directed for the first two weeks. After two weeks, begin to feed plants in either type of growing medium as established plants.

Keep Them out of the Limelight

Newly transplanted or repotted plants should be kept out of bright lights for about a week, until they've gotten over the shock of their move.

Starting New Plants from Old

At one time or another most of you have probably placed the stem and leaf of a house plant into a glass of water and watched roots develop. What you were doing is rooting a cutting. Most house plants can be propagated using some form of this technique.

Never throw away a healthy leaf that falls or breaks off a plant. Instead, water-root it. Fill a shallow cake or pie tin with perlite (the spongy, white pebbles used in growing mixes) and spray it with enough water to wet it through.

Take cuttings for propagation

Transplant cuttings when their roots are big enough

Place the stem of the leaf into the wet perlite so that the underside of the leaf touches the perlite. Leave it there until small plantlets form where the stem joins the leaf. When these plantlets are as large as your thumbnail, check to see if they have grown healthy roots. When it looks to you as if their roots are big enough to survive in soil, transplant them into a 2¼-inch clay pot filled with a soil or soilless mix and treat as a normal house plant.

Some plants, like geraniums, Chinese evergreens, jade plant, dumb cane, velvet plant, and prayer plant, can be propagated with stem-tip cuttings. Take cuttings 3 to 4 inches long from the ends of branches. Remove all of the leaves except the ones on the very end. Dip the cut end of each stem into Rootone rooting powder 1 to 1½ inches deep. Fill a 2¼-inch clay pot with growing medium and pack down firmly. Poke a hole in the center of the planter mix with a pencil, all the way to the bottom of the pot. Set the Rootone-covered stem into the hole and press soil or soilless mix around the stem. Place these new plants in a dim place and keep damp for a week. Then move them to a spot that provides normal light for that variety of plant and treat as an adult house plant.

Pinch back house plants to thicken

African Violets

The Girls in the Bridge Club

That's how we refer to our African violets. Believe me, there are times when we have so many of them on hand that it looks like tournament time at Great Oaks. African violets are the most popular flowering house plant, and they should be. There is one of these beauties to suit anyone's fancy, and they don't take that much special care.

Show Them Off

Don't try to hide your violets in a shady corner or you can kiss them good-bye. Every one of them is a show-off and expects a spotlight from Mother Nature. If you place them on a stand or table, try this rotation: north in the summer, south in the winter, and west only if you have no other choice. East is good anytime. Use a sheer curtain to keep them from cooking in the sun.

Keep Them Comfortable

You ought to take a lesson on how to cut down your heat bill from your African violets. They like it 65° F at night and 72° F during the day.

Keep Them Moving

Keep an inexpensive oscillating fan moving the air around your violets. You can leave it on all day, or just from 3:00 P.M. to 9:00 P.M. Don't expose them to drafts or unexpected temperature drops.

Whence They Came

They came from the jungle, so they like it humid, 50 percent humidity to be exact. If you have more than a few, a small cool-water humidifier will do the job. For just a few, set them on a tray or saucer of gravel and keep the gravel damp.

Dress Them Right

You know my feeling about clay pots. It should come as no surprise that that's their preference. To maintain moisture, set the clay pot inside a decorative plastic planter or wrap it with Saran Wrap. Don't cover the bottom of the pot.

Soil Is No Big Thing

Violets don't like rich soil, so get an inexpensive soil test kit at the garden shop. This kit comes in handy for all your garden needs. Test for pH, nitrogen, phosphorus, and potash. Violets want 7.0 on the pH scale. You can raise pH with 1 teaspoon of white vinegar per gallon of water and lower it with 1 teaspoon of lime per gallon.

Feed Them Anything Their Little Hearts Desire

Or feed them whatever you can afford. I haven't found much difference between African violet foods, so use any brand. The fish foods are good but they stink—the complaints from your family may not be worth it. Let your violets diet during the hot summer.

Water Them but Don't Drown Them

Use the best water you can fill your watering can with, and make sure it is at room temperature. Remember to feed each time you water and remove excess water from the pots.

What's Bugging Them?

To get rid of bugs, use Kelthane for the tops, Diazinon for the bottoms, and Benomyl for the fungus problems.

A Final Word

I've written this book on the "need to know" principle. If I thought a certain step would make your gardening chores faster, easier, safer, or cheaper, I've explained why it's important and how to do it. Right now you may feel that I expect you to know a lot more than you have the time or patience for, but when you get out your spade and hoe you'll see that every step is simple and logical, and the effort is rewarded a hundredfold by the results. As the basic procedures become second nature, you'll grow in confidence and start to develop your own gardening style. You'll experiment with new plants you always thought too difficult before, you'll try out new ways of doing things, maybe you'll even get involved in some of the more sophisticated garden activities, like greenhouse growing or local competitions. You'll find out how much fun gardening can be—and you just may find that you're not so impatient after all.

Index

ABOUT THE AUTHOR

America's foremost gardening authority, Jerry Baker is known to millions through the success of his best-selling books, PLANTS ARE LIKE PEOPLE and TALK TO YOUR PLANTS. He appears frequently on TV's *Daytime*, *P.M. Magazine*, and *America Overnight*.